D0094765

SPIES
IN THE
VATICAN

SPIES
IN THE
VATICAN

THE SOVIET UNION'S COLD WAR
AGAINST THE CATHOLIC CHURCH

JOHN O. KOEHLER

PEGASUS BOOKS
NEW YORK

SPIES IN THE VATICAN

Pegasus Books LLC
80 Broad Street, 5th Floor
New York, NY 10004

First Pegasus Books edition 2009

Interior design by Maria Fernandez

Library of Congress Cataloging-in-Publication Data is available.

ISBN: 978-1-60598-050-8

10 9 8 7 6 5 4 3 2 1

Printed in the United States of America
Distributed by W. W. Norton & Company
www.pegasusbooks.us

*I dedicate this book to those who
paid with their lives or suffered imprisonment
for defending their religious beliefs
against communist tyrants*

CONTENTS

1 A BRUTAL WAR AGAINST RELIGION

*A fight to the death must be
declared upon religion . . . take
on religion at the tip of the
bayonet . . .*

—Nikolai Bukharin,
editor of *Pravda* 1918–1929

Before dawn on Easter Sunday 1923, Monsignor Konstantin Budkiewicz kneeled on the steps leading to a row of cells at Moscow's infamous Lubyanka Prison. A single bullet fired from a communist executioner's Nagant revolver shattered the back of the 65-year-old Monsignor's head. The Catholic Church in Russia had its first 20th-century martyr. His crime? Resisting religious persecution by the Bolsheviks, thus "committing a counterrevolutionary act." The Monsignor was a defendant in the first major show trial in the Bolsheviks' quest to destroy the Catholic Church in Russia. The chief target, Polish-born Archbishop Jan Cieplak, and more than a dozen priests were also convicted. The archbishop was sentenced to death as well, but was quietly exiled after intervention by the Holy See and a number of Western governments, winding up in Latvia and eventually in Rome. In ill health, he later moved to the United States, where he died in Passaic, N.J., in 1926 at the age of 68. The others were given long sentences they served in Gulags, the communist concentration camps where many died. Four years earlier, after the Bolsheviks pledged to "liberate the toiling masses from religious prejudices and organize the broadest scientific, education, and anti-religious propaganda," Archbishop Baron Edward von der Ropp of the Mogilev diocese was arrested on trumped-up charges of engaging in "illegal economic speculations."[1] He undoubtedly escaped a bullet in the head when the Bolshevik leadership decided to exchange him for Karl Radek, the Ukrainian-born Bolshevik confidant of Vladimir I. Lenin who was imprisoned in Germany. He had entered the country illegally on a mission to determine whether the Bolsheviks could expect support from German politicians and intellectuals. And so Radek was sent to Moscow and Archbishop von der Ropp to Warsaw.

At the time of Monsignor Budkiewicz's execution, the Catholic hierarchy had known for some six years that their Church was slated for decimation by watching the brutal war against the predominant Russian Orthodox Church, whose disciples in 1917 numbered roughly 118.24 million out of a population of 147.8 million. There were 5 million Catholics in Russia at the time.[2] Olga Vasilieva of the Russian Orthodox Church periodical *Halicize* wrote that between 1917 and 1920, the repression "took away about 9000 lives," adding: "The Russian church had entered the path to the Calvary."

---

1. Rev. Christopher L. Zugger, *The Forgotten* (Syracuse University Press, 2001).
2. Ibid.

Churchmen did much to prevent civil disorder during the tumultuous years immediately after the November 1917 seizure of power by the Bolsheviks. Execution and imprisonment without trial was their reward. Archpriest Ioann Kochurov of the St. Catherine Cathedral in the village of Tsarskoye Selo near St. Petersburg was seized by a mob of Red soldiers, taken to an airfield, and shot without a trial. His school-aged son was forced to watch. Many hours later, Father Ioann's parishioners were allowed to bury the body in a vault beneath the cathedral. The sight of his body was no doubt a warning to the parishioners about the price for their continued faith.

Behind this terror was none other than Ilyich Ulyanov Lenin, the Bolshevik leader who not only commanded the Red Army but also the first communist secret police organization, the Cheka. While the Red Army was busy murdering real or suspected opponents to communism, the Cheka under its first chief Felix Dzerzhinsky was establishing a vast network of spies in all corners of Russia to ferret out "counterrevolutionaries" which, of course, included all religious leaders. To avoid arrest or worse, church leaders often met in secret. One such group consisted of both Catholic and Orthodox clergy, including Dominican monks. It met at the home of Father Vladimir and Anna Ivanovna Abrikosov in Moscow. Within that group, the Cheka had planted a "voluntary collaborator" described as a young man who had "professed his intention of becoming a Catholic monk and indeed had impressed the nuns as 'especially pious.'"[3] This may well have been the communists' first spy against the Catholic Church. In April 1922, the Cheka, later renamed GPU and OGPU, began arresting members of that group. Even though there had already been an orgy of executions and imprisonments without trials in the early years of communist rule, in 1922 the authorities in Moscow made the

3. Irina I. Osipova, *Hide Me Within Thy Wounds*, Germans from Russia Heritage Collection, North Dakota State University Libraries, 2003.

pretense of fairness due to international pressure and resorted to "trials." Needless to say, these trials were little more than a show. One of the first involved the Abrikosov group for anti-government and counterrevolutionary activities. Father Abrikosov was lucky. After a trial, he was ordered expelled from Russia and settled in Rome. Dozens of others, including Abrikosov's wife, wound up in prison with average sentences of ten years.

A civil war between the White and Red armies was raging between 1918 and 1920, and the one-year Soviet Polish war (1919–1920) brought the Soviet Union economic disaster. A drought, low agricultural yields, and failure in industrial production created a horrific famine. Millions of Russians faced starvation. The American Relief Association came to the aid with $66 million worth of food. Because of the generous spending on relief for refugees and the displaced during and after World War I by Pope Benedict XV, the Vatican was facing bankruptcy. Nevertheless, the Holy See provided $2 million in aid.[4] But little reached the most needy, such as farmers, as most of the funds went to the Red Army and the government functionaries. The Vatican's generosity meant nothing to the communists as the campaign to smother religion continued unabated. Lenin paid the Vatican back by ordering the looting of the churches and monasteries of their sacred treasures and real estate.

On March 19, 1922, Lenin wrote a top-secret letter to members of the Politburo: "Now and only now, when people are being eaten in famine-stricken areas, and hundreds, if not thousands, of corpses lie in the roads, we can (and therefore must) pursue the removal of church property with the most frenzied and ruthless energy and not hesitate to put down the least opposition." The goateed master criminal ordered "the removal of church property by any means necessary in order to secure for ourselves a fund of several hundred million

4. Fr. Zugger, *The Forgotten*, (Syracuse University Press, 2001).

gold rubles (do not forget the immense wealth of some monasteries)." He wrote that without these treasures, any government work in general, and economic buildup in particular, would be impossible. Thus, **"in order to get our hands on this fund of several hundred million gold rubles (and perhaps several hundred billion), we must do whatever is necessary"** [emphasis added]. He urged the passing of a secret resolution that the removal of property of value, especially from the very rich lauras,[5] monasteries, and churches **"must be carried out with ruthless resolution, leaving nothing in doubt, and in the very shortest time"** [emphasis added]. In other words, Lenin told his cohorts to steal as quickly as possible before the world could react with condemnation when the communist lies— that the proceeds from the looting would go to the starving population —were exposed. Father Edmund Walsh, an American Jesuit who led the Papal relief mission, estimated the minimum value of the stolen church treasures at 250 million United States dollars. Not a ruble was spent on the starving peasants, of whom more than 5 million died. "All the unique features of the system were displayed: cruelty, vengefulness, and obstinacy. Lenin was willing to sacrifice a substantial section of the peasantry as long as the industrial centers were kept in food," wrote Mikhail Heller and Aleksandr Nekrich in their book *Utopia in Power*.

The campaign to eradicate religion began under Lenin who, in 1922, ordered the establishment of a giant SLON (a special camp on the Archipelago Solovki) on five islands in the White Sea. One of the largest cloisters was located on the main island and became a prison. By 1928 the camps held about 38,000 clerics and intellectuals who became slave laborers. With the accession of the Red throne by Josef Stalin after Lenin's death in 1924, it became even bloodier. In 1930, the NKVD, successor to the GPU, revealed that since 1917 the Russian

5. A term for large monasteries.

Orthodox Church lost 42,800 clergymen, monks, and nuns who had, perished in labor camps and prisons from hardships and executions.[6] During the "Great Purge" of 1936/1938, 100,000 clerics and laymen were shot.[7] Only 5,665 remained at liberty in 1941. The much smaller Catholic Church had 1,000 of its clergymen executed. By 1932 the Soviet authorities had arrested 19,812 priests and nuns.[8] Stalin's secret police were not only bent on eradicating religion: they were waging an even grislier war against the Kulaks, the farmers who resisted the government collectivization of their lands. About six million deaths through execution and starvation were recorded. Four million alone were in the "Breadbasket of Russia," the Ukraine.[9] Along with decimating the Russian Orthodox and Catholic dioceses and all other religious groups such as Baptists, Lutherans, and Muslims, the communist authorities also destroyed thousands of churches, monasteries, and mosques. But Stalin not only wielded his deadly power over the various religions, he also hauled Party officials and high-ranking military officers before show trials. Hundreds were found guilty on trumped-up charges and torture-induced confessions. Most were shot. The last trial in 1938 was that of Nikolai Bukharin, a brilliant economist and friend of Lenin who, as editor of the Party newspaper *Pravda*, called for the extermination of religion "at the tip of the bayonet." From 1926 to 1929, he was head of the Communist International. He broke with Stalin over "market socialism," which was eventually pursued by Mikhail Gorbachev 27 years after Bukharin's execution. And the bloodbath was only going to continue.

6. Archpresbyter Mikhail Polsky, *The New Martyrs of Russia* (Monastery Press, Montreal, P.Q., Canada, 1972).
7. Olga Vasilieva, "The Church of New Martyrs," Pravoslavie.ru, 2003.
8. Irina I. Osipova, *Hide Me Within Thy Wounds*, (Germans from Russia Heritage Collection, North Dakota University Libraries, 2003), citing the records of the "organs," meaning secret police.
9. Courtois, Werth, Panne, Paczkowski, Bartosek, Margolin, *Das Schwarzbuch des Kommunimus* (Piper Verlag, Muenchen, 1998).

By 1941, when the Nazis invaded the Soviet Union, only two of about 1,200 Catholic churches remained active. Whatever was left of Catholic believers practiced underground—or, as surviving priests would call it, in catacombs. Although burdened with searching for German spies, the NKVD kept secret agents inherited from the GPU imbedded with church groups. At the same time, Stalin made nice to the Russian Orthodox Church, whose patriotic support he needed in light of the war with Germany. However, were they still unaware of this infiltration? Or aware, but unable to figure out who the infiltrators were? After the war and until the collapse of the Soviet Union, the Russian Orthodox leadership was under total secret police control. Numerous clergy became agents, the most prominent being the Patriarch Aleksi II whose code name was Drozdov, or Blackbird.[10] While the Catholic Church remained stuck with only two places of worship, the Russian Orthodoxie was duly rewarded for its subservience to the state. By the time of Stalin's death in 1953 and before Nikita S. Khrushchev came to power in 1958, 22,000 Orthodox churches had been reopened. In 1954 the secret police was reorganized and renamed Committee for State Security, KGB for short. Two years later, speaking as Party leader during the 20th Party Congress, Khrushchev denounced Stalin for committing crimes during the Great Purge and the "cult of personality" in which Stalin had wallowed. He pressed for reforms. But when he replaced Nikolai Bulganin as prime minister in 1958, Khrushchev launched a new campaign against religion. The Orthodox hierarchy lost its prominent members—those not already secret KGB officers—to imprisonment or forced resignations. Submissive clergymen totally obedient to the ruling authorities took over the administration of the remaining places of worship. Taming the various religious groups was

---

10. Keith Armes article "Chekists in Cassocks: The Orthodox Church and the KGB," Institute for the study of Conflict, Ideology and Policy, Boston University.

just one item on Khrushchev's plate. Why was he so eager to start this initiative against religion again? Because he viewed it as a threat to Soviet hegemony and, as was the case with Lenin, an enemy of Marxist doctrine.

Ever-increasing dissatisfaction with communist rule after the war by the people in Moscow's satellites first resulted in the bloody 1956 squelching of the Hungarian revolution. To save the communist regime of East Germany, the Soviet leader approved the building of the Berlin Wall in 1961 to stem the flow of escapees to West Berlin. More than 5,600 had fled five days before the border was sealed on August 13. Within the Central Committee, members began to exhibit misgivings with Khrushchev's mismanagement of foreign policy, including the 1962 Cuban Missile Crisis, as well as with a deteriorating economy. There was also consternation over Khrushchev's continued handling of religious issues, particularly as it concerned the Catholic Church. Pope John XXIII had received Khrushchev's son-in-law in the Vatican in an attempt to determine if there could be some accommodations for improving conditions for the church. Discussing the Second Vatican Council,[11] scheduled to convene in October 1962, Pope John agreed to accept an offer by Khrushchev to allow the attendance of two Orthodox prelates, Metropolitans Borovoy and Kotlyrov, both of whom were KGB agents, if no attacks against communism were made at the conclave.[12] After the opening session, the conclave was adjourned to prepare for the general meetings, which were postponed briefly after the death of Pope John XXIII in June 1963. Pope Paul VI was elected two weeks later and ordered continuation of the council.

---

11. Also called Vatican II, this was an ecclesial, theological and ecumenical congress aimed at modernizing the Church, especially issues regarding liturgy affecting Catholics throughout the world. The Council voted to allow the use of vernacular language in celebrating the mass, instead of the traditional Latin.
12. Malachi Martin, *The Keys of This Blood*, (Touchstone, New York, 1991).

In the meantime, all was not tranquil within the Soviet Communist Party's leadership ranks. Dissatisfaction with Nikita Khrushchev's performance had been mounting steadily for some time. Finally, the Central Committee staged a bloodless coup in 1964. KGB chief Vladimir Semichastny, who was part of the conspiracy against Khrushchev, was tasked to meet the Soviet leader on October 13 at Moscow's Vnukovo Airport as he returned from vacation at the Black Sea to tell him he had been removed as head of the Party and the nation. He was rewarded with full Central Committee membership. Comrade Nikita was fortunate that his opponents had decided to act "humanely." Instead of shooting him, as had been past practice in such cases, he was allowed to live out his days at his seven-acre country dacha Petrovno Dalneye on the Moskva River, 18 miles west of Moscow, where he died of natural causes in 1971.

Leonid Brezhnev was installed to lead the Communist Party and to head the Soviet Union after the coup. His policy toward religion was less restrictive. Rather than imprison or exile clerics, he waged a campaign of attrition: i.e., let religion die on the vine, as new appointments would not be approved. Brezhnev, who owed his position in a large part to Semichastny, became weary of the KGB chief's increasing penchant for boosting the popularity of the service and his own stature as well as neglecting the surveillance of anti-government suspects. He was sacked in 1967 and replaced by Yuri Andropov, who was ambassador to Hungary when the anticommunist uprising erupted in 1956. He was promoted to the Central Committee for his part in suppressing the revolt. Like his predecessor, he had no secret police or intelligence experience. But he was a quick study. Under his command, control over dissidents was tightened by using more subtle measures such as issuing domestic travel restrictions to prevent demonstrations and relieving some pressures by permitting some of the more vocal and well-known dissidents to leave the Soviet Union. In other words, good riddance—let them scream on the outside.

Vatican II concluded in December 1965. By that time, the KGB's Fifth Directorate, which, among other tasks such as guarding against ideological subversion, was responsible for surveillance of all religious groups, had received the first top-secret 27-page report on the council from the Polish security service SB.[13] Thus, one must conclude that the treachery was carried out by a Polish priest. The spy wearing the clerical collar was most likely the late Bishop Jerzy Dabrowski of Gniezno, who died in 1991 at the age of 61. His collaboration with the secret police was not exposed until January 2007, when the Institute of Remembrance, which is charged with investigating Poland's communist past, opened his secret police file IPNBU 01940/74. In 1963, the bishop, whose code name was "Ignacy," was assigned to Rome, where he was active for seven years. Later, he became a deputy to the president of the Polish Episcopate. A source, who asked not to be named, told this writer of a conversation with a former secret police official who said the bishop had supplied secret and confidential documents from Vatican II to the KGB. "It was a nice surprise for us what Ignacy brought us and he assured us about regularly supplying us protocols from meetings of representatives of the Polish Episcopate which had operational value." Details of the bishop's recruitment were not found. One document, however, showed that that on November 9, 1965, his SB handler paid him 70,000 Italian lire, worth about 112.05 U.S. dollars—not a significant amount, but good pocket money for someone whose living expenses were paid for by the Church. After his return to Poland, Bishop Dabrowski, who was a close associate of the Primate, Josef Cardinal Glemp, negotiated with the communists during the 1980s to secure a Catholic mission to the Soviet Union. What a catch he was for the KGB!

Dabrowski's initial report on Vatican II opened with organizational

---

13. Polish security services coverage of the meetings of the 2. Ecumenical Council October 1–21, 1963, classified top secret. Copy of KGB report furnished the East German Ministry for State Security (Stasi). BSTU No. 000001-27.

aspects of the council, including the participation of 2,300 priests from throughout the world. One of many recommendations for changes in church structures was to restore the lay deaconry without adhering to celibacy so as to at least partially overcome the serious shortage of priests due to men willing to become priests in Europe and Latin America. While many delegates voiced opposition because this would demoralize the clerics, the motive of the Polish bishops was purely political. Bishop Mazur said: "The Polish bishops are opposed to restoring a lay deaconry because the communist regime in Poland would exploit this institution to try and divide the unity of the Church from within. The Polish bishops are of the opinion that the state would find it easier to gain influence over married lay deacons with families than over independent clerics who accordingly live in celibacy." An astute observation, as family members would be prone to blackmail and in danger of arrest and imprisonment. A sad thing, indeed, that they had to be viewed as collateral.

Finally, Dabrowski wrote the last section of his report, which he titled "Anticommunist campaigns apparent at the council." The report lamented the "serious increase" in anticommunist propaganda in the general Catholic press and the Vatican press prompted by official declarations by representatives of the Vatican. "One recognizes a tendency (among officials) to search for theoretical evidence to be applied for fostering anticommunism." Following the Pontificate of John XXIII, who had ordered the scaling back of attacks on communism in hope of easing the plight of his Church behind the Iron Curtain, the Vatican, according to the spy's report, found it difficult to return to "primitive anticommunist propaganda which condemned any ideas of societal progress under Marxism." No matter how Soviet politicians, by stressing their desires for world peace, had contributed toward persuading the Catholic world that the communist danger was at present less threatening, communism changed its tactics but not its aims, as per the report quoted by the Jesuit monthly *La Civiltà*

Cattolica. "The danger for the Church remains the same. Therefore it is necessary to again develop an active battle against communism and not to go into negotiations with it." In discussions within the conclave, according to the report to the KGB, it was emphasized that "the Catholic anticommunism must not be a blind conservatism based on fear. On the contrary, it must fight against the societal injustices."

A comprehensive report on the conclave reached Moscow within six months after its conclusion.[14] In a preamble, the spy wrote: "The decision to convene the Second Vatican Council was prompted by a number of elements arising from the internal situation of the Catholic Church as well as her position in the world. But without a doubt, the essential external reason was the necessity to solidify Vatican policies in view of the fact that the socialist camp [Ed.: communism] has strengthened its position as well as the spread and deepening of the Marxist ideology. The latter applies not only in Europe but also in Third World countries which the Catholic Church has selected as the territory for its future ideological expansion." The Vatican held to the promise of Pope John XXIII to Nikita Khrushchev that there would be no attack on communism at the council in exchange for allowing officials of the Russian Orthodox Church to attend the Rome proceedings. However, the report mentioned the Croatian Bishop of Split-Markaska Frane Franic using "the old term 'aggressive Church' so as to emphasize his demand for an active battle against atheism. In this connection he recommended the establishment of a special secretariat in combating unbelievers."

The report stressed that an "influential group in the Vatican made demands to search for new methods in the battle against materialism and, specifically, the communist social order since the old methods of ignoring the socialist countries and the total condemnation of all

14. Information of the security organs of the People's Republic of Poland classified top secret. Russian translation dated 23 October 1966. MfS Department X document No. 3088.

progressive movements had in praxis proved less effective." The Vatican acted expeditiously on this demand. It ordered the establishment of the Secretariat for Unbelievers eight months before Vatican II came to a close. Franz Cardinal Koenig of Vienna, an expert on Eastern Europe, was named to head the secretariat with its seat in the Austrian capital.[15]

In an obvious effort to stress its importance, the Polish spy Dabrowski prepared a separate top-secret report titled "The anticommunist centers of the Vatican." He wrote:

> Up to the end of the Vatican Council one was able to observe a dual activity against the socialist countries and also against the progressive and communist movements in other countries. This double game consisted of the Vatican using all official institutions and Church institutions for the propagation of its politics and attaining certain objectives in relation to socialist countries. However, independent of this "official" activity, the Vatican, with the help of various orders and even government of a few capitalist states, created an extensive network of covert propaganda and subversive centers in a number of West European countries. These centers, operating under various guises such as scientific, cultural and welfare institutions, conducted "unofficial" activities which will be continued in the future, aimed especially against the socialist countries.

15. Cardinal Koenig was seriously injured in an auto accident while traveling to Zagreb, Yugoslavia, to attend the funeral of Cardinal Stepinac. He was taken to a local hospital. As he was recovering, he noticed a portrait of Marshal Tito hanging on the wall of his room. "Then it came to me that after getting well, the Archbishop of Vienna must pay more attention to the neighboring countries in the East." He did and became known as "a man of the East," regularly visiting Cardinal Mindszenty at the American embassy in Budapest, where he had sought asylum from communist authorities who wanted to imprison him.

The "official" activities are carried out by various trustees. During council session, and especially after Vatican II closed, Vatican circles were active to centralize these hitherto dual activities. At this point we do not have sufficient information regarding the conception of this planned organ. Nevertheless, one can already observe a rivalry between various institutions of the Vatican as to who would lead this center. In this regard, the Jesuits have displayed particular interest in assuming a leading role in the activities of the Secretariat for Unbelievers, especially in centralizing the anticommunist activities. Independent of the secretariat, existing Vatican centers continue their activities aimed chiefly against the socialist countries. *For this reason, further Bearbeitung (i.e., infiltration) of these centers is absolutely essential"* [emphasis added].[16]

The report closed with notes on the behavior of Vatican II participants who were members of the Ostakademie, a Catholic Institution in Koenigstein, a town near Frankfurt in West Germany. [Editor's note: The Ostakademie was formed at the height of the Cold War in 1958. It dealt with problems of the Church in communist countries, including persecution of believers and refugee problems.] "These participants are of the opinion that any type of diplomatic relations of the Vatican with East European countries contribute to complications within the Catholic Church. Therefore it was decided to actively contravene in the progressive trends within Catholic movements. Besides the main task of battling communism and against the so-called 'leftwing Catholicism' decided upon in Koenigstein, must be the study of relations between the Soviet Union and the rest of the

---

16. Annex 1241/66 to report on Vatican II, top secret translation from the Russian. BSTU No. 000207-000214.

East bloc countries as well as the deepening discrepancy between the communist leaders and the masses."

The Vatican II reports arrived at 12 Ulitsa Lubyanskaya in Moscow, the KGB headquarters, just a few months after the takeover by Yuri Andropov in 1967. Andropov immediately ordered an extensive re-organization of directorates of the KGB. Responsibility for keeping tabs on anti-government and communist party activities, as well as surveil-lance and control of religious groups, was taken out of the Second Directorate, which was generally responsible for internal security. These tasks now became the responsibility of a newly created Fifth Directorate. Andropov appointed V. F. Kadyshev, a party hack with no security experience, to head the new operation. Kadyshev had been propaganda secretary in the provincial party committee of the Stavropol region, the same area where Andropov came from. The organizing of the new directorate as well as preoccupation with increas-ingly vocal political dissidents apparently delayed for some months the analysis of the Vatican II spy reports. When Andropov was finally briefed, he could not help but weigh the possibility that the Vatican's attempts of improving relations with the Soviet Union and the entire East bloc was part of a well-thought-out disinformation operation. It seemed to him that two could play the same game of espionage and subversion. Thus, in early 1969, Yuri Andropov ordered intensifying espionage operations against the Holy See.[17] Besides the prime target, the pope, he was particularly interested in the activities of Archbishop Agostino Casaroli, who was known as the Vatican's "secret agent" for his travels to European communist states, arriving at borders in civilian clothes for meetings with communist officials. Eventually, every department of the Church had been infiltrated.

---

17. Christopher Andrew and Vasili Mitrokhin, *The Sword and the Shield* (Basic Books, New York, N.Y., 1999).

2 THE VATICAN'S OSTPOLITIK

President John Kennedy told the embattled people of West Berlin on June 26, 1963, that he was one of them. "Ich bin ein Berliner," I am a Berliner, he exclaimed to the roar of several hundred thousand as he spoke in front of city hall flanked by Chancellor Konrad Adenauer, Gen. Lucius D. Clay of Berlin Airlift fame, and Berlin mayor Willy Brandt. It was a tough anticommunist speech. The people were so fired up that authorities feared they might just head for the Wall less than a mile to the east and tear it down with bare hands. It could have been a bloodbath, as East German border guards were always quick to shoot at those trying to escape or anyone climbing over it from the west. But after the president signed the Golden Book, the city's record of its most distinguished visitors, the crowd dispersed peacefully.

In the afternoon, President Kennedy addressed the students at the Free University in West Berlin. As he stood in the university garden, he looked at his speech, which had already been distributed to the press, then put it back into his jacket pocket and spoke off the cuff. It was a display of political resoluteness but dampened by a desire to find a way to end the Cold War "by taking small steps" toward conciliation.[1] "The shield of the military commitment to guard the freedom of West Berlin, which I confirmed this morning, will not be lowered or put aside so long as its presence is needed," the president declared. "But behind that shield it is not enough to mark time, to adhere to a status quo, while awaiting a change for the better."

Less than a month later, Egon Bahr, a confidant and adviser of West Berlin's Mayor Brandt, a ranking Social Democrat, lectured at the Evangelical Academy in Bavaria on West Germany's future foreign policy vis-à-vis communist Eastern Europe. Bahr echoed Kennedy's "small steps" theory, calling for "Wandel durch Annaeherung," change through rapprochement. Bahr's lecture became Brandt's policy when he was elected as West Germany's first socialist chancellor, and in January 1970 he announced his "Ostpolitik," Eastern Policy. This was a policy of détente with the Soviet Union and its East European satellites, resulting in treaties renouncing the threat of force, recognizing the East German communist government, and expanding commercial relations. Brandt's most immediate task was to "seek an act of conciliation" with Moscow. But before making his trip to the Kremlin scheduled for August 12, he traveled to Rome for an audience on July 12 with Pope Paul VI. Thus, receiving a copy of the 10-page stenographic transcript of the meeting from a KGB spy, the Polish priest Dabrowski, was like manna from heaven. The discussion between

1. I covered the event as an AP correspondent. In a conversation after the speech, McGeorge Bundy, one of Kennedy's advisers, told me that he sensed the tension at city hall and that he had told the president that "he went too far" and that he needed to tone down the university address.

the pope and Chancellor Brandt was also attended by Archbishop Casaroli.[2] The archbishop, who had years of experience in the Vatican's Department of Extraordinary Affairs, had studied Bahr's lecture. Although he was the already the emissary of Pope John XXIII to communist regimes, he pursued even more actively a policy of closer contacts with authorities in Eastern European nations in an effort to lessen repression of his Church after the election of Pope Paul VI. His activities even became known as the Vatican's Ostpolitik. Recognizing the archbishop's experience in dealing with communists, highlighted by his successfully reaching a partial accord between Hungary and the Holy See and his efforts during the unrest in Poland, Pope John Paul II promoted him to Cardinal and in July 1979 appointed him to the second-highest office, secretary of state.

Before reporting the questions and answers from the pope's session with Chancellor Brandt, the introduction said the information was furnished by a "vetted source from which we have previously received valuable information." The report said that the analyses of previously obtained documents "gave no rise to suspect disinformation," but cautioned that "this cannot be completely discounted." It was the first time such caution was noted in the nearly one thousand documents examined by this writer. In other words, Dabrowski's information furnished in the past was judged as "genuine," but he was not yet completely trusted. The topic of the meeting, the KGB was told, concerned questions regarding Chancellor Brandt's Ostpolitik, the internal situation in West Germany, as well as questions regarding relations between the Bonn government and the Western allies. After the usual polite exchange of greetings, Brandt said: "Your Holiness knows what I am pursuing. The government for which I am

---

2. MfS Document X/2265, top-secret translation from the Russian dated September 14, 1970. BSTU No. 0002217-226.

responsible, and which represents the German people, is seeking peaceful paths with our East European neighbors." Pope Paul replied that any activity for "fostering peace enjoys the pleasure of the heavens." Brandt replied that he "wished that the words of his Holiness could be heard by the gentlemen Kiesinger, Barzel, and Strauss," prompting the pope to respond: "All are good Christians. I am not talking about them as politicians, that is another question. I am fully informed about them." The chancellor was referring to three of his major political opponents of the conservative Christian Democratic Union (CDU). Kurt Georg Kiesinger preceded Brandt as Chancellor of West Germany, Rainer Barzel was head of the CDU parliamentary faction, and Franz Josef Strauss was defense minister, all staunch anti-communists and opposed to détente with the Soviets.

Chancellor Brandt, who fled to Norway after the Nazis seized power, remarked that he wanted to draw the attention of the pope to the fact that "no one is quite clear how high the cost is that our people need to bear for the crimes committed by Hitler and his supporters." He told the Holy Father that "as far as the West is concerned, we have become allies, but with the East we have no peaceful ties." Brandt was obviously wrestling with the fact that his unilateral dealings with the Soviets at the height of the Cold War might be construed by the West as a sellout. Pope Paul assured Brandt that he viewed the German people as a "civilized and Christian people." The West German chancellor replied: "We must show the people of Eastern Europe and the world the new face of Germany, our real face." The pope said he had been informed that the negotiations with the Soviet Union "are approaching a positive conclusion." Chancellor Brandt replied that there were still "a few questions which need to be clarified, not only with the Russians, but also with our English and American friends." He added that his foreign minister, Walter Scheel, would be traveling shortly to London, to Washington, and after that to Moscow. "I would like to convince our allies that all that we are doing, as well as the selflessness we are exhibiting, is to serve the peace for all."

The ensuing conversation between the pope and Chancellor Brandt was of such great value to the Moscow negotiators that it must have moved KGB boss Andropov to send a glowing note of thanks to his Polish colleagues who had recruited Dabrowski. Pope Paul VI asked whether the agreement to be signed with the Soviets would be "of great significance," to which Brandt replied: "Yes, very great." He explained that coming to an agreement would signify that Moscow no longer viewed West Germany as an enemy state and would thus establish a "new type of relationship with other East European nations and a new climate for Berlin." The pope said he had been told that there were differences of opinion between the Brandt government in Bonn and the Western allies because "some initiatives [Ed.: by the West German side] had not been coordinated." The chancellor's answer:

> I have personally informed our allies thoroughly, but the fact is that because of technical and timely reasons, we could not always inform them immediately. Earlier I was told that especially we Germans should ease the contacts with the big powers, meaning between the USA and the USSR. Mr. Wilson [British prime minister Harold Wilson] agreed with me. But Mr. Pompidou [French foreign minister Georges Pompidou], it seems to me, does not wish that our initiatives dominate European diplomacy. I told him that we are doing the ground work. I feel that if they [Ed.: the Western allies] are no longer forced to concentrate on the German Question, then it would be easier for them to concentrate on other questions. Mr. Pompidou told me that he looks favorably at this way of thinking. He wanted my guarantees concerning the Berlin Question and I gave them to him.

President Pompidou's reference to Berlin echoed the concern voiced by West Germany's Western allies that the socialist chancellor might go it alone to reach an agreement with the Soviet Union over easing relations with the other communist bloc countries, especially with East Germany and Poland. As mentioned earlier, this same concern was voiced often, at times vehemently, by the conservative opposition of Brandt's Social Democratic Party (SPD). Considering that one of Brandt's closest confidants and assistants, as well as other members of the SPD, were spies for the Stasi, the East German secret police which shared pertinent information with the Soviet KGB, this dissention was not news for the Soviets. However, coming straight from the horse's mouth, so to speak, solidified the information for the Soviet negotiators and gave them an edge. One of their most valuable sources was Günter Guillaume, a Berlin photographer who was recruited by East German intelligence and trained as an espionage agent specifically to infiltrate the Social Democratic Party. He managed to ingratiate himself so well with top party functionaries that he became a paid functionary and in short order attracted the attention of Brandt. After his election as chancellor, Brandt brought Guillaume to his Bonn chancellery and got him a top secret security clearance. He rose to become a personal assistant to Brandt with access to the highest government secrets. In 1973, an investigator for the federal counterespionage agency was working on a case in West Berlin involving a photographer who had "defected" from the East. When the detective noticed that his suspect had close ties to Guillaume, he opened a second investigation. After nearly a year under tight surveillance, Guillaume was arrested, charged with high treason, and sentenced to a mere 13 years in prison. He was released in 1981 and exchanged for Western spies caught in Eastern Europe. Chancellor Brandt was forced to resign.[3]

3. John O. Koehler, *Stasi: The Untold Story of the East German Secret Police*, pp. 151–163 (Westview Press, Boulder, CO, 1999). Guillaume died in 1995 at the age of 68.

Following the papal audience on July 12, 1970, the chancellor met with Jean Villot, Pope Paul's secretary of state, and archbishops Giovanni Benelli and Agostino Casaroli, both members of the state secretariat. This meeting was separately reported to the KGB via Polish intelligence by an agent ensconsed in the secretary of state's office.[4] Brandt was quoted as expressing satisfaction that Pope Paul VI said he would use his influence to assure that the Christian Democratic Party opposition would not obstruct the Ostpolitik of the government. Brandt said the pope told him that "Mr. Kiesinger is a good Catholic and, if necessary, I am ready for a dialogue with him." Though it was known that there were differences among the Western allies over Brandt's dealings with the Soviets, coming directly from a report which had the chancellor lamenting to the Holy Father that the Ostpolitik of his government "has met with resistance" in Washington and Paris. He accused the U.S. and France of playing a double game. "While on the one hand the USA and France are supportive of our policies, one the other hand, however, they support my opposition. President Pompidou is afraid that the BRD [West Germany] could move to spearhead the easing of international tensions as a result of achieving better relations with the East." Chancellor Brandt spent some time pontificating on internal West German politics, saying that any agreement with the Soviets on normalizing relations with the East European communist countries would be viewed as a great triumph of his Social Democratic Party. Needless to say, the Soviets would go to great lengths in accommodating the leader of a Western socialist political party. Brandt signed the non-aggression

4. Italian Security Service Report No. 260 titled KGB Residentura in Rome charged with assisting a KGB agent to infiltrate Vatican objectives. The report, labeled "Delicate Source," surfaced during the assassination attempt investigation. It read in part: "Of incalculable interest were the interpreters who worked at the Office of the Secretary of State and at the Office of Public Affairs where they had access to a concentration of essential information on political affairs and they could be contacted through advertisement of job offers such as teachers and translators—jobs that did not pay very much."

treaty with the Soviet Union a month after his visit with the pope, on August 12. The accord called for normalization of diplomatic relations as well as confirming the territorial status quo between West Germany and the Soviet Union. Four months later, on December 7, the West German chancellor signed a non-aggression treaty with Poland, abandoning all territorial claims and recognizing each other diplomatically.

Chancellor Brandt's visit with Pope Paul VI prompted Archbishop Casaroli, who had years of experience in the Vatican's Department of Extraordinary Affairs, to restudy the 1963 lecture of Brandt's adviser Egon Bahr, who espoused a policy of "Wandel Durch Annaeherung," change through rapprochement, which formed the basis for West Germany's Ostpolitik. Although he had already been the emissary of Pope John XXIII to communist regimes, he pursued an even more active role in maintaining even closer contacts with authorities of Eastern European nations in an effort to lessen repression of his Church after the election of Pope Paul VI. After Chancellor Brandt's meeting with the pope, the cardinal's activities even became known as the Vatican's Ostpolitik around the world. Recognizing the archbishop's experience in dealing with communists, highlighted by his successfully reaching a partial accord between Hungary and the Holy See and his efforts during the unrest in Poland which began with anti-government riots in 1956, Pope John Paul II promoted him to cardinal and in July 1979 appointed him to the second-highest office, secretary of state.

Some unimaginative arch-conservative churchmen viewed Cardinal Casaroli's activities as overly pro-communist. He was even called the "Red" cardinal, which he totally ignored. The KGB and the "brother organs," as Moscow used to call sister services on the satellite countries, thought otherwise. Spies were planted in the cardinal's office, the Vatican's most sensitive group next to the pope's. East bloc intelligence services never lacked ingenuity and resourcefulness in their penetration efforts. A couple employed as the secretary of state's housekeepers were a particularly valuable KGB asset. They were Irene Trollerova, a native of Czechoslovakia, born in 1933, and her Italian-born husband Marco Torreta, a nephew of the cardinal. According to a 1990 statement by SISDE, the Italian Security Service, both were moles for the KGB, Marco Torreta since 1950. Irene returned from a visit to Czechoslovakia in the early 1980s with a ceramic statue of the Virgin Mary, about 10 inches high, a beautiful work of renowned Czech ceramic art. The couple presented the statue to Cardinal Casaroli, who accepted gratefully. What a betrayal by his own nephew! Inside the revered religious icon was a "bug," a tiny but powerful transmitter which was monitored from outside the building by the couples' handlers from the Soviet Embassy in Rome. The statue had been placed in an armoire in the dining room close to Cardinal Casaroli's office. Another eavesdropping device inside a rectangular piece of wood was hidden in the same armoire. Both were not discovered until 1990 during a massive probe initiated by Magistrate Rosario Priore in the aftermath of the assassination attempt on Pope John Paul II. The bugs had been transmitting until that time.

Communist secret police interest in the Vatican's Ostpolitik strategy regarding their churches and diocese in Eastern Europe had intensified in the early 1960s, as Archbishop Casaroli traveled frequently in Eastern Europe, including Czechoslovakia, Hungary, and Poland, to meet with church leaders and municipal and party officials. In July 1971, the East German secret police, the Stasi, circulated a 12-page top-secret and closely held analysis of the papal Ostpolitik, based on information furnished by a spy with access to the State Secretariat. The Vatican's policy is, it said, "to use all means—including the activities of the national churches—to foster 'liberalization' in the socialist [read communist] countries." These "means" include: "1. Gathering of information on the situation of Catholics as well as on

the political situation in the socialist countries through the strengthening of contacts to the national churches. Simultaneously, the Vatican relies on information, which it has obtained through its special
secretariats, the Institute for Church Sociology as well as through
emigrants. 2. Support foreign policy activities initiated by socialist
countries in the interest of raising the international prestige and the
role of the Vatican (i.e. European Security Conference)." With these
means, the spy opined, the following was to be achieved: "To undermine the community of socialist states by differentiating in dealings
with the various socialist countries. This includes development of
official relations, such as establishment of diplomatic relations with
Yugoslavia, signing of agreements with Czechoslovakia and Hungary.
Undermine the Marxist ideology and propagate the proposition that
religion stands outside the social system." Finally, the spy said that
the Vatican's effort includes compromising the Movement of Clergy
for Peace, the so-called liberation priests who were ardently pro-communist, a subject for a later chapter.

This analysis is the first I saw that dealt extensively with Casaroli's
activities. It said that the pope was personally most interested in the
development of the Vatican's Ostpolitik. "However, Casaroli's Moscow
visit in February, 1971, showed that difficulties [Ed.: in dealing with
communist countries] still need to be overcome." Citing an internal
Vatican report, the analysis said "in Moscow it became clear to him
that Moscow is interested in contacts, though less on concrete agreement with the Vatican on matters of interest to the Church." In Moscow
he relayed the Vatican's declaration on joining any nuclear weapons
nonproliferation agreement. The paper said reports from inside the
state secretariat reported considerable differences over how Ostpolitik
should be conducted between Casaroli and Archbishop Giovanni
Benelli, who was responsible for diplomatic relations with other countries. Casaroli's office at the time was charged with maintaining contacts with nations with which the Vatican had no diplomatic relations,

including China, North Korea, Myanmar (Burma), and Vietnam. "Casaroli maintains that the efforts to develop a Vatican Ostpolitik depended mainly on normalizing relations with the Soviet Union. Benelli, however, argues that normalizing relations with the People's Republic of China should take priority because of China's influence in Latin America and Asia which is being totally underestimated by Casaroli and other influential Vatican officials." At the time of this writing, the Holy See still had no diplomatic relations with Peking, although Pope Benedict XVI had dispatched Vatican officials for intermittent negotiations. The major stumbling block is the Vatican's refusal to renounce its relations with Taiwan. China's influence in Latin America is chiefly limited to trade which has had no apparent effect on the standing of the Catholic Church.

The East German secret police analysis concluded that Casaroli's "first step toward activating official international relations with the socialist countries has been successful vis-à-vis Yugoslavia because that country is, on its own, very interested in improving its relations with the Vatican because Tito, in the view of Vatican officials, feels it would improve relations between 6.5 million Croats and other Slavs. By establishing such official contacts, the Vatican's aims are to exploit them in its offensive against other socialist countries. Yugoslavia, according to Vatican views, is particularly suited to achieve those aims because of its significant Catholic population and because its government is pursuing an independent [Ed.: from Moscow] foreign policy." The identity of the source in the Vatican of the information used in the analysis was extremely sensitive, as the document cautioned: "This information is intended only for personal edification and, in the interest of source security, can not be utilized for publicity purposes."

It was to be expected that the Kremlin hierarchy would be shaken by the election of the Polish Cardinal Karol Wojtyla on October 16, 1978, as Pope John Paul II, as well as Pope John Paul's elevation of Archbishop Casaroli to lead the State Secretariat. A top-secret KGB report in June 1979, based on "sources" inside and outside the Vatican, said: "In view of the anticommunist views of John Paul II, who in his function as Archbishop of Krakow often sharply criticized socialist [Ed.: communist] society, the Catholic upper strata places great hope that he will be successful to re-establish the Vatican's anticommunist unity and to organize a new ideological offensive against the international communist movement. With his extreme anticommunist views, the new Pope will attempt to toughen the Vatican's Ostpolitik, especially through a more active campaign for 'the protection of human rights and religious freedom in socialist countries'." How Moscow misjudged the position of Cardinal Casaroli was evident when the report said that Pope John Paul II would encounter opposition from his new secretary of state, Cardinal Casaroli.

Another unidentified mole reported to the Soviet intelligence service, upon the change of personnel in the Vatican: "The personal secretary of the pope, the American priest John Magee, was transferred to the State Secretariat. He was replaced by Mons. Kabongo, a priest from Zaire who, despite his young age, has diplomatic experience. He previously served in the Secretariat for Public Affairs. The reason for the change is that the leadership of the American Church had tried, through the former personal secretary, to convince the pope that he should pursue the American policy in the Polish question and to practice more restraint in critiquing Western lifestyle. According to the pope's view, changes in the social system could be achieved under the leadership of the Church without bloodshed, because the Party is not in a position to lead the process of renewal, and because the Soviet Union is not able to interfere from a position of strength. Such a radical position forced upon the Vatican could lead to a confrontation between Church and State in Poland, something which the pope wants to avoid at any cost. Magee's transfer is aimed at weakening the American pressure." The report closed with a remark that the information was furnished by "competent sources" within the Vatican. Those competent sources were not just incompetent, but dead wrong. George Weigel, the author of the excellent biography of Pope John Paul II *Witness to Hope*, who knew Father Magee well, told me that the report illustrates the incompetence of the KGB and its sources. "Magee is a pure-bred Irishman. Kabongo had minimal diplomatic experience. Neither one of them had anything of consequence to do with the pope's interface with Solidarity or with the U.S. government." John Magee was promoted to serve as a bishop in Ireland. What, then, was the basis for the spy's report? Was it a deliberate effort to feed misinformation to lead the KGB analysts astray, or simply a desire to tell the spymasters what they wanted to hear?

The espionage penetration of Cardinal Casaroli's department did nothing to save the Eastern European communist parties from becoming history. One man who steadfastly ignored those of the Vatican hierarchy and who felt the secretary of state had been too accommodating to the Soviet Union, the Church's ideological foe, was Pope John Paul II. There is no question that Casaroli displayed enormous diplomatic skill, especially during the turbulent times in Poland during the 1970s and early 1980s. When he reached age 75 in 1989 he tried to retire, but the pontiff persuaded him to remain in office for another year in light of the fall of Communism in Eastern Europe and the ensuing diplomatic action the Vatican would be required to perform. Cardinal Casaroli died in 1998.

3 SPIES PENETRATE THE PAPAL SANCTUM

The efforts of East European communist governments and the Soviet regime to burrow their way into the inner workings of the highest level of the Church certainly were to be expected, as they viewed people's loyalty to the Church a direct betrayal of their loyalty to the Party and, therefore, "subversive activity" that had to be stopped. How well they succeeded, however, would not have been believed had the collapse of the regimes not occurred so rapidly that their intelligence services did not have sufficient time to destroy all of their explosive documents. Unfortunately, the documents obtained by me only date back to the late 1960s and cover merely a bit over a decade. Nevertheless, had the East European communist bloc managed to hang tough and overcome its domestic difficulties, the opponents of democratic nations would have had valuable tools for managing their foreign policy. Operating within the secretariat of the Holy Father were at least two spies who were able to provide the Soviet KGB with information on secret Vatican policies and actions.[1]

1. Copies of stenographic transcripts of private discussions are in possession of the author.

In addition, as Vatican officials cooperated with Western governments and revealed the Vatican's perspective, Western diplomats often reciprocated by revealing much to the Vatican about their policies and actions. Such revelations from Washington, London, and Bonn, intended only for Vatican ears, were reported to the KGB by its agents in the Holy See. Examples of this are described below.

On May 29, 1970, French foreign minister Maurice Schumann had a lengthy audience with Pope Paul VI. It was at the height of the Vietnam War, and President Richard M. Nixon was already weighing a U.S. withdrawal. The pope told Schumann he felt that he was worried about something. Schumann replied: "Worried? No. But I can not say that I am satisfied. We are very disturbed over Washington's mistakes. Cambodia—that is nonsense, pure nonsense."[2] He added that French president Georges Pompidou met with President Nixon in February to discuss the situation in Vietnam; they "agreed with all aspects, but then . . . your Holiness has seen [what happened]." Pope Paul VI, known as a close friend of the United States and a staunch anticommunist to the point that Polish authorities would not allow him to enter their country during the unrest, responded: "The President of the United States is convinced that this is the last, necessary effort."[3]

The French foreign minister then criticized the Americans for not sufficiently studying history, noting: "They should at least read their own newspapers of a few years ago, at a time when we entertained the same illusions vis-à-vis Indochina." The pope asked if this meant a negative assessment on the part of his visitor. "Yes, of

2. President Nixon, to prevent a total takeover of Cambodia by the communists, ordered U.S. forces to move into that country on April 30, 1970. See also: Henry Kissinger, *White House Years* (Little, Brown & Co., 1979).
3. Top-secret report to the KGB from Polish security service, dated August 13, 1970, including a copy of a stenographic report of the meeting. KGB provided a copy of the report to East German secret police register No. 2039/70—XX/4/1363/70. BSTU No. 000443.

course. I have personally spoken with Mr. Rogers [Ed.: U.S. secretary of state William P.] who talked about 'necessities,' but did not want to hear any advice. That doesn't mean just Asia, but in general." Seemingly puzzled, the pontiff inquired just what he meant. "Lately we have talked about the situation in Europe. It seems to me that the Americans don't comprehend it. They have their own world strategy. For them Europe is only a portion of the world, while for us it is everything. I have grasped for the first time that America, without realizing it, is apprehensive about her own responsibilities."[4]

Again, the pope seemed perplexed, if not exasperated: "I don't seem to understand." France's highest-ranking diplomat replied with a lengthy, convoluted explanation about a recommendation for an international conference which the U.S. government was ignoring while conducting clandestine talks in Paris with the Vietnam communists. "The Americans want negotiations within the framework of blocs which would mean recognition of [Ed.: communist] satellite states and not only because of the Soviet Union. Thereon rests the problem. The Americans say they that they do not wish to consider such a question, but the Washington diplomacy is working toward it. The mistake is that the negotiations would not take place between states but between blocs and in that way everything is to be decided between Washington and Moscow. This means robbing all peoples of hope, and I don't speak only about the peoples of the Soviet bloc." It became clear that the French government felt aggrieved that it was left out not only by what it perceived as the Nixon administration's "aggressive go-it-alone diplomacy" as it concerned relations with communist states, but also by the fact that West Germany's socialist chancellor Willy Brandt had announced his Ostpolitik on January 14, 1970. Regarding Brandt, the French minister told the pope: "We have reservations as to the method he selected. In reality, we do not

4. Ibid.

know very much about what he is doing. Brandt has reached the conclusion that it would be difficult to coordinate with us regarding measures which he perceives must be taken immediately. We demand more from Mr. Brandt. There exists between our states bilateral agreement which, however, now appears worse than it was in the past." In other words, "don't do anything that involves foreign policy, Herr Brandt, unless we have debated it."[5] Again the pope countered the complaint, saying "but I have been informed that certain results have been achieved, at least as it pertains to the general atmosphere." The French foreign minister disagreed and continued his complaints about carrying on four-power (U.S., Great Britain, France, and Soviet Union) talks "without knowing what the Germans in Bonn and the Poles in Warsaw are saying to each other, the Germans and the Russians in Moscow and the Americans and the Russians in Vienna."

And so the document went on in this vein for more than 1,100 words. How Soviet foreign minister Andrei Gromyko in Moscow must have been gleefully rubbing his hands when he read the transcript! Incidentally, the letter of transmittal for the transcript said the information came from the security services of Poland. The mole was undoubtedly a Polish priest assigned to the pope's secretariat.

While his French visitor unburdened himself of the dilemma facing his nation's international diplomacy and the frustrations with the Nixon administration, Pope Paul VI was reticent. He asked a question here, offered a terse comment there, but without ever revealing any substantive knowledge he had concerning President

5. On January 22, 1963, French president Charles de Gaulle and German (then West German) chancellor Konrad Adenauer signed the historic Franco-German treaty in Paris. Article II, paragraph 1 says: "The two governments will consult before any decision on all important questions of foreign policy and, in the first place, on questions of common interest, with a view to reaching as far as possible an analogous position." I was Associated Press chief correspondent in Bonn at the time and can attest to the consternation and dismay this paragraph created with U.S. ambassador to Bonn Walter C. Dowling, who told me angrily that the Bonn Foreign Ministry had not informed him ahead of time. Dowling retired shortly thereafter.

Nixon's effort to extricate the U.S. from the Vietnam conflict which he had learned a few months earlier.

Shortly before Christmas 1969, the pope received a special emissary from President Nixon, John A. Volpe, a former governor of Massachusetts who was then serving as secretary of transportation.[6] Volpe told the pope that President Nixon was engulfed by work, which is the reason why he sent him to the Vatican. "In this," the pontiff responded, "all are heartily welcome. The president knows exactly what I think about the necessity of an exchange of our views. We have achieved very normal and very close relations. You know about that, Mr. Minister." At the time, Italy's domestic political situation was in flux, with the Communist Party and its union constantly stirring up trouble with strikes that erupted into riots. Secretary Volpe told the pope that he had meetings with a series of industrial and political leaders, including President Giuseppe Saragat, "who is a true friend of the American people and he told me he was worried." The pope said everyone was worried, to which his visitor replied that he was not. "But if we are not successful to find a road to peace! In Vietnam, the war continues. In the Middle East, tension is increasing."

Secretary Volpe responded: "Holy Father, Mr. Nixon has instructed me to tell you that he has a direct, secret contact with the government in Hanoi. He is a great optimist. I assume, however, that the road to peace will neither be easy, nor short. The relations with Moscow have improved as well. Our government will discuss the arms race with the Soviet government. That is now certain." The pope then remarked that, regarding a solution of the Vietnam conflict, "the Chinese also wield important influence." Secretary Volpe agreed and pointed out that the problems between China and the Soviet Union "have changed many matters in favor of the United States . . . Mr. Nixon has

6. Copy of stenographic transcript labeled "Top Secret—Translation from Polish" dated Dec. 12, 1969, transmitted to MfS International Relations Dept. X. BSTU No. 000247.

told me that perhaps in one, or at the latest two years, he will find a
solution [Ed.: for improved China-U.S. relations]. We also have contacts in Peking." Actually the "China Solution" was found even more
quickly. Henry Kissinger, the national security adviser to the president, made a secret trip to China in June 1971 to prepare the way for
the president's visit in February 1972. Evidently, Pope Paul VI and
President Nixon had established a great measure of mutual trust
when one views the sensitivity of the information relayed by the secretary. Such information would have hardly been shared with the Vatican had Washington known about the communist espionage
infiltration of the Holy See's most sensitive office. And here was the
Polish espionage agency's brilliance: they infiltrated the party which
the West would have least suspected.

On June 6, 1970, President Nixon appointed a confidant and vet-
eran diplomat, Henry Cabot Lodge Jr., as his especial envoy to the
Holy See.[7] Later, on July 3, Lodge had a lengthy meeting with Cardinal Jean Villot, the Vatican secretary of state, and his deputy Archbishop Giovanni Benelli.[8] Lodge touched upon a variety of
potentially volatile East-West problems. He informed the cardinals
that "the U.S. government views the situation in the Middle East as
very disquieting and considers the presence of the USSR in this region
as a fact of great significance. Washington believes there are two
groupings within the Soviet Union hierarchy—the moderates and the
irreconcilable, the viewpoints of which are split on questions of
Middle East policy and which influence interchangeably the foreign
affairs ministry. In this situation, it is difficult to predict when one
can achieve a settlement of the conflict." He opined that the disquiet

---

7. Formal diplomatic relations between the Vatican and the United States were not established until 1984 when President Ronald Reagan appointed William A. Wilson, a prominent California business executive, as the first U.S. Ambassador Extraordinary and
Plenipotentiary to the Holy See.
8. Top-secret KGB report based on information from Polish intelligence dated September
2 and transmitted to East German intelligence, log No. 2170/70, BSTU No. 000240.

besetting both governments stemmed from the activities of Arab military factions. "This creates a climate which can be politically exploited by Peking." Washington, he explained, was worried. China, in view of its tensions with Moscow which had already escalated to skirmishes along their borders, might meddle in the Middle East.

The ambassador, like Secretary Volpe before him, touched upon the Vietnam conflict and reiterated that "President expects to reach an agreement with Hanoi and will shortly launch important diplomatic initiatives," adding that "its results, however, are difficult to predict since the DRV [Democratic Republic of Vietnam] is interchangeably either under the influence of Moscow or of Peking, and between them there exists no uniform thoughts on how to handle this question."

Ambassador Lodge spoke at length about efforts to ease East-West tension, including the Strategic Arms Limitations Talks (SALT) in Vienna. "President Nixon believes that the negotiations in Vienna are proceeding in the right direction, but that the results will depend on the totality of relations between Moscow and Washington. He again brought up proposals for a European conference on security questions." But chances of holding one "still are very far in the future." Among other considerations "is the fact that the Soviet Union does not want, or are afraid, to pull their troops out of countries of the Warsaw Pact."[9] Soviet military presence "is not only significant from a military point of view, but they are also the support of communist

9. The Soviet Union had first proposed such a conference in 1954 but it was dismissed by the Western powers as a mere effort to stabilize the status quo, i.e., Moscow's grip on its satellite states, preserving the division of Germany. In 1969 Finish President Urho Kekkonen, whom some U.S. diplomats believed was being manipulated by the Soviets, revived the proposal and sent it to other governments. After many tedious multi-national consultations and preliminary meetings, the Conference on Security and Cooperation in Europe (CSCE) was held in Helsinki, resulting in the Helsinki Accord, dealing with security and border issues, issues of cooperation, free movement of people and information, and the future of the CSCE. (Some of the information in this note was contained in a July 31, 2005, article published by the Helsinki Sanomat newspaper.)

power which, in the event of a Soviet troop withdrawal, would disin-
tegrate." It would be another 20 years before this analysis came true.

In his talk with Cardinal Villot and Archbishop Benelli, Ambassador Lodge, as did French foreign minister Schumann during a talk
with Pope Paul VI, also mentioned West German chancellor Brandt's
Ostpolitik, which he said was being supported by President Nixon,
albeit with some reservations. "An improvement of relations between
the BRD [Federal Republic of Germany] and the communist countries is in the interest of all Western nations. The president, however,
is of the opinion that Bonn's initiatives need to be in tune with all
allies, especially with the United States, which does not intend to
relinquish the responsibilities and rights inherent when it concerns
the area of creating a future Germany." Ambassador Lodge emphasized that Washington "supports the recognition of the Oder-Neisse
border [Ed.: Poland's once-disputed Western border recognized by
Chancellor Brandt] on condition that the Soviet Union recognizes
the existence of the special relations between West Berlin [Ed.: then
under control of the Soviet Union and the Western allies] and the
BRD." The memorandum detailing Ambassador Lodge's summation
of such sensitive U.S. foreign policy consideration reaching the
Kremlin via the spies in the pope's office certainly was an incredible
security breach, to say the least.

The following day, on July 4, Pope Paul VI received Ambassador
Lodge for talks which generally centered on the previous day's report
to his secretary of state.[10] The Holy Father reiterated the Vatican's anxiety over the war in Vietnam, to which the ambassador replied that
President Nixon was working hard to find an equitable solution. The
pope responded: "Mr. Ambassador, I would like to mention at this

10. Top-secret copy of stenographic transcript headed "translation from the Russian
language—information obtained from the security organs of the VR (Peoples Republic)
Poland and transmitted to East German intelligence," Log No. X/2172/70 dated September 2, 1970. BSTU No. 000233.

point that without a realistic study of the China question, one can search in vain to find a different path to peace in Asia. President Nixon knows how I feel about the question." How right he was, upon reviewing history with the benefit of hindsight. Ambassador Lodge reassured the pope that the U.S. government was aware of the pontiff's interest in this question. "The question is the establishment of a connection to Peking. Please believe me, Your Holiness, I know the Asian questions, but neither I nor other members of President Nixon's staff have been successful in completely understanding how one should proceed with Peking. England and France have ambassadors there, but they are in the same position." Nevertheless, replied the pope, "Something needs to be done. Let God enlighten us . . . perhaps together we will find the proper way."

Ambassador Lodge told the pope that Washington felt that one needed to wait for the results of negotiations between Moscow and Peking.[11] The pope voiced his usual skepticism when it came to questions involving relations between Peking and Moscow. "Many think

11. Tension between the Soviet Union and China surfaced in early 1969 along the Ussuri River running between the two nations in northeast Asia. It began with a Chinese ambush of a Soviet border patrol in which at least 30 Russians were killed. There were other skirmishes over islands in the Argun and Amur rivers. However, Soviet actions began in the early 1960s. At a reception in West Berlin in the fall of 1963, the author had a conversation with Andrei Smirnov, Soviet ambassador to West Germany who was on a visit to the divided city. Smirnov expressed concern over Peking's belligerency toward the USSR and mentioned, as if almost in passing, that some Soviet troops would be transferred from East Germany to the Chinese border. This was not a slip of the tongue. The ambassador knew full well that this would be a news item for the Associated Press. In fact, the author was able to establish within days that the Soviet's had already vacated a tactical nuclear missile facility near the town of Halle on Route 6, which was off limits to the U.S., British, and French military liaison missions accredited to the Soviet commander in East Germany. Dropping tidbits as Smirnov did was common for Soviet diplomats as a way of fishing for reactions from other governments. Another example was when William L. Stearman, a State Department Soviet affairs expert then dealing with North Vietnam affairs, was asked, in a most casual manner over lunch, by a Soviet embassy official how the U.S. would react if the USSR were to attack Chinese nuclear plants at Lop Nor. Dr. Stearman said this resulted in formulating contingency foreign policy plans in the event of a Sino-Soviet war.

so, but I am of the opinion that it would be a mistake to view Peking as the sole alternative to an agreement with Moscow. I even believe that Moscow can not view an agreement with Peking, which in any case would be difficult enough to achieve, as the only way for the future. You see, we in the Vatican are convinced that Moscow wishes for an agreement with the West European states and, on a broader level, with you, the Americans. However, the Russians are mistrustful. That is their shortcoming, perhaps their worst. Nevertheless, the greater their problems with China, the more they turn to the West. Let me say it bluntly: also toward us, here in the Vatican, in a variety of ways and means." The latter statement seemed to indicate that he suspected that his office had been infiltrated. Ambassador Lodge gave assurances that he would inform President Nixon of the Holy Father's opinions.

As the audience neared its end, Pope Paul VI made some remarks which must have puzzled the ambassador. "Mr. Ambassador, my worry is not over. I know that God will not allow me to witness peace on earth. I feel distinctly that the end of the mission, with which I had been entrusted, is nearing. But I wish that you, Mr. Ambassador, should know that even in the hour of death, I will sacrifice myself for peace on earth. I beseech you to repeat this to the president." This statement was a poser, indeed. The pontiff was 73 years old and there was no indication at that time that he was seriously ill and near death. In fact, he lived another eight years, though he was frail toward the end. Was it a premonition that prompted his remarks? Just over four months later, on November 27, Pope Paul VI was on a pilgrimage to Southeast Asia. When he stopped at the Manila airport, he faced an assassination attempt. A Bolivian communist artist and member of a movement called Surrealism, Benjamín Mendoza y Amor Flores, lunged at the pope with a knife. He was quickly subdued. Although it was first denied by the Vatican, it was later learned that he did suffer a minor stab wound, but he was able to continue his travels. There was no evidence that the attack was more than a "random event," although the painter's group was associated with the so-called liberation theology.

In the pope's absence, the communist spies, embedded within the ornate offices of the Holy See and performing their treacherous deeds within walls adorned by crucifixes, were working like vacuum cleaners purloining the secrets that Western governments, especially Washington, shared with the pope. Their "handlers" most likely used enciphered cables transmitted from their respective embassies in Rome, as the material wound up with their intelligence services in less time than it would have taken the postal or even courier routes. At a time of a volatile Cold War period—the Vietnam War heading toward a solution and the Middle East still a powder keg—time was of the essence. For example, a top-secret outline of a meeting between Pope Paul VI and U.S. president Richard M. Nixon at the Vatican on September 28, 1970, reached the KGB in Moscow via the Polish intelligence service within a few days and was distributed to the East Germans and translated by October 19.[12] Incredible!

Contrary to the usual stenographic recording of the discussions at meetings between the Holy Father and important political visitors, President Nixon's visit was noted with a mere one-page report, saying the information was supplied "by a believable source." It said the pope "demanded from Nixon the assurance that the USA will not start a new conflict in the Near East." This means that the two men discussed the ongoing tensions between Israel and the Arab countries. The report said the pope "informed the president about his upcoming trips to Australia, the Philippines, and New Zealand, where he *will more sharply criticize the continuation of the war in Vietnam which, in turn, will contribute toward solidifying and expanding the influence of the Church*" [emphasis added]. Mr. Nixon then informed the pope

12. Ministry for State Security (MfS) document No. X/2597 titled "Regarding the Audience of Nixon by Pope Paul VI." BSTU No. 000216.

that he would shortly announce a further and more significant reduction of U.S. troops in Vietnam. Indeed, President Nixon announced two weeks later, on October 12, the withdrawal of 40,000 American military personnel. The president, according to the spy's report, emphasized his continuing interest in the Vatican's liaison effort in the exchange of prisoners. "The pope also encouraged Nixon to carry out arms reduction so that in this way money could be saved for use in liquidating illiteracy in South America," the report concluded.

Egyptian president Gamal Abdel Nasser, whose blockade of Israeli shipping through the Gulf of Aqaba led to the Six-Day War and the disastrous defeat of Egypt in 1967 and a Soviet military alliance, died in September 1970 and was succeeded by Anwar Sadat.[13] In a renewed effort to at least stabilize the Middle East, U.S. secretary of state William P. Rogers made an extensive trip visiting, among other countries, Saudi Arabia, Jordan, Lebanon, Egypt, and Israel before meeting with Pope Paul VI on May 8, 1971.[14] Rogers briefed the pontiff on his trip, explaining that he told the respective governments the United States would support credits of "several billion dollars" for the economic development which would also help to solve the problem of Palestinian refugees to "forestall the necessity of their return to Israeli territory." As the quid pro quo, he said, Washington wished the recognition of Israel. "Israel says it wants guaranties for secure borders, but in reality it wants to annex part of the occupied territories which we oppose." In closing, the secretary told the pope that Israel opposed the massive financial aid because it feels it would "merely deepen the tendency for the liquidation of Israel."[15]

13. Sadat, following the Camp David talks with Israeli prime minister Menachem Begin, signed a peace treaty with Israel in 1979, for which both men were awarded the Nobel Prize. Sadat was assassinated by Muslim fundamentalists in 1981.
14. A year earlier, Rogers had promoted a cease-fire in the Middle East which lasted until the 1973 war. He signed the Vietnam Peace Agreement.
15. Top-secret KGB memorandum, based on information from Polish intelligence, to the Stasi. Log No. X/1539/71. BSTU No. 000201.

Because the Soviets still maintained a military and intelligence presence, such information must have been shared with the Egyptian government, which reacted within four months. President Sadat dispatched his special envoy Antoine Canaan to Rome for four days of meetings with the hierarchy of the Vatican, including cardinals Johannes Willebrands, Fuerstenberg, and Gaspariego. Ambassador Canaan briefed them on the political situation in the Middle East. The top-secret memorandum, which the Soviet KGB obtained from a Polish spy via Warsaw's intelligence service, said the discussion centered on assistance to Egypt "by the Vatican as well as various Catholic nations, particularly South American." The Vatican officials promised Egypt political support. "The Vatican will *above all* [emphasis added] support the rapprochement between Egypt and the USA in order to accelerate the change in domestic politics [Ed.: Egyptian] *to the right* [Ed.: from socialist]. However, as a "quid pro quo the Vatican demands Egypt's interference in Libya, where the present government is waging an open struggle against Catholicism, and the reduction of the influence of 'the Muslim brothers' in this battle." Canaan replied that in his opinion this would not be feasible.

In digesting this information, as well as the effort of U.S. secretary of state Rogers, the Kremlin surely must have been rattled. Whatever apprehension ensued was not misplaced. Less than a year later, in July 1972, the quest for diminishing Soviet intentions to control Middle East political affairs was dealt a major blow. President Sadat, tired of high-handed meddling, ordered the immediate withdrawal of about 5,000 Soviet military advisers as well as all combat air force personnel numbering more than 10,000.

While President Nixon was preparing for his June 1972 trip to Moscow, the pope met briefly with Ambassador Lodge, whom he told that he was pleased that the president would meet with the Soviet leadership. "It is my opinion that the Soviet leadership *honestly* [emphasis added] wishes to achieve useful agreements with the West on the whole, and with the USA especially." The ambassador might well have been astounded by the pope's use of the word "honestly" as, judging by past Soviet actions, that word hardly fitted the Kremlin's vocabulary. Thus, Lodge replied that the American government was "not completely convinced . . . President Nixon wants to use his visit to examine the good intentions of the Soviet leadership and, according to our view, our contacts with Peking will be useful in negotiations with the Soviet Union." The pope's response was not recorded by the spy who reported on this meeting to East German intelligence.[16] He either did not hear it himself to accurately record it, or found it not worth reporting. As the report was not based on a stenographic transcript as was usual, and since it was transmitted to East Berlin instead of Moscow, it is highly likely that the spy was a Benedictine monk on the Stasi payroll code-named "Lichtblick," whose activities will be examined in a later chapter. Of course, the report, labeled "Top Secret—Return all copies," indicating the stringent compartmentalization of such communications, was duly handed over to the Stasi's KGB liaison officer.

On January 27, 1973, a week after the inauguration of Richard Nixon for his second term as president, the Vietnam War cease-fire agreement was signed in Paris after prolonged negotiations. While the talks were in progress, thousands more from both sides of the conflict died.[17] The agreement provided that all foreign combat troops, except nearly 10,000 military advisers and civilians, would be out of the country within 60 days, while North Vietnam forces would

---

16. Stasi report log No. XX/4/669/72 dated May 4, 1972. BSTU No. 000293.
17. Signers for the U.S.: Henry Cabot Lodge, Jr., delegation head; William P. Rogers, secretary of state. For the Republic of (South) Vietnam: Tran Van Lam, foreign minister. For the Democratic Republic of (North) Vietnam: Nguyen Duy Trinh, foreign minister. For the Provisional Revolutionary Government of the Republic of South Vietnam: Nguyen Thi Binh. By the time of the signing, more than 58,000 Americans and well over 3 million Vietnamese, military and civilians from both sides, had died.

remain in the south but could not be reinforced. South Vietnam was to remain an independent entity. It was in this emotion-laden atmosphere, particularly acute among the Southern officials and most of the population, that South Vietnam foreign minister Tran Van Lam visited the Vatican for an audience with Pope Paul VI. The poignancy of the conversations between the pontiff and the anguish voiced by both men is heart rending at times. To get a better understanding of the feelings of both men, it is worth transcribing the entire document that the spy passed on to his communist handlers, and how the text of the conversation encouraged Hanoi to violate the agreement practically before the ink was dry. The document translated verbatim as found in the Stasi archives:

Department X

Berlin March 29 1973
Log No. X/ 980/73
Translation from the Russian

TOP SECRET!

INFORMATION FROM THE SECURITY ORGANS OF THE PEOPLES REPUBLIC OF POLAND

Stenographic transcript of negotiations between Paul VI and the Foreign Minister of South Vietnam, Tran Van Lam

VATICAN, FEBRUARY 22 1973

POPE: I greet you, Mr. Minister. May God bless you.

T.V.LAM: I thank your Holiness. I have the honor to deliver to you a letter and greetings from our President, Mr. Van Thieu.

POPE: That is very kind of him. We are thankful to President Thieu that he also thought of us. We must thank the merciful God that he has given us hope in these hours.

L.: Your Holiness, we are very worried. We feel ourselves as betrayed and abandoned. So many of our young people have perished for nothing.

P.: Only God knows the value of self-sacrifice, and not a single sacrifice offered to God will have been in vain.

L.: Our people now are experiencing hours of suffering. We became an object of barter in the hands of the great powers, and we believed that the United States is our friend.

P.: This they are, Mr. Minister. When they can maintain the peace, then your sacrifices will not have been in vain. Please believe us . . .

L.: For us this war has not yet ended.

P.: Mr. Minister, you surely mean the struggle for a free and peaceful development of your wonderful people. Should that be so, then we share your fears and those of President Van Thieu. The important factor is to put an end to this fratricidal war, a war not only between the children of one and the same God, but of one and the same home land as well.

L.: But we are still fighting.

P.: We know about that. We pray often to God that he spare the people, who are so dear to our hearts, of further sacrifices and pain.

L.: Mr. Nguyen Van Thieu instructed me to thank Your Holiness for the help which during all these years you have provided us either direct through the Papal Throne, or through representatives of various Catholic organizations.

P.: We thank you. We wanted to do much more, but unfortunately we are also dependent on the generosity of others.

L.: Our government entertains the hope that, in these difficult minutes, it will not also be abandoned by the Catholic Church.

P.: Our heart beats for you. We will never abandon you, but as you know, Mr. Minister, our voice does not always find resonance.

L.: However, in spite of this, the diplomacy of the Papal Throne favors the agreement between the United States and the government of Hanoi.

P.: Yes, that is true. In various circumstances we gave you to understand that above all the firing must cease. Those on the other side were your foes, but at the same time also your brothers. We told the same thing to Mr. Xuan Thuy.[18]

L.:   We felt very disappointed, and it was for us a great surprise, when we heard that Your Holiness wished to receive this communist.

P.:   We always receive all. This house is the House of God.

L.:   But they are the enemy of the Church and the enemy of all religions. They are the enemy of humanity.

P.:   We have nothing in common with their ideology, but we worry over the question of peace and the discontinuation of firing.

L.:   In our country we have almost one million of refugees from North Vietnam. In many cases they are Catholics and clergymen, who fled to us to escape communist persecution.

P.:   That is well known to us. God values the good that you have done. Who knows, perhaps today's happenings are the days of God's mercifulness. Please believe us, believe us, that most importantly is the seize fire.

L.:   But we already no longer feel safe from new communist attacks.

18. Le Duc Tho and Xuan Thuy, both high-ranking members of North Vietnam's Politburo, were Hanoi's primary alternating negotiators beginning in 1970, with Xuan Thuy the chief negotiator vis-à-vis Henry Kissinger at the Paris talks.

P.: Mr. Minister, God's mercifulness is unending. I beg you not to forget that times have changed.

L.: Our Catholic Bishops also are full of fear and are worried.

P.: We know that, Mr. Minister. But, look, it is necessary that one must trust in God in whose hands one must place oneself of his own free will.

L.: But I am talking about politics, and not about theology.

P.: Yes, indeed. The will of God shows itself in all spheres.

L.: But we cannot simply give in to the communists who occupy our Catholic soil.

P.: We have provided you help in every possible way. And despite that, we must jointly think about God's will and bow to it even then when it seems to us that things are not going well for us.

L.: Does that mean that the Papal Throne will also forsake us?

P.: What are you saying, Mr. Minister! We already have pulled together all of our resources in order to participate in the reconstruction of your glorious country.

L.: But still, the help is for those from the North.

P.: In your case the Papal Throne does not divide people according to borders. For us they all are children of a heavenly father.

L.: We are a people fighting for freedom.

P.: That makes us very happy, Mr. Minister. We wish to believe that it will help in freeing the political prisoners which are in your hands.

L.: When it comes to that question, we have the best intentions. However, the opponent has no political prisoners of ours since almost all were murdered.

P.: A fratricidal war is the most horrible of all wars. This time you are doing your duty. Somebody has to make the beginning.

L.: In a few days in Paris I shall see the good will of our foe.

P.: Mr. Minister, if you do all that depends on you, you will achieve peace and receive God's blessings.

L.: But we are threatened by communism.

P.: According to our opinion, you now have exactly the possibility to push ahead with the question of neutralization of Vietnam, first in a divided, then in the united Vietnam.

L.: By the communists? No!

P.: We mean that such a process will be carried out by the sons of the Vietnam people.

L.: However, Your Holiness, we are of the opinion, that the decision on this question is, at this point, not even close.

P.: The developments of the events will be shown. God will decide.

L.: Before I travel to Paris, I wish to beg your Holiness to exercise your great authority to influence Washington not to allow any communist aggression against my country and the neighboring states.

P.: Our staff maintains a steady contact with the staff of Mr. Nixon. We believe we have already used all of the means available to us.

L.: Allow me to remark that you have already used these means in favor of our opponents.

P.: For peace, Mr. Minister. Be so kind and relay to President Van Thieu our heartfelt best wishes and assure him of our fatherly understanding for all of the Vietnamese people and for your state in the South.

L.: I thank Your Holiness.

P.:   And we wish to also add our apostolic blessing for all
      those in Vietnam who expect justice, freedom and a
      free dissemination of the truth.

L.:   I thank Your Holiness.

The reader will surely have felt Foreign Minister Lam's frustration,
impatience and, at times, despair over the fate of his country. He was
certainly correct in expressing his doubts about the integrity of any
agreement with North Vietnam. While the United States fully complied, the North was in blatant violation virtually from day one. The
fact that the pope's hands were also "tied" from providing aid that
came off as too biased politically is also clear. The axiom that ALL in
need must be helped was clearly a source of vexation to Foreign Minister Lam as well. The war-weary South and its leadership was no
match for the communist invaders who continued to enjoy the support of the Soviet Union and China. And, of course, when this transcript reached Hanoi, the communist leadership could not have
harbored any doubts that their resumption of armed aggression
would go unopposed by any Western government.[19]

Less than a year after the pope's fateful meeting with the South
Vietnamese foreign minister, the Holy Father met with U.S. secretary of state Henry Kissinger, who succeeded William Rogers in
1973. Apparently the communists' mole in the pope's secretariat
had no opportunity to copy the usual stenographic transcript.
However, he did furnish the KGB with a two-page report of the
most important subjects touched upon during the discussions in

---

19. Intermittent fighting racked the South until a full-scale invasion, ordered by Hanoi's
Politburo, began in March, 1975 and culminated with the fall of Saigon on April 30
when U.S. Army Capt. Stuart A. Herrington was the last person boarding the last
U.S. helicopter lifting off the roof of the U.S. Embassy. President Thieu had accused the
U.S. of betrayal and left the country for Taiwan, later settling in England.

which Cardinal Casaroli, the Vatican's foreign policy expert, also participated.[20] The conversations centered on President Richard Nixon's meeting in Moscow with Soviet leader Leonid Brezhnev June 27 to July 3, 1974, during which a number of agreements and protocols were signed, including one limiting underground nuclear testing, between the U.S. and the Soviet Union.[21] The United States considered the Moscow agreements of such importance that the pope was briefed three days later by Dr. Kissinger, who had accompanied the president to the Soviet capital. "According to Nixon's judgment, Kissinger reported, the leadership of the USSR is striving for a continuation of peaceful cooperation with the West, particularly with the USA, and that the latest meeting was an important step toward achieving significant agreements," the spy reported. Cardinal Casaroli was reported to have remarked that he noted that the Moscow talks failed to reach any agreement regarding the plan for military security. "Kissinger emphasized that there had been discussions regarding that question and, though no final results were reached, the talks were viewed as positive." The KGB was told that Kissinger told the pope that the Soviet Union "was very interested" in economic cooperation with the USA as well as in a "quick and positive" conclusion of the European Security Conference.[22] "While discussing the Near [Ed.: Middle] East question, Kissinger said the

20. East German MfS translation of KGB document based on information obtained through the Polish intelligence service. Document No. X/2700 dated August 20, 1974. BSTU No. 000110-111.

21. Other agreements and protocols: Long-term Economic, Industrial, and Technical Cooperation; Anti-ballistic Missile Treaty (ABM); Energy Cooperation Agreement; Housing and Construction Agreement; and the Scientific Research and Development of Artificial Hearts Cooperation Agreement.

22. Talks toward establishing the Organization for Security and Cooperation in Europe (OSCE) began in 1972 at the suggestion of the Soviet Union with the aim of using the talks to maintain its grip on the Eastern European communist nations. The Western nations, however, saw the talks as an effort to reduce tension, furthering economic cooperation, and obtaining improvements for the people of the communist bloc. (Reference: Wikipedia.)

USSR can very quickly resume diplomatic relations with Israel. But he said the Near East problem still is extremely difficult and so far no concrete formula has been found that could be accepted by the Security Conference." Dr. Kissinger's timing was way off. The Soviet had broken its relations with the Jewish state in 1967 at the outbreak of the Six-Day War, and these were not renewed until 1991. And the Middle East problem, rather than being settled, or at least diminished, continued on its bloody course. While the report may not have been of significant import to the Kremlin as had been previous information culled from the pope's meetings with foreign officials, it at least provided some snippets useful in formulating the Soviet's stance in further dealings with the United States.

In September, 1999, I myself visited Archbishop John P. Foley[23], a wonderful man whom I first met in the mid-1980s. The archbishop is president of the Pontifical Council for Social Communications. I discussed with him my project of exposing communist espionage against the Vatican and gave him copies of sensitive Vatican documents that inside spies had passed on to the enemies of the Church. When I translated the transcript of Pope Paul's audience with Minister Lam, Archbishop Foley was astonished. "But these are copies of the real conversation," he exclaimed. He was visibly dismayed by this betrayal. It was obvious that he had had no idea of the espionage problem. The archbishop passed the documents on to Secretary of State Cardinal Sodano, along with my request for a meeting with the cardinal or his deputy. In a letter to Archbishop Foley, Cardinal Sodano acknowledged receipt of the documents and wrote "I would appreciate it if you were to express my thanks to Mr. Koehler. At the present time, in fact, it is not necessary to disturb him further."[24] Did the cardinal already know about the incredible extent of the Vatican's

23. He was elevated to cardinal on November 27, 2007.
24. I have a copy of Cardinal Sodano's letter dated September 20, 1999.

espionage infiltration during communism's relentless efforts to oppress—i.e., destroy—Catholicism? I believe he did. On the other hand, he may have been simply too distraught and unwilling to face it as too upsetting.

While in Rome, a source told me, on condition of anonymity, that a laic attorney, Dr. Gianluigi Marrone, whose office at the time was in Vatican City, dealt with matters involving foreign espionage against the Vatican. I requested a meeting with Dr. Marrone by telephone and by letter. I never received an answer, which did not surprise me. It was par for the course that the Vatican would remain silent on matters so distressful to the Church.

The conversation of Pope Paul VI with Dr. Kissinger is the last spy report I found in the Stasi files. It is likely that other documents, including those recording the audiences granted later by Pope John Paul II to President Jimmy Carter, President Ronald Reagan, and other top U.S. officials were destroyed when East Germany collapsed. But it is just as possible that the Vatican spy-catchers had successfully sanitized the pope's secretariat. However, terse paraphrased reports of secret papal conversations with U.S. officials continued to be provided the KGB via the Hungarian and Polish services, likely by agents in other Vatican offices.

4 PRELUDE TO ULTIMATE EVIL

The pope's visit was a lance head that went straight
into the bowels of the whole Soviet Empire
and gave it a wound from which it
simply didn't recover.

—British historian Neal Ascherson
on Pope John Paul II 1979 visit to Poland

In the spring of 1979, Major Victor Sheymov of the KGB, the Soviet Committee for State Security's 8th Chief Directorate, was dispatched from Moscow to Warsaw, on an ultra-secret project. Outfitted with the highest security clearances, Sheymov was the KGB's chief expert on cipher technology and had been tasked with installing a new high-security computer system as added security for the Soviet embassy's encoded communications with KGB headquarters known by insiders as "the Center." The project was ordered by the all-powerful Politburo of the Soviet regime as a general effort to upgrade all communications facilities to strengthen security in light of the growing unrest in Poland.

It was Sheymov's first visit to Poland, nine years after the nation's communist regime was shaken by major unrest among workers at the Lenin shipyard in Gdansk on the Baltic Sea, where 44 workers were killed before order was restored. They were irate over increases in food prices, so much so that they marched on the local Communist Party headquarters, which subsequently went up in flames. The action spread to other ports, with workers battling police and resulting in numerous deaths. The price of food continued to rise, with no comparable compensation in wages. And in 1976, dissident workers and intellectuals banded together in the Worker's Defense Committee (KOR) and periodically staged numerous strikes. Subsequent clashes prompted communist authorities to finally agree to negotiations. On the surface, this calmed the tensions. But beneath this veil, the population was restive while the government wrestled with economic problems that had driven the nation into a foreign debt of 16 billion dollars, worth nearly 50 billion dollars in 2008.

But an extraordinary event in the lives of the Polish people lifted their spirits, at least for a while. On October 16, 1978, Cardinal Karol Wojtyla of Krakow was elected pope, succeeding Pope John Paul I. He took the name Pope John Paul II. According to a report by an agent of the East German State Security Ministry—the Stasi, as the East German people had pejoratively nicknamed them—the entire country erupted with jubilation. "On the streets of Krakow, people embraced each other and got on their knees on the streets. Celebrations lasted throughout the night, and small masses were conducted impromptu throughout the city. The next day, a solemn service was held on the square before the cathedral of Krakow. A giant photograph of the new pope adorned the outside wall of the Bishop's Palace.

Once Sheymov got settled in at the Soviet embassy, he was joined by his companion Valery Titov, the embassy security officer, for a glass of brandy.[1] After some small talk, Titov asked Sheymov what he had learned about Poland so far. The major replied that he was surprised that the Poles were so poor, that it seemed the entire country was sliding down hill. The security officer agreed that Sheymov was right and that it was getting worse, that the people were barely able to survive. If this was not changed, chaos would ensue. In response, Sheymov said he was also surprised by the people's "obvious hatred of us."

On October 19, 1978, just three days after the election of Karol Wojtyla as the first Polish pope, the U.S. Central Intelligence Agency's (CIA) National Foreign Assessment Center circulated a four-page classified assessment on the impact of a Polish pope on the Soviet Union. It said that this papacy would "undoubtedly prove extremely worrisome to Moscow, if only because of the responsiveness his papacy is likely to evoke in East European communist societies. The selection of a Polish Pope, which reflects the uniquely vital Polish church, will make even more difficult Moscow's traditional attempts to bind culturally Western Poland more closely to the East, to integrate the Poles more closely into a Soviet dominated bilateral and multilateral system of alliances, and to foster greater social and political discipline in Poland by consolidating the power of the Polish communist party."

The assessment went on to say that "the impact of Pope John Paul II would make it even more difficult for the Soviet regime to check and to counter Poland's instinctive cultural and political gravitation to the West. The Soviets have never been able to cope successfully with the legacy of Polish nationalism, particularly Polish opposition

1. The entire episode of Major Shemov's mission to Warsaw and his encounters with KGB officers assigned to the embassy is based on the major's recollections recounted in his fascinating book *Tower of Secrets* (Naval Institute Press, Annapolis, 1993). Major Sheymov wrote that names of Soviet personnel were changed. After exfiltration, he continued his studies at a U.S. university and holds an MBA. He was awarded the CIA Distinguished Service Medal for his contributions to the national security of the U.S.

to foreign occupiers and alien political systems." The CIA opined that the "potential spillover effect of the East European nationalism to the USSR is also considerable, particularly in the Ukraine where the Uniates Church, as the Byzantine-Rite-Catholics called themselves, has many adherents, in Byelorussia which includes former Polish territories that were once heavily Catholic, and in the Baltic countries where there are several million Catholics. The Soviet leadership is probably already anxious about how to cope with the ultimate impact of a Polish papacy on East European nationalism as well as such derivative issues as Euro-communism and Soviet dissidence." Thus, the Soviet Union's history of hostility toward the Church was given even more motivation to continue to grow.

The CIA assessment coincided closely with the issuance of a top-secret report by communist East Germany's Ministry for State Security (MFS), responsible for internal security—i.e., counterespionage and oppression of dissidence—as well as for foreign espionage. The report of April 4, 1979 was titled "information on questions regarding the Vatican's political positions following the election of Pope John II." It was so sensitive that only eight copies were distributed to the most senior officials, and all needed to be returned to its originator, Chief Directorate XX, who was responsible, among others, for church affairs and underground activities.[2] As the relationship between the MFS and the Soviet KGB was symbiotic, the report was surely shared with Moscow.

"The pope, who had been confronted directly with Marxist practices toward which he maintained an unyielding position, will represent the interests of the Catholic Church vis-à-vis the governments of socialist [i.e., communist] states more decisively than his predecessor," the report said.

---

2. Report No. 228/79, kept in the Berlin Archive of MFS files (BSTU) and numbered BSTU 000340.

"Within the framework of the Vatican's endeavors toward achieving legally binding resolutions with socialist states, he will not sacrifice his mission of 'defense of the Catholic Church and the principles of Christian morality against the expansion of state atheism.' In this regard, the pope will also take a stand for human rights, personal rights, human dignity, and religious freedom, as well as against discriminations.

"In connection with the pope's aim to secure religious freedom in all countries, also in the socialist [read communist] states and to expand the effectiveness of the Catholic Church is being meticulously pursued by the Vatican to determine which concrete steps the various socialist states are undertaking relative to their policies toward churches. This aspect will determine what other measures the Vatican will take toward socialist states. The Vatican has numerous other possibilities in its policies toward other states."

The report by the East German Ministry for State Security, the Stasi, describes Pope John Paul II as viewing the Polish episcopacy as "more aggressive" than, for example, the Hungarian and portrays him as being an "anticommunist but, above all, a Pole." In the specific case of Poland, based on her history of fervent nationalism, this was almost as dangerous to the Soviets as raw anticommunist sentiment. An agent for the MfS, a former seminarian and member of the Berlin Conference of Bishops code-named "Clemens," was in Krakow the day of Karol Wojtyla's election. Describing the jubilation of the population, the agent added: "Nationalism celebrated enthusiastically and one heard such opinions that Poland, with Zbigniew Brzezinski, the security adviser of the U.S. president [Carter], will determine worldly power and, with the new pope, the spiritual power."

The CIA assessment on the tribulation of the Soviet regime as well as the East German report were incredibly on target, so much so that it is as if the CIA had planted a bug at the Soviet embassy to listen to KGB Major Sheymov's conversations with the security officer Titov, during his Warsaw visit, and all the East German information came from a spy in the Vatican.[3] When speaking about the various political situations within the East bloc, the major also mentioned Czechoslovakia. "They are not that friendly an ally either, but the individual Czechs are not as openly hostile as I've found the Poles. This feels personal. Everywhere we've been so far, the moment we've been recognized as Russians, people have turned sullen. They look at us the way they must have eyed the Nazis." Titov agreed about the hatred and remarked that if the Poles had "the slightest chance to kick our butts, you'd better believe they'll take it," adding that they were not cowards, and recalled how their cavalry had attacked German tanks when World War II began in 1939. Sheymov responded that he imagined the Polish people's morale received a "real boost" when their cardinal was elected pope, as Catholicism had always played a central role in Poland's national identity.

Titov thought that if the pope were to give the signal, "every Pole would be in the streets, fighting our tanks with whatever he has. Then our choice would be to kill all of them or get the hell out. As a matter of fact, he is our biggest headache." Since history showed that the Soviet leadership would have no compunction to act so aggressively to preserve their empire, they feared the pope would act likewise.

The two KGB officers felt that the Soviets had only two options. One would be to kill the pope, which both agreed would be a "huge mistake." The other would be to support the tough Polish defense minister, General Wojciech Jaruzelski, who would know how to deal with his rebellious countrymen. "Besides, he knows all too well where his bread is buttered. If we go, he would be hanged." The major wondered if Moscow understood this situation. "Not really,"

3. The author will deal with this aspect in a later chapter.

said the security officer. "They certainly don't have any idea how deeply rooted the problem is [Polish hostility]."

The next day, Major Sheymov was summoned to the office of General Nikolai Pavlovich Kuritsyn, the KGB representative to the Polish State Security Service (SB), for a detailed discussion on how his mission to upgrade the ultra-secret communications equipment was progressing. While chatting about a recent security faux pas at the KGB technical directorate, they were interrupted by the Counselor of Embassy, named Solovyev, who in fact was the "resident," as the heads of clandestine KGB stations were called. It irritated the general, who demanded to know what was so important. "It's about the pope," the resident answered. He eyed Sheymov as if questioning his presence. Noticing Solovyev's hesitation, General Kuritsyn told the resident that the major knew more secrets about Poland and the pope than they did.

"The center wants all the information you have on the pope," Solovyev said, adding that it was urgent. General Kuritsyn expressed his irritation, as such information had already been sent to Moscow twice.

"No, they mean all of it. All personal acquaintances, and anything derogatory on them [Ed.: on the pope and his acquaintances] . . . anything that could get us close to him. Physically! Moscow also prohibited us from opening inquiries. No footprints. What do we do?"

Major Sheymov recalled that Solovyev's revelations prompted a sudden silence. They looked at one another, knowing that "getting physically close" could only mean one thing: assassination. Major Sheymov said he felt light headed as he watched the two KGB officers obviously calculating the political consequences of a murder that would rock the civilized world in horror and disgust. As the cable was placed on the general's desk, Sheymov noticed that instead of the code name Svirido, it bore the name Andropov, the chairman of the KGB. General Kuritsyn was ready to explode: "Idiots! This is political suicide. Not just political, either. If we take the pope out, our days in

Poland are numbered. Even if we tried to hold on, we'd have to wipe out the Poles—every last one would die for him. This is likely to start something I'm scared even to think about. Yes, a while ago we could have pulled off the quiet liquidation of a cardinal and gotten away with it, but not now. It's just too late." He knew the volatile situation in Poland, and knew that things were already on the brink of eruption.

The men surely knew that losing Poland would severely test the continued existence of the Warsaw Pact, the defense organization of the communist bloc. It certainly would have seriously impeded the continued maintenance of 380,000 Soviet troops in communist East Germany, as their direct supply routes led through Poland. To prevent this, the Brezhnev Doctrine, which called for armed intervention if communist rule in any Warsaw Pact nation was threatened, would surely be applied, as it had been a few years earlier to beat down the unrest in Czechoslovakia during the "Prague Spring" in 1968.

The KGB boss in Poland told the resident to comply and dig up the information. "Do it yourself; don't involve anyone else. As they said, no footprints, especially not yours or mine."

Sheymov, 33 years old at the time of his Warsaw experience, relayed in his book *Tower of Secrets* how this incident changed his life. A graduate of Moscow's Technical University, he worked for the Soviet Space Initiative program until he joined the KGB in 1971. Already dismayed by the amorality of the Soviet regime and its disdain for the freedoms of the individual, he decided to turn his back on tyranny and defect after learning of a possible plot to assassimate Pope John Paul II. He managed to contact an officer of the U.S. Central Intelligence Agency and in 1980 he and his wife and eight-year-old daughter were smuggled out of Moscow to the West.

Trouble for Moscow Intensifies

In early April, 1979, the Vatican announced that Pope John II would make an eight-day pilgrimage to Poland beginning on June 2.

Judging by the reaction in Moscow, one would have thought that Leonid Brezhnev, the powerful Soviet Communist Party chairman, imagined he was facing the apocalypse as he knew it. Already facing widespread anti-government unrest, his reaction was one of maniacal rage. What had exacerbated the apprehension among East European communist leaders was the encyclical *Redemptor Hominis* (Redeemer of Man) Pope John Paul II had issued a month earlier. A top-secret analysis prepared for the East German leaders pointed out that the pope called for peace, disarmament, and overcoming hunger and damage to the environment, "although it also contains remarks aimed at the countries of the socialist community. This refers mainly to the so-called human right campaign with which imperialism attempts to put fascism and communism on the same level when referring to totalitarian state systems."[4] And yet Brezhnev was powerless to stop the pope from visiting. Why? Fearing international backlash? Realizing that the Polish people would man the barricades in protest more violently than ever, if their beloved and revered pope was stopped from visiting the brethren in his homeland?

In his biography of Edward Gierek, the First Secretary of the Polish Communist Party, Janusz Rolicki wrote that Brezhnev telephoned Gierek, saying he had been informed that Pope John II had been invited by the Polish Church diocese to visit Poland, and asked what his reaction was. Gierek replied that he would get the reception "he deserves." Brezhnev countered "take my advice, do not give him any reception, it will only cause trouble."

The Polish party chief stood his ground. "How can I not receive a Polish pope when the majority of my countrymen are Catholic? They view his election as a great achievement. Furthermore, how could I justify why we are closing the border to the pope?" Brezhnev, already

4. Analysis by Ministry for State Security Chief Directorate XX No. 243/79, dated March 27, 1979. It was so secret that only five copies were distributed. BSTU No. 000151.

in ill health and short-tempered, persisted. "Just tell the pope, who is a wise man, to say publicly that he is ill and can't make the trip."

When Gierek said that political considerations dictated that the pope be admitted, Brezhnev grew even testier, saying "you were a better communist when you refused to admit Pope Paul VI and nothing terrible happened." He added: "The Poles survived that, and they will survive a second time." One must wonder whether Brezhnev was still compos mentis, considering that Wladyslaw Gomulka had been fired as party chief and replaced with Gierek when the unrest erupted in 1970—although, to Gierek's credit, he realized that John Paul II was Polish and had a huge following, whereas Paul VI was "just" a pope.

Gierek was undoubtedly more sophisticated and worldly than perhaps any other leader within the communist bloc. He was raised and schooled in France, where his Polish parents had immigrated, and later returned to the homeland. When he did not relent, the bushy-browed Brezhnev became threatening: "Well, do as you want, but be careful that you won't regret it later." Brezhnev's consternation undoubtedly was aggravated not only by the ongoing workers' unrest, but also by Foreign Minister Andrei Gromyko's report on his visit in Rome with Pope John Paul II eleven weeks earlier. In his autobiography, Gromyko wrote that he described to the pope "major Soviet initiatives" in securing world peace and "as far as I can judge the Catholic Church accords great importance to strengthening peace, to disarmament, and to the liquidation of weapons of mass destruction. The Soviet leadership believes that this position has great value. As for ideological or religious differences, they must not be allowed to stand in the way of collaboration on this noble goal." To which the pope replied: "It is possible that the obstacles to freedom or religion have not been removed everywhere." Gromyko said he replied that such accusations are "not new to us," maintaining that such misinformation was spread by the West, adding that "from the first days of its existence, the Soviet State has guaranteed freedom of religious belief."[5] Of course, the pontiff knew that this was a blatant lie. Being Polish, he would have been witness to decades of Soviet hostility toward organized religion—Orthodoxy, Catholic, Jewish, and Muslim alike.

While the KGB contingent in Poland moved into high gear, as Polish security had already shown that it was practically helpless in countering continued anti-government stirrings among workers and many intellectuals, consternation became acute within the neighboring East German communist regime as well. Party boss Erich Honecker was as alarmed as Moscow that the papal visit might well spark increased tensions within the Polish population which could spill over into the German Democratic Republic (GDR). Honecker remembered the 1953 unarmed revolt which was brutally put down by the Soviet Army and police, killing 21 civilians, wounding 343, including 191 policemen, and sending nearly 2,000 to prisons. Among post-revolt defections to West Germany were about 8000 riot police officers and 2,718 members and candidates of the ruling communist Social Unity Party (SED).[6]

Honecker called on Erich Mielke, a convicted murderer of two Berlin police officers in 1931,[7] and ordered that his secret police, the Stasi, be put on high alert leading up to the pope's visit. On April 17, 1979, Mielke issued a two-page secret order to all subordinate units to mobilize their spies—i.e., secret informers, or IM (unofficial coworkers)—"to reconnoiter and prevent negative enemy activities." These IMs had been planted in virtually all public institutions, schools, universities, churches, and factories. They spied on their friends, many

5. Gromyko, *Memoirs* (London, Hutchinson, 1989), pp. 212–213, quoted by George Weigel in his biography of Pope John Paul II, *Witness to Hope* (New York, HarperCollins, 1999), p. 298.
6. John O. Koehler: *Stasi: The Untold Story of the East German Secret Police* (WestView Press, Boulder, CO, 1999), pp. 59–60.
7. Ibid., chapter 2.

of whom wound up in prison after merely hinting that they would prefer the West to the East. Now, their assignments were to accompany and spy on all Catholic pilgrims to Poland for the pope's visit.

"The head of Department XX has the operational obligation to report any planned hostile actions in connection with the ceremonies of the papal visit to the head of Department X who, in turn, will coordinate with the security organs of the People's Republic of Poland (VRP). Particularly significant operational information, which would necessitate central decisions, must immediately be reported to me or to my deputy Major General [Rudi] Mittig."[8] Department XX was charged with increasing the observation of religious institutions and underground activities. Department X was tasked with handling international connections, meaning the sharing of information with the Soviet KGB in Moscow.

The Mielke order was accompanied by a two-page list of information requirements, which included: "Indications about provocative or hostile actions in the VRP; problems and behavior of DDR (East German) citizens and other political/operational actions during the papal visit; meetings between DDR citizens and Poles; behavior of priests and leading Catholic lay persons; indications of major gifts and establishment of official contacts between communities; all political/operational knowledge which needs immediate reporting— e.g., terrorism, catastrophes, etc.; what influence does the papal visit have on the religious life; any indications on partnerships between communities of the VRP and the DDR.; what is known about enemy contacts to community representatives from the BRD (West Germany) or single persons from the BRD Catholic Church was observed."

The initial analysis sent to Stasi chief Mielke described the general church situation in connection with the Polish pope's visit. "Since

8. MfS Nr. 102554/338. Kopie BSTU AR 8.

Wojtyla has become pope, the political situation has become aggravated. He knows the socialist countries and is a stronger ideological foe than Paul VI. The comrades of Poland are not pleased by this development. They expected anticommunist moves, but the pope is smart enough to avoid them." It seems like all their suspicions of hostility against the Church had borne fruit in a round-about way.

Preparations for East German secret police activities in Poland mirrored *Deutsche Gruendlichkeit* (German thoroughness), often viewed as bordering on the maniacal. The Stasi's final report was more than an inch thick, 214 pages. It listed the regional headquarters located in each of the 15 East German provinces which were ordered to assign their secret informers, some of whom were classified as IMV, meaning unofficial collaborator, specifically asssigned to expose "persons suspected of subversion," to pre-selected areas of Poland. For example, the regional headquarters at the Baltic Sea city of Rostock dispatched six of its IMVs to the city of Gdansk to report on any "enemy activities, even though the pope was not scheduled to visit the city but where workers at its major shipyards have been increasingly voicing their anti-government sentiments." In all, the final report listed the assignments and code names of more than 100 spies, perhaps even 200, with detailed timetables. Their reports were in writing or tape recordings for delivery by special couriers to their handlers in East Germany. They wormed their way into groups of hundreds of East German Catholic pilgrims, including priests and nuns, took hundreds of photographs of visitors and the license plate numbers of all vehicles bearing non-Polish plates. At least 25 spies were women, and a half dozen were journalists from both sides of the Iron Curtain. About a half dozen were residents of West Berlin. Most importantly, there were certainly a number of priests and laypersons among the horde of spies, considering that the East German secret police had more than 54 priests and 64 laypersons on its payroll, a fact which will be explored in a later chapter.

A month before the pope's scheduled arrival, Stasi spies were dispatched to Poland on reconnaissance missions, particularly to cities on the Holy Father's itinerary. They reported on preparations for the historic—and, for the Polish Communist Party, threatening—visit. Unrest, of course, was growing. The spies reported that the government was trying to alleviate problems with an increase of food supplies to major locations such as Warsaw and Krakow while at the same time placing police and militia units on high alert. Early in May, one agent spent three days in Krakow and nearby Nowa Huta, Poland's "first socialist city" with its giant V.I. Lenin steel plant where workers had been voicing their dissatisfaction for many years. He reported that about three weeks earlier, an attempt had been made to blow up the life-size statue of Lenin. "The explosive was fastened on a foot of Lenin and detonated. The heel was torn off. The culprits escaped without a trace." The spy added: "The mood of the people is not the best. There is great dissatisfaction in connection with meat and sausage supplies and if something is offered, the quality is poor. On the other hand, one can buy almost anything on the black market and all prices are 100% higher [than in stores]."[9] The situation was bleak.

As customary, this report was shared with the Soviet KGB in Moscow. It is easy to imagine how it rattled the Kremlin crowd to the core. After all, Nowa Huta came to life with massive Soviet aid for building the giant I.V. Lenin steel plant in 1949, supplying more than 500 engineers and technicians to train Poles, and massive steel-making equipment. No doubt they viewed this as an instance of the Poles "biting the hand that fed them."

The day before the arrival of Pope John Paul II, thousands of white-and-yellow flags of the Vatican flew alongside the red-and-white

9. Stasi archive No. BSTU 000299. There is no identification as to the recipient department. But since the body of the report indicated that he had contacted Polish acquaintances he had known for 15 years, it is likely that he was an agent for the HVA, the foreign espionage department.

Polish national banners outside private and factory buildings. Apartment dwellers had draped them out of their windows. And a number of Poles affirmed their fiery nationalism by displaying the outlawed red-and-white flags bearing the eagle and crown of the former Polish kingdom. Authorities estimated that more than 10 million pilgrims were en route to Warsaw and to the other four cities and towns to be visited—Gniezno, Czestochowa, Krakow, and Karol Wojtyla's birthplace Wadowice. Fearing possible violent demonstrations, the government had planned to station militia units in the city. However, the venerable Stefan Cardinal Wyszynski was able to persuade the authorities to keep them outside the city. Thus, according to an East German spy, "formidable militia units with water cannons and other equipment were camped in tents in the outskirts. They rarely appeared in the city itself." The pontiff also wanted to visit the Baltic Sea city of Gdansk, where the formidable anti-government protests by shipyard workers erupted in 1970. The communist government, fearing more unrest, banned that visit as well as trips to Katowice and Wroclaw. The monthly dissident bulletin *Glos*, produced by Catholic intellectuals, opined that the communist government was bent on limiting the pope's visit to "keep him from being seen by believers of the working class."

At 10:05 on a sunny morning at Warsaw's Okecie airport, Karol Wojtyla walked down the ramp of his Alitalia plane, knelt, and kissed the soil of his beloved motherland as church bells throughout this troubled nation rang in welcome. He rose and waved to an estimated 20,000 of his countrymen who had braved the unusual 90-degree temperature to greet the man now named Pope John Paul II. A solid wall of humanity, waving Vatican and red-and-white Polish flags, cheering and chanting "Sto Lat" (May You Live 100 Years), lined the seven-mile route into the center of the Polish capital. It was a seminal moment in human and political history. It signaled the liberation of Eastern Europe from communist tyranny a decade later.

The Cathedral of St. John in Warsaw's town square was the Holy Father's first stop for a brief welcoming ceremony—attended by the country's entire episcopate—and private prayers, then on to the residence of Stefan Cardinal Wyszynski, the Polish primate whom the communist authorities persecuted for his unwavering battle against oppression, including three years imprisonment without a trial.

Belvedere Palace, the residence of the figurehead president Henryk Jablonski, was the last stop for Pope John Paul II before being driven to Victory Square for his formal mass. The welcoming party also included Communist Party leader Edward Gierek. It was a cordial, but not a warm, encounter. Gierek had voiced his apprehension over the visit of a man who, as Cardinal Karol Wojtyla, was openly anticommunist and had often clashed with authorities. And now he did so again. "The Church wishes to serve people also in the temporal dimension of their life and existence. By establishing a religious relationship with people, the Church consolidates them in their natural social bonds."[10] Note that the pope said "social," not "socialist," bonds. Conspicuously missing was Prime Minister Piotr Jaroszewicz, a virulent Stalinist. A Stasi[11] agent reported that "one rumor is chasing the other from authorities expecting chaos, hundreds of deaths and militia units dressed disguised as priests in black robes." Regarding the prime minister, the agent wrote that when, contrary to protocol, Cardinal Wyszynski boarded the pope's plane on arrival, one assumed that Jaroszewicz had died just before and that he was to inform Pope John Paul II about it, but that this would be secret until after the pope had departed. It must be emphasized, however, that even before the pope's arrival, the people were shaken by rumors, one of which said that during the pope's visit a leading politician would die. Jaroszewicz was one of the last old communists and

10. Vatican press release.
11. Agent report of June 4, 1979. BSTU No. 000246.

was considered a "rigid supporter of Leonid Brezhnev. Considering the open hate exhibited by a large part of the intelligentsia and farmers vis-à-vis the SU [Soviet Union], making public a report confirming the rumor would have resulted in ecstasy." In truth, he did not die until 1992, when he and his wife were murdered. Four suspects were tried and acquitted. Attempted robbery was suspected.

Pope John Paul II arrived at Victory Square at 4 P.M. where a nearly 40-foot-high wooden cross had been erected. Joyous cheers and applause of nearly 300,000 fellow Poles greeted the man whom they considered their staunchest ally in the quest for liberation from communism, which had produced nothing but economic disaster and personal deprivation. An estimated one million, authorities estimated, had come to the city and jammed the streets near the square. Cars were not allowed into the city, and reports said roadblocks by police and militia units on roads leading to Warsaw turned back millions more. Associated Press special correspondent Hugh Mulligan told the author that at that time, the mass congregation was the largest religious gathering ever held behind the Iron Curtain. As the pope was speaking, thousands of pilgrims raised their arms high with crucifixes, some small, some large, clasped in their hands. Pope John Paul stopped speaking, looked fondly at his flock, and said: "I hope you will always be faithful to this sign, always."

In his homily for Mass, Pope John Paul II made it clear that the Church would not be cowed by communist doctrine. ". . . man cannot be fully understood without Christ, or rather, man is incapable of understanding himself fully without Christ," he declared. "Therefore, Christ cannot be kept out of the history of man in any part of the globe, at any longitude or latitude of geography. The exclusion of Christ from the history of man is an act against man." The pope continued: "Today, here in Victory Square, in the capital of Poland, I am asking all of you, through the great eucharistic prayers, that Christ will not cease to be before us an open book of life for the future, for our Polish future." One can only imagine how Soviet party leader Leonid Brezhnev and his minions interpreted these thinly veiled words of courage to his fellow countrymen who remembered his words after his election in 1978 at St. Peter's Square, when he said: "Be not afraid." In closing, the pontiff prayed:

> *Let the Spirit descend*
> *Let the Spirit descend*
> *And renew the Face of the Earth,*
> *The Face of this Land.*

That prayer surely must have resonated with apprehension among the Soviet hierarchy. It certainly did with Lech Walesa, who interpreted it as daring the Polish people to "change the face of the Earth." The Nobel Peace Prize laureate and founder of the Solidarity anti-government trade union in 1980 said "We had no strength, no great will, I had only 10 people who were willing to work along with me and fight for freedom in a nation of 40 million."[12] Mr. Walesa continued: "The Holy Father told us: 'Don't be afraid, change the face of the Earth, be strong believers.' Then all of a sudden people thought about his words and woke up. They regained the will for action. If this had not occurred, communism would have fallen in some 50 or 60 years. Communism did not fall because of the words, but the words helped. As it is said, 'first there was the Word and then it became flesh'." Solidarity was finally officially recognized by the communist government as a full-fledged trade union.

From Warsaw, the pope traveled by helicopter to the town of Gniezno, the first Christian outpost in Poland, established in 966. The town, some 150 miles west of Warsaw, had swelled to more than 300,000 people who again braved the 90-degree heat to cheer and to

12. Interview with the Associated Press, April 3, 2005.

hear the man whom they later would consider their redeemer from a despotic regime. Not only was the visit a special day for Poles, but it also was the feast of Pentecost, the fiftieth day after Easter commemorating the descent of the Holy Sprit upon the disciples. Before visiting with the pilgrims gathered in a lush meadow just outside of this provincial town, Pope John Paul II spoke to the faithful assembled at the Cathedral of Gniezno. He said he was pained that many brethren could not hear his voice, an obvious reference to the tight control over the media by the communist regimes of Eastern Europe. An East German secret police spy reported on May 5 to his control officer in Dresden, Major Schurz, that despite the heat which caused many people to faint, no one "even thought about leaving early and despite the great strains the enthusiasm held no limits. The pope spoke in Polish and the speech contained a few veiled attacks against the Polish government. He said at one point: 'Allow the children to come to me and do not stand in their way.' This biblical citation obviously referred to the Polish government's alleged curtailment of religious instructions for children. This citation prompted an incredible applause of the masses."[13] Another spy, whose code name was "Karaat," highlighted in his report a banner carried by pilgrims from Czechoslovakia. These pilgrims obviously had not forgotten the brutal 1968 invasion of their country. In Czech, it read: "Holy Father, think about your Czechoslovak children!" Another banner read: "Three Cheers for Him—He is Our King." The pope's day ended with a prayer at the tomb of St. Adalbert. This patron saint of Poland, martyred by the Prussians in the 10th century, was interred in the town's 14th-century Gothic cathedral.

A white helicopter brought Pope John Paul II to the city of Czesto-chowa, 138 miles southwest of Warsaw. Since the Middle Ages, the

---

13. District Administration for State Security Dresden, Department XX, report 4/1755, June 5, 1979. BSTU No. 000065. The agent's cover name was Werner Albrecht.

city has been considered by the Polish people as their county's holiest city, visited by millions of pilgrims each year. Pope John Paul II himself called Czestochowa the "spiritual capital of Poland." Some 500,000 joyous Poles, double the number of the city's residents, greeted him with cheers, chants of Sto Lat, folk songs, and the waving of the Vatican and Polish flags. The pontiff sat beneath a canopy of red and gold glittering under a bright sun. As he spoke, many of the pilgrims' cheeks were moistened by tears as he spoke outside the Basilica of the Shrine of The Black Madonna[14] at Jasna Gora (Shining Mountain) Monastery that dates back to the 14th century. In 1655, despite a long and bloody siege, the monastery became the only stronghold with defenders marching along its wall carrying the Black Madonna portrait and defeating the Swedish invaders. Thus, the Black Madonna became the Poles' symbol of freedom, and the pope, while a bishop, then a cardinal, often visited the shrine to display his firmness against communism. During this visit, the Holy Father appealed for religious unity and "justice that satisfied the peoples' needs and guarantees the rights and duties of each member of the country to prevent disharmony and opposition arising from evident privileges of some and discrimination against others." Signifying comprehension of the meaning of the pope's words, the pilgrims responded with deafening applause.

In his address of 78 bishops assembled for the Polish Bishops' Conference at the Jasna Gora Basilica, the pontiff appealed to the

---

14. According to historians, the painting, also known as Our Lady of Czestochowa, was given to a group of Paulite monks from Hungary for safekeeping by Prince Wladislaw of Opole, who built the monastery for the Paulites. The 15th-century historian Jan Dlugosz wrote that the icon was painted by St. Luke on wood. Candles burning for centuries in front of the painting produced the soot that discolored it and gave it its name. It was damaged by robbers in the 16th century. During the 17th-century Swedish-Polish war, 3,000 Swedish soldiers besieged the monastery for more than a month. But the monks, led by Prior Augustyn Kordecki, had fortified Jasna Gora and, joined by local peasants, stood fast and forced the withdrawal of the attackers. The Jasna Gora victory, and thus the protection of the icon, was viewed by the Polish people as a miracle.

Polish regime to recognize "fundamental human rights, including religious freedom," something guaranteed by the nation's constitution but which in fact was sharply curtailed by the government. Addressing the churchmen, he was not as restrained as he was in his public remarks. Apropos Christianity vs. Marxist ideology, the pontiff, who became an expert in dealing with the communist functionaries in his days as one of Poland's leading clergymen, said that any genuine dialog "must respect the convictions of believers, ensure all citizens' rights as well as for the religious community to which most of the Polish people belong. This will not be easy because it occurs between two diametrically opposed concepts." It seemed at this stage well-nigh impossible, seeing as the church had been infiltrated for decades and used as a gateway to spying on the West.

As the pope departed Shining Mountain, United Press International reported that militia men attacked a number of spectators and two photographers. The news service noted that reporters witnessed nothing that might have provoked the action. However, UPI pointed out that the atmosphere around Czestochowa was strained, as thousands of miners and factory workers from the Silesia region had come to greet the pope and they were angry because the pope had not been allowed to visit their region, where tensions were bound to erupt.

The Holy Father's next stop was Krakow, Poland's third-largest city with about 1.5 million people living within its metropolitan area. The Vistula River runs through the medieval city graced by the magnificent Wawel Cathedral—its Zygmunt bell, cast in 1520, is one of the world's largest—the magnificent Gothic structure of the Basilica of the Virgin Mary, the Basilica of the Holy Trinity, and 19 other Catholic churches, the oldest of which dates to the 11th century. Until his departure from Poland, the city was the pope's base, from which he made a number of side trips.

Well over 800,000 Poles gave the pontiff as joyous a welcome in Krakow as he had received wherever he appeared since setting foot in his homeland four days earlier. One open-air mass at Blonie meadow drew an estimated one million devotees. Militia units blocking all vehicles trying to enter the city were jeered by hundreds of students of Krakow University, Poland's oldest, where the great astronomer Nicolaus Copernicus once studied. The students were venting their anger over non-residents being prevented from entering the city to worship their Holy Father. For Karol Wojtyla, the return to Krakow as pope was a highly emotional experience that often was mirrored in his face as well in the cheers and applause of the people. After studying in secret during the Nazi occupation, he was ordained in 1946, served as a parish priest in Krakow, and eventually was appointed Archbishop of Krakow by Pope Paul VI.

On June 7, John Paul II was flown by helicopter to his birthplace, Wadowice, a town of nearly 20,000 established early in the 11th century, where he delivered a brief homily at the Basilica and visited the home where he was born. Again, he was cheered not only by the townspeople, but also by thousands who had come to pay homage from surrounding villages. Then he added another historic papal event: a pilgrimage to the former Nazi concentration camp of Auschwitz and its nearby Birkenau annex. Surrounded by barbed wire and watchtowers, the complexes of wooden barracks had been preserved as a stark reminder of the incredible inhumanity perpetrated by Adolf Hitler's Nazi hordes.

After walking through the Auschwitz camp entrance beneath a wrought-iron arch bearing the slogan "Arbeit Macht Frei"—Work Liberates—fashioned by inmates, he spoke again to another 600,000. He began his emotional speech by comparing the camp, where four million were slaughtered, with the hill outside Jerusalem where Jesus was crucified. "This is the Golgotha of the modern world," he told the silent, solemn crowd. Of the total number killed there, some 2.5 million were Jews—men, women, and children. The other victims were Christians, including hundreds of priests, nuns, and laypersons of many Central and East European nationalities. As he did in his many other speeches and homilies, the pontiff again implored his fellow Poles to resist whatever they are told to the contrary: "You are not who they say you are, so let me remind you who you are." In a special tribute to murdered Jews, he said: "In particular, I pause here with you, my dear pilgrims in this encounter, before the inscriptions in Hebrew." Pointing to a stele inscribed in some 20 languages spoken by those who perished in the death chambers, he declaimed that the Hebrew inscription "awakens the memory of the people whose sons and daughters were chosen for extermination." Before leaving the death camp, Pope John Paul II met with a number of survivors, including about 200 priests, who displayed the numbers tattooed on their forearms by the Nazis. For the rest of his time as pope, it seems that John Paul II paid special attention to memorializing the Holocaust. Perhaps this visit to Auschwitz was a watershed for that as well.

By evening, when he returned to Krakow, the pope was visibly tired when he reached his quarters at the stately bishop's residence on 3 Franciszkanska, where he had lived from 1963 to 1978. But outside, the crowd kept chanting "Sto Lat," forcing him to appear on a balcony in shirtsleeves. After giving his usual blessing, the pope asked: "Do you really want me to live a hundred years?" The pilgrims shouted "Yes!" Displaying his now-famous smile, he said: "Dobrze, good; then allow me to get some sleep."

A morning helicopter flight brought the pontiff to Nowy Targ, a town of 34,000 in the foothills of the pope's beloved Tatra Mountains where he had often vacationed, skiing in winter and hiking through scenic meadows and up rocky hills in the summer. During the World War II Nazi occupation, it was the home of partisans covertly battling German troops. Tens of thousands were again gathered at the small airstrip to welcome the Polish pope. Many were clad in native costume, women in bodices and long skirts emblazoned with flowery patterns, men in colorful embroidered breeches with long knit stockings and wearing wide-brimmed black hats. Before he began the mass, the ceremony was opened by John Cardinal Krol of Philadelphia, whose parents had immigrated to the United States from Tarnow, a town 40 miles east of Krakow. He told the crowd that the pope had come to Poland to pay homage to St. Stanislaus, the missionary who was martyred by King Boleslaw 900 years earlier, and that the Holy Father was seeking to follow the example of the saint by "speaking the truth with courage." Pope John Paul II reiterated what he had said in all of his speeches, that his wish was that his visit would "help the great, great cause of peace, friendship in relations between national and social justice." The pope's words were duly recorded by East German secret police spy "Stephan" on tape for his handler, 1st Lieutenant Michler, at MfS district headquarters in Cottbus, a town close to the Polish border.[15] This spy apparently was the most active of all during the pope's visit, having traveled to Warsaw, Czestochowa, and Krakow while most of the other Stasi moles were assigned to only one destination. On June 15, 1979, "Stephan" recorded his observations, the transcript of which covered seven single-spaced pages.[16] His account was highly literate, pointing to a man educated at a university level.

The pontiff's day ended with a visit to the majestic Wawel Cathedral on Wawel Hill overlooking Krakow. The cathedral actually is one of three churches built there, the first in the 11th century, while its present structure was completed in the mid-14th century. It stands next to the Wawel Royal Castle. As the newly ordained Father Karol Wojtyla in 1946, he had said his first mass at the cathedral in a tribute to his parents. Pope John Paul II spoke at the crypt of St. Stanislaus, who was interred in a side chapel of the cathedral which is also the burial site of many Polish royals, churchmen, and prominent intellectuals.

On returning to the bishop's residence, the East German spy

15. Report dated June 15, 1979. BSTU No. 000204-210.
16. Transcript of recording by IMV "Stephan" by 1st Lt. Michler, Regional Office Cottbus. BSTU 000204-000210.

"Stephan" observed the pope speaking to a number of Poles who had gathered outside. He collared a man and questioned him about his conversation with the Holy Father. "I was told that the pope had said that humanity should unite into a peaceful family but that the border between the DDR and the BDR [Deutsche Demokratische Republik, East Germany; Bundesrepublic Deutschland, West Germany] is playing a negative role. One must do away with the border. I was told that this was what the pope said word for word."[17] These words, as well as those of Cardinal Krol earlier in the day, no doubt were alarming not only to the tyrannical East German regime, but also when they reached the Kremlin via the KGB.

The day before his departure, the pontiff journeyed to Mogila, a small town on the northern outskirts of Krakow with a population of 38,000. Just southwest lies the steel town of Nowa Huta, which an apprehensive government fearing anticommunist disturbances had placed off limits to the pope. Once again, communist heavy handedness backfired. They simply failed to comprehend the religious fervor of the workers and their families. They had obviously forgotten that, as Archbishop of Krakow, Karol Wojtyla had listened to his flock and defied the atheist rulers by asserting his will and built the first church, the Ark Church, in a city which was supposed to be the first truly communist settlement not in need of a house of religious worship. It took nearly 20 years to get the building permit. Now, on this warm June Saturday two years later, tens of thousands left their town, many wearing typical steelworkers' clothes such as leather aprons, to welcome Pope John Paul II outside their neighborhood. If he couldn't come to them, then they would come to him.

The pilgrims from Nowa Huta joined their Mogila brethren to cheer the pontiff and hear his words in the picturesque Park of the 13th-century Cistercian Abbey with its Shrine of the Holy Cross.

17. Ibid.

Joined by eight cardinals and 18 archbishops and bishops atop a huge outdoor altar, the pontiff blessed the crowd and reminded them that the sanctuary he built in "the first socialist city" was prompted by "a living awareness and responsible awareness and responsible faith and must continue to serve that faith." Comprehension of the words' meaning was signaled by thunderous response. And the secret police spies mingling with the crowd had another ominous report for their handlers which, when passed on to Moscow, must have raised a few more beads of sweat above Leonid Brezhnev's bushy eyebrows. Especially alarming must have been another of the veiled references to his view of communist ideology. "I am asking this labor system to allow the church to love man and man's dignity and dignity of his labor that Christ gives us by his presence." After some lighthearted banter with some pilgrims, he departed for Krakow and a stop at Rakowicki Cemetery, where he kneeled before the tomb of his family and prayed.

The pope returned to his old residence, where he hosted a reception for visiting dignitaries and bishops. His day closed with attending a historic concert at the 17th-century Baroque Church of St. Casimir's next to the Franciscan Monastery, the premiere of the choral work *Beatus Vir* by Polish composer Henryk Gorecki, some of whose earlier compositions had been interpreted by the regime as having anticommunist overtones. The concert took place just after Gorecki had resigned as provost of the State Higher School of Music to protest the government's ban of the pope's visit to the mining town of Katowice.[18] The choral

18. John Litweiler in *Encyclopedia Britannica*. After Gorecki's resignation, his passport was confiscated and, he said, "I was treated as through I was dead." After the collapse of communism, be became an international celebrity, traveling throughout Europe and to New York, earning high praise for his Symphony No.3: "Symphony of Sorrowful Songs" (composed in 1976), which by 1993 had sold 150,000 copies in the United States alone. Gorecki's earlier works were based on tragic scenes in which he wanted to "express great sorrow—the war, the rotten times under communism, our life today, the starving, Bosnia . . . this sorrow, it burns inside me."

work contained Latin psalm texts he found in the official liturgical book of the Roman rite, the missal, lent to him by Piotr Malecki, Karol Wojtyla's first altar boy at St. Florian's Church, which had been given to him by Father Wojtyla in the 1950s. When the concert ended, the composer, one of whose legs is shorter than the other, limped toward the pontiff, whom he embraced as tears streamed down his face.[19] It really was as if they viewed him as their savior, both spiritually and socio-politically, from the Soviets.

Mid-morning on Sunday, June 10 found two million—some sources said it was close to three—crowded into the 120-acre grassy Blonia meadow and its adjoining Jordana Park, both favorite recreation sites for the people of Krakow. From the meadow, one has a spectacular view of the majestic spire of Wawel Cathedral and the towers of the castle. Again there was a sea of Polish and Vatican flags, large ones and small ones being waved by countless children, and the ever-present cheers welcomed John Paul II for the mass ending his historic pilgrimage which spurred an oppressed people toward seeking freedom even more intensively. The usual contingent of East German secret spies with such codes names as "Fruehling," "Fritz Schulz," "Lehman," the accredited journalist from Interpress news service "Georg," and, of course, the prolific "Stephan," were on hand to keep their eyes and ears open.[20] There were no unruly demonstrations that would have resulted in intervention by communist security force.

The arrival of the pope and his entourage was signaled by a trumpet sounding what seemed like the welcome hymn for kings and queens centuries ago. Contrary to previous appearances, he was received with reverential silence by the people in deference to the Pontiff's Mass in honor of the martyred St. Stanislaus, who was hacked to death with a sword in 1079 by King Boleslaw II, who had accused the bishop of

19. George Weigel, *Witness to Hope* (New York, HarperCollins, 1999), p. 318.
20. MfS Register No. XX/4/781/79. BSTU No. 000321.

treason. According to one version, the bishop had severely criticized the king for treating his soldiers' faithless wives cruelly; another holds that the king himself was guilty of sexual misconduct and the bishop and the bishop excommunicated him. Stanislaus was canonized in 1253. Wawel Cathedral holds St. Stanislaus's sarcophagus, which is why the pope had chosen to hold his Papal Mass within its view. A choir of more than 300 voices provided a beautiful musical rendition of a hymn while Pope John Paul II mounted the high altar. As was often the case during this visit, he was accompanied by high-ranking churchmen who came from neighboring countries like Germany and Latvia—and from as far away as Brazil.

Before heading for the airport, the pope met briefly with several hundred journalists from around the globe. The AP's special correspondent Hugh Mulligan recalled the Holy Father speaking in Polish, English, Italian, and French. Standing on the balcony of the archbishop's residence, Mulligan said, the pope responded to a question about his visit by saying that his spirit had been lifted by visiting his home land. "I thank God for his benevolence in enabling me to make it," he said.

As his motorcade to the Krakow airport wound its way through the center of the city, thousands again cheered and chanted "Sto Lat." Thousands more had gathered at the airport. The AP's Hugh Mulligan said he was astonished when Polish president Henryk Jablonski, who had come to say farewell, hugged the pope and kissed his hand, duly recorded by East German spy "Stephan," who called it a "Bruderschaftskuss,"[21] or Brotherhood Kiss, clearly an act of subversion in the eyes of the Stasi. Before kneeling and kissing his homeland good-bye, he said to the president that "this journey mobilizes men but saps their energy." Stefan Cardinal Wyszynski, Poland's Primate, smiled and said "The love of one's country boosts his energy."

21. June 15 report by "Stephan." BSTU No. 000204-210.

More than 50,000 faithful welcomed the pope's return to the Vatican. He told the people that "the faith of Poland is a reality, living and pulsating. It contained, like all authentic expressions of faith, a message of optimism."[22]

Moscow's Conundrum

Meanwhile, back in Moscow, KGB specialists were studying and analyzing the agents' reports on the papal visit, relying more on the East Germans than on Polish security officials, whom they considered as being untrustworthy,[23] based on the "nationalist sentiment" they were sure a Polish pope would ignite. They also dug through Western press comments and of prominent Poles. *Time* magazine of June 11, 1979, quoted the editor of Poland's Catholic monthly publication *Wiez* (The Link) as saying: "The pope's visit will inject new energy into society. The masses will feel stronger, they will understand that they should demand more. These nine days will be a religious event, of course, but they will also shape the consciousness of the people."

U.S. News and World Report commented on June 18 that "John Paul sought throughout his scheduled nine-day stay in the country to lay out a broader area of church responsibility than is now acceptable to Communist leaders in Eastern Europe." The magazine pointed out that the Polish regime has "long held that church and state can coexist only if the church restricts itself to moral and spiritual questions."

Kenneth A. Briggs wrote in the *New York Times* on June 11, 1979: "With the church morale so high and the pope pressing harder than

22. Vatican press office.
23. During a series of interviews with the author in 1990 and 1991 in Munich, former Colonel Rainer Wiegand of the Stasi's counter espionage department, who defected to the West before East Germany's collapse, told of his visits with high-ranking KGB officers in Moscow to discuss the Polish situation. "They told me 'you Germans and the Bulgarians are okay, but we can forget the others, and the Poles we can forget altogether'." And when visiting with Polish security officials, Wiegand said, he was told: "The KGB gets nothing from us."

expected for government concessions on religious rights, what is the likely outcome for Polish Catholics? First, there is every indication here that the church, newly conscious of its power, will flex its muscle in an effort to win certain demands from the state. The pope has shifted the grounds of the debate. Until now, the state has acted as if it dealt the cards. But in his address to the Polish bishops, the pope firmly declared that mutual recognition would be contingent on the church's insistence that the state grant fuller human and religious rights. The bishops are expected to lead a prudent but bolder fight now on such issues as greater access to public media and the right to have Catholic schools." In light of the communists' past reaction to Catholicism, this seemed unlikely, unless they could construe it to serve their own ends, as in the case with past Vatican infiltration.

Pondering the Western interpretations of the significance of the Polish pope's visit, the KGB surely must have also reviewed previous major workers' protests such as the 1956 bread riots, the Gdansk shipyard strikes in 1970, and others. And, of course, in view of earlier revolts in Czechoslovakia, Hungary, and East Germany, all brutally put down by Soviet arms with loss of lives and many wounded, this would have been studied and evaluated along with the current situation and the impact of the pope's visit.

When the analysis reached the Kremlin, it ominously added to the other woes that had befallen the leaders of the workers' paradise over the past decade. A new storm had arisen in Afghanistan, which for years had had significant economic and infrastructure support from the Soviet Union. Engineered by former prime minister Sardar Mohammed Daoud, a coup in 1973 demolished the monarchy. Daoud proclaimed the Republic of Afghanistan and installed himself as its president. At first, he remained on good terms with Moscow. But soon the Afghan leader cooled toward the Kremlin, and in April 1978, he was overthrown with Soviet help by the communist People's Democratic Party of Afghanistan (PDPA). Daoud and his immediate family were murdered. Nur M. Taraki took over as president, but his regime was opposed at once by resistance fighters.

Karol Cardinal Wojtyla was elected pope five months later, and things got only worse. A Polish pope! Zchto delatj? What to do? That's what First Secretary Brezhnev and his cohorts must have asked themselves. First, the trouble in far-off Afghanistan, a land that they hoped would eventually provide the Soviet Union with a route, through disputed Baluchistan, to the strategic Arabian Sea.[24] And now, a Polish pope at a time when his land was on the verge of chaos with ever-increasing anti-Soviet sentiment among the people, especially the working class. Had the masters of the Kremlin not been alleged atheists, they might have exclaimed: "Bozche moio! My God! And judging by the reaction of the Poles when the visit did commence, their reaction certainly was on the mark.

The Soviet leadership decided to tackle both problems almost simultaneously and aggressively. When the visit of John Paul II was announced in April 1979, General of the Army Alexei Yepishev, head of the Soviet Army's Main Political Directorate, was sent to Kabul to assess the situation, just as he had done in 1968 when he visited Czechoslovakia before the invasion[25] as a result of the Prague Spring.

And after the pope's triumphant June visit, decision time was at hand.

November 13, 1979, the Moscow weather was as dreary as must

24. From discussions with Mohammad Gailani of Mahaz-e-Milli Islami (mujahideen group), Engineer Ishaq, member of the political committee of Jamiat-e-Islamia (mujahideen) and Prof. S.B. Majrooh, director of the Afghan Information Center, at Islamabad, Pakistan, September, 1985, while on a fact-finding mission for the U.S. Information Agency. All pointed out that the area through which the Soviets would need to move to the Arabian Sea was severed from Afghanistan and taken over by Pakistan in 1893 by the Durand Line, which was never recognized by any Afghan government.
25. *Military Review*, September/October 1995: History of the Soviet War In Aghanistan: History and Harbinger of Future War? By retired general Mohammad Yahya Nwroz, Army of Aghanistan, and Lester W. Grau, Foreign Military Studies Office, U.S. Army Command and General Staff College, Ft. Leavenworth, KS.

have been the disposition of the Soviet leadership, temperatures hovered near freezing with a drizzly rain alternating with snow. Nine members of the Secretariat of the Communist Party Central Committee met at their headquarters on Staraia Ploshchad 4, a nondescript concrete building in the center of Moscow. The tenth member, Leonid Brezhnev, did not attend, as he was ill. Their deliberations most likely included the Afghanistan problem, as the Soviet invasion began on December 24, Christmas Eve,[26] but things were most definitely centered on how to counter the impact made on restless Poland by Pope John Paul II. When the meeting ended, the Secretariat issued the following order to the KGB:

> Use all possibilities available to the Soviet Union to prevent the new course of policies initiated by the Polish pope; if necessary with additional measures beyond disinformation and discreditation.
>
> The order was signed by Mikhail A. Suslov; Andrei P. Kirilenko; Konstantin U. Chernenko, Konstantin V. Rusakov, V. N. Ponomarev, Ivan V. Kapitonov, Mikhail V. Zimianim, Vladimir I. Dolgikh, and Mikhail S. Gorbachev.

In layman's terms, this was an order for assassination, foreshadowed by the need to "get physically close" with the pope that had resulted in KGB Major Sheymov's defection.

I obtained what appeared to me to be the partial text of this order during an interview in Rome with a high-ranking Italian official close to his country's security services. While discussing the attempted assassination of Pope John Paul II, he extracted a paper from a file,

---

26. Ibid. Soviet airborne troops had already arrived in October at Bagram airport to secure passage of land forces through the Salang Pass and its 8,910-foot tunnel providing passage of a major Kabul-Tashkent highway over the Hindu Kush mountains at 12,800 feet.

On Easter Sunday, March 31, 1923, Mosignor Konstantin Budiewicz was shot and killed at the Lubianka Prison in Moscow at the age of 56. One of Russia's most prominent Christian leaders, he became the first 20th century Catholic Martyr for "committing a counterrevolutionary act" by being an advocate for building a Christian Democratic movement. *1906–Photo Archive, SPB, St. Petersburg, Russia.*

Archbishop Jan Felix Cieplak. In 1917 he was named Bishop of the archdiocese of Mogilev, one of the oldest Roman Catholic Churches in Russia. In
1923 he was put on trial alongside Budkiewicz and 14 other priests in what
became known as the Cieplak Trial. Narrowly escaping execution, he was
sentenced to prison for ten years and then expelled from the Soviet Union.
He fled to Rome and later emigrated to the United States after being named
the Archbishop of Vilnius, Lithuania.

Drawing of a chaotic scene at the 1923 Cieplak Trial by Francis McCullagh, an Irishman who rode with the Cossacks in the Russo-Japanese War. McCullagh became a British intelligence agent, and, disguised as a journalist, reported on this and other communist-era activities. He is the author of several books, including *The Bolshevik Persecution of Christianity*, published in London, 1924.

Prisoners from the Cieplak Case. *Source unknown.*

Father Jerzy Popieluszko with flowers from parishioners.

Father Popieluszko after an evening mass in Warsaw on Sunday, July 29, 1984. Shortly thereafter he was kidnapped by secret police, bound and gagged and thrown into a river, where he drowned. The main perpetrator, Grzegorz Piotrowski, was released from prison after serving 15 years, shortened from the original 25 by lingering communist-era amnesties. *Associated Press/Czareksokolowski*

Former union official Luigi Scricciolo, who was arrested along with his wife Paola as alleged members of the Red Brigades, stand behind Lech Walesa in Rome, February, 1981. *Associated Press*

A huge crowd welcomes Pope John Paul II with cheers of "Sto Lat," may you live a hundred years, on June 4, 1979 at Czestochowa near the famous Monastery Jana Gora. This was his third day of his nine-day visit to his home-land. *Associated Press*

Pope John Paul II and President Ronald Reagan in a private meeting on June 7, 1982, at the Vatican, discussing the recent anti-communist uprising in Poland and how to subvert the Soviet domination of Easter Europe. *Osservatore Romano*

handed it to his secretary, and instructed her to translate portions of it. Then he handed me the paper. Beneath the translated text, it added: "SISDE says document found in Moscow points to plan for the 'physical elimination of JP II'." SISDE is the acronym for Servicio per le Informazioni a la Sicurezza Democratica, the Italian government's security service. Needless to say, I was thunderstruck. The official, who asked me not to reveal his name or position, would not say exactly how this order had been obtained. However, I surmised that it was part of the treasure trove of KGB documents handed to the British Secret Intelligence Service (SIS) by KGB Colonel Vasili Mitrokhin when he defected in 1992. I will deal with this document, and Russian reaction to it, in another chapter.

KGB chief Yuri V. Andropov now had a full plate. He not only had to keep his spies in Poland working overtime, but he also needed to devise a scheme to make sure that the days of the Polish pope were numbered "if necessary."

5 A STYMIED KREMLIN

After more than a decade of occasional lethal turbulence in Poland, the New Year of 1981 did not augur a lessening of strife. As if it did not have enough on its plate—Polish battles for freedom, the Afghan war, and jittery leaders of their East European minions—the Kremlin now faced an anticommunist workers' movement called Solidarnosc, Solidarity, that had grown to 10 million members, 700,000 of whom had belonged to the Communist Party. Then, in what must have seemed to the Soviet tyrants like the massing of new storm clouds, the Italian Socialist Party's Trade Union had invited a delegation of Solidarnosc for a five-day visit to Rome starting January 14. Reacting with inordinate speed, the Central Committee's Secretariat met a day earlier in a top-secret session to plot counteraction. Unquestionably, agents of the KGB had already informed home base that the 18-member delegation would be led by Solidarnosc leader Lech Walesa, the pesky electrician from the Lenin Shipyard, and joined by a founder of the Free Worker's Union, Anna Walentynowicz, the fierce welder from Gdansk, and Andrzej Gwiazda and Krzystof Wyszkowski, both prominent functionaries of the KOR, the Workers' Defense Committee. How was the Soviet Secret Police being kept informed at such a high level? Through their mole, Luigi Scricciolo, who had been an agent since 1976 for Ivan Tomov Dontchev, the Bulgarian intelligence chief in Italy. And, of course, the Bulgarians were under virtual control of the KGB. Scricciolo, the head of the foreign department of the Italian Social Labor Federation, traveled several times to Poland during the late 1970s, advising Walesa and delivering radios and printing equipment to Solidarnosc. Thus, he was able to keep the communist intelligence services abreast on the underground activities in Poland. And so it made perfect sense that Scricciolo was assigned, or that he assigned himself, as the guide of the Polish delegation.[1] He was a consummate agent.

The Central Committee's deliberations on the danger to "socialism" by the Walesa delegation, resulted in the decision to cable top-secret instructions, on January 14, to Nikolai Lunkov, its ambassador to Italy. It outlined the Kremlin's concern about the visit and instructed the ambassador to meet with the head of the Italian Communist Party, Enrico Berlinguer, or his deputy. Stressing the Soviet leadership's concern about the Walesa delegation's anti-Soviet influence on Western labor groups, the missive ended: "Evidently, from the above-mentioned facts, based on the interests of the Polish people and the interests of PLP (Polish Labor Party), it would be wise for you to *neutralize* [emphasis added] Mr. Walesa and his accomplices from using the trip to Italy to promote anticommunist, anti-Socialist, and anti-Soviet views."

1. Claire Sterling, The Times of the Assassins (Holt, Rinehart and Winston, New York, 1983), and Paul Henze, The Plot to Kill the Pope (Charles Scribner's Sons, New York, 1983).

Neutralize how? Killing them? That was the plan, but a former CIA officer, who asked that he not be named, told the author that authorities believed the killing was cancelled when those in control realized that murdering the popular Polish labor leader would arouse the indignation of the free world and further strengthen anticommunism. But more importantly, Italian authorities would surely strengthen domestic security so severely that it might well make further pro-communist operations impossible. Although there had been killings of dissidents, as explained in a later chapter, doing away with someone of Walesa's stature and influence surely would have ignited a civil war with massive human casualties. Only a Soviet invasion could have quelled it, but not without causing indignation in the Western world with ensuing consequences beyond even Moscow's control.

Lech Walesa and his delegation were received on January 15 by Pope John Paul II at a "solemn investiture for the first institutionalized free trade union in the worldwide Communist order, conducted with the ceremony usually reserved for a visiting head of state."[2] The Holy Father then met with his Polish brethren alone, no one else present. No evidence has come to light that the tete-a-tete was bugged.

The union's canonization was completed in the public part of the audience: an exchange of gifts and speeches by the pontiff and Walesa. And Walesa made obvious efforts to emphasize the nonpolitical nature of the fledgling trade union. "We are not interested in political problems," he said. "We are interested in the rights of man, of society, of the faith. . . . If these human rights will be respected, then man will feel himself a human and help others. These truths we have learned from you, Holy Father, and from the Church. They will be our orders."[3]

2. Claire Sterling, op. cit.
3. *Il Messsagero*, Rome, January 16, 1981, as quoted by Claire Sterling.

Pope John Paul II replied: "There does not exist, because there must not exist, a contradiction between the workers' independent social initiatives and the structure of a system that considers human labor the fundamental value of social and civic life. To undertake such an effort is a right confirmed by the entire code of international life. We know that the Poles have been deprived of this right more than once in the course of their history, a fact that has not made us lose our faith in divine Providence, and in ever beginning again."[4]

Before the delegation departed Rome, the pontiff personally celebrated mass for them in his private chapel. "I want to gather around this altar all working men, and all that their lives contain. If on this altar we can place all Polish labor, the strength which derives from on high will be restored to us, and man will become the son of God and give dignity to his labor. I beg you to carry my words to all working men in Poland."[5]

The Solidarity delegation returned to Poland without incident, but to unabated unrest despite a "fact-finding" Soviet government delegation which crisscrossed the beleaguered land, haranguing national and local Communist Party functionaries to take radical action against the recalcitrant workers and private farm owners advocating their own Rural Solidarity. The farmers had the firm backing of Walesa and the Catholic Church. Despite this open alliance with the anticommunists, the authorities took no punitive actions against the farmers, fully aware that the already-serious food shortages would have become more acute had they done so.

Four days after Walesa's return home, the Soviet Politburo met in Moscow to discuss the delegation's findings. Reporting was Leonid Zamyatin, head of the Central Committee's International Information Department, who once served Nikita Khrushchev as press spokesman.

4. Ibid.
5. Ibid.

He bewailed that the "group around Walesa backed by the Church wields great strength" with which the Polish Communist Party leadership "must come to terms."[6] Wielding especially dangerous influence are the "counterrevolutionary forces" of the KOR, the Committee for Workers' Defense, said Zamyatin. "These include Jacek Kuron, Adam Michnik, Andrzej Gwiazda, Bogdan Lis, and Anna Walentynowicz," naming a group of Poland's most vocal anti-government activists who had been imprisoned from time to time. "Solidarity is now essentially a political party, which is openly hostile to the PZPR (Polish Communist Party) and the state," Zamyatin lamented. He added that the Polish Communist Party was attempting to form a third trade union loyal to the state. "What we have in mind is to sever the KOR from Solidarity." The attempt failed. Obviously, the Polish communists had become weary of Moscow's constant pressure, and they were aware that the non-communist international community had become more vocal in their support for dissidents in the communist world. Furthermore, the Polish people knew that the Soviets had a "full plate" in maintaining their authority over other East European countries such as East Germany, Czechoslovakia, and the Baltic states.

The Kremlin's extreme nervousness over the ever-increasing possibility that a civil war might erupt if the Polish regime did not react more forcefully was apparent in every session of the Politburo. In the top-secret minutes of the April 8, 1981 session, Leonid Brezhnev exclaimed: "All of us are deeply alarmed by the further course of events in Poland. Worst of all is that the friends [Ed.: a term frequently applied to the Polish leadership] listen and agree with our recommendations, but in practice do nothing. In the meantime the counterrevolution is on the march all over."[7] Foreign Minister Andrei

---

6. Session of the CPSU CC Politburo, 22 January 1981, classified top-secret working notes. Translation by Cold War International History Project (CWIHP), George Washington University (GWU).
7. Politburo session April 8, 1981, working notes. Translated by CWIHP, GWU.

Gromyko, whose facial expressions always seemed as if he were suf-fering from severe acid reflux, told the session that his ministry was receiving a "huge" amount of information about the situation in Poland. He accused the United States and West Germany of "greatly distorting the true state of affairs." He made this statement at a time when protesting workers in the town of Bydgoszcz were brutally beaten and, in three cases, seriously hurt, merely for seeking to speak with party officials about continuing food shortages, an incident which resulted in a four-hour nationwide strike. "In addition, they speak a great deal about the Soviet Union, as though warning us that the Soviet Union must not use its armed forces to interfere in Poland's affairs."[8]

The tenor of the meeting, especially Gromyko's remarks, was one of apprehension about the Polish crisis and the reaction to it by Western nations, especially the United States, which had permeated both Politburo and Central Committee sessions for at least a decade. Back in 1977, President Carter was persuaded to make a demonstra-tive visit to Poland by his national security adviser, Zbigniew Brzezinski. The trip was viewed as too provocative by Secretary of State Cyrus Vance who, along with his Soviet affairs adviser, Marshall Shulman, opposed it.[9] Brzezinski, a native of Poland, was particularly tough on the Soviets' adherence to the accords of the Helsinki Final Act of the Conference on Security and Cooperation in Europe (CSCE). Moscow, along with 35 other nations, had signed and pledged to uphold respect for human rights, expansion of contacts between Eastern and Western Europe, freedom of travel, and the free flow of information across borders. By ignoring the wishes of the Polish workers, the Soviet regime systematically violated the agree-ment, as did other European communist regimes, particularly East

8. Ibid.
9. Zbigniew Brzezinski, *Power and Principle* (Collins, New York, 1985).

Germany. A visit by Carter to the Polish primate, Stefan Cardinal Wyszynski, who had endured three years of imprisonment for his valiant and passionate defense of civil liberties and religious tolerance, was cancelled at the urging of the State Department. Thus, Brzezinski took it upon himself to visit the indefatigable cardinal with the president's wife Rosalynn. It should be noted that Brzezinski was thoroughly detested by the Soviets not only for his stand on Poland but also for persuading his president to assist the Afghan anti-Soviet resistance and supplying the mujahideen with Stinger anti-aircraft missiles, which practically rendered Soviet air support ineffective.[10] It must be pointed out that presidents Richard Nixon and Gerald Ford had visited Poland years earlier to find peaceful solutions to the ever-burgeoning crisis.

Now, three years later, the Politburo had to deal with a most formidable exponent of anticommunism, the newly elected President Ronald Reagan, who was making an excellent recovery from the assassination attempt months before. Some of his closest advisers were practicing Catholics, such as Secretary of State Alexander Haig, his deputy William Clark, CIA Director William Casey and his deputy General Vernon Walters, and National Security Adviser Richard V. Allen. And the KGB had already a sizable dossier on the president, in which he was characterized as a "died-in-the-wool anticommunist who engaged in a campaign to drive progressive people out of the film industry and the unions. As a presidential candidate he promised to regain the international leadership position the United States forfeited under President Carter."[11] The KGB said President Reagan would reverse this "weakened United States' position worldwide"

10. Conversation with Richard V. Allen, former National Security Adviser to President Reagan, who said he esteemed Brzezinski highly for his devotion to national security and for freedom-seeking people behind the Iron Curtain.
11. John O. Koehler, *Stasi: The Untold Story of the East German Secret Police* (Westview Press, Boulder, CO, 1999).

and quoted him as saying during his campaign: "No one wants to use atomic weapons, but the enemy should go to sleep every night in fear that we could use them." The tone of many KGB reports was one of reluctant respect: "Reagan is a firm and unbending politician for whom words and deeds are one and the same." One report in the dossier emphasized the president's "incessant attacks on the lack of political freedom, prohibition of free speech, restriction of religious worship and travel, and economic failures of the socialist countries." And, of course, the Soviets were acutely aware of the intimate relationship between the Reagan White House and the Catholic hierarchy, especially with Philadelphia's John Cardinal Krol, the main advocate of Pope John Paul II and a Polish lobbyist, and John Cardinal O'Connor of New York

While facing formidable Western support for the obstreperous Polish workers, including the Italian Communist Party and the huge American AFL-CIO under the leadership of its staunch anticommunist president, Lane Kirkland, KGB agents were busy in West Germany trying to sniff out financial aid flowing to Solidarity. A top-secret KGB report of April 8, 1981, which was shared with the East German secret police, said the West German embassy in Vienna had organized a drive during which 200,000 Austrian shillings (about $13,440) was collected and sent to the West German embassy in Warsaw for delivery to Solidarity.[12] The report also said the West German Bishops Conference had called for a collection drive and that the Hans-Seidel Foundation of the Christian Democratic Union had delivered 60,000 DM ($24,429) directly to Lech Walesa during his visit to Rome in January. It pointed out that according to sources within the Catholic Church, the collection system was "functioning well and the activities of Solidarnosc have been secured chiefly because of the contributions." The

---

12. Report No. 2282.81, labeled "translation from the Russian—Top Secret, to Ministerium fuer Staatssicherheit (Stasi)," BSTU No. 000157.

report credited a mole buried within the West German Foreign Ministry in Bonn for the information.

With all this information pouring into the Kremlin, high-ranking Soviet functionaries kept roving across Poland, cajoling Communist Party officials to take tougher action against strikers and their leaders. Their appeals and threats fell on deaf ears. Resurgent nationalism was trumping their loyalty to their Soviet "comrades." During the April 2, 1981 Politburo session, many complaints were voiced about hollow promises by Communist Party leader Stanislaw Kania. Brezhnev decided that Defense Minister Dimitriy Ustinov and KGB chief Yuri Andropov should travel to the city of Brest on the Soviet border for a meeting with Kania and Wojciech Jaruzelski for another tough talk, which included the proclamation of martial law to cope with Solidarity and, in Brezhnev's words, "economic chaos and confusion," adding: "An absurd situation has emerged."[13] Andropov remarked that "Jaruzelski has gone soft, and Kania recently has begun to drink more and more excessively. This is a very pathetic situation." The KGB chief also expressed alarm that the Polish events were "influencing the situation in the western provinces of our country, particularly in Byelorussia. Many villages there are listening to Polish-language radio and television. I might add that in Georgia, we have had wild demonstrations. As in Tbilisi not long ago, groups of loudmouths have been gathering on the street, proclaiming anti-Soviet slogans, etc. Here, we must also adopt severe measures internally."

The Brest meeting was held, but nothing favorable toward quieting the Polish climate emerged. With ongoing Soviet pressure, Jaruzelski became prime minister and retained his post as defense minister. In March, another intimidating major Soviet-led maneuver was held in areas surrounding Poland. It changed nothing inside Poland and,

13. April 3, 1981 top-secret Politburo meeting. Virtual Archive, CWIHP, GWU, document No. 11.

realizing that an invasion by Soviet military forces would create a dangerous confrontation with the Western powers, Brezhnev and his cabinet continued voicing their demand for the imposition of martial law by native Polish forces.

6 MOSCOW'S DESPERATION INTENSIFIES

I was particularly interested to read your comments about the resurgence of religion. I have had a feeling, particularly in view of the pope's visit to Poland, that religion might very well turn out to be the Soviets' Achilles heel.

—President Ronald Reagan replying to
the author's report on a visit to Hungary
and Czechoslovakia, July 6, 1981

Erich Honecker, the Communist Party leader of East Germany, and his Politburo viewed the ongoing anti-government turmoil with consternation. They all remembered that if it had not been for armed Soviet intervention when the workers rebelled in 1953, their "workers' paradise" would have disappeared. Now, fearing Moscow's possible indecision and the Polish party's readiness for compromise with the Solidarity movement, the German Democratic Republic would be next. After all, the country was held together solely by the of the Ministry for State Security, the Stasi. Hundreds of thousands of dissidents suffered in its penitentiaries, and executions were still carried out for capital crimes, including "resisting the powers of the state," and so-called economic crimes, including black marketing.

Thus, Honecker ordered Stasi chief Erich Mielke to ready his minions, who had already gained experience in Poland during the visit of Pope John Paul II, for further assignments in the troubled eastern neighborhood. While Honecker was clearly concerned, his secret police boss displayed a disdain for "Polish habits" as he and other functionaries perceived them. They blamed events on *polnische Schlamperei*—Polish sloppiness, on the part of their communist comrades in Warsaw.[1] A special counterintelligence task force was established at Stasi headquarters in East Berlin. Mielke personally traveled to Warsaw to oversee the establishment of a Stasi war room at the East German embassy in Warsaw. Stasi officers were assigned to consulates throughout Poland to act as handlers of their spies in the field. In addition, KGB and Stasi officers collaborated about recruiting informants among military officers and officials of the Sluzba Bezpieczenstwa, the SB, the Polish secret police. One of the East German "IMFs," as the civilian spies with "enemy" contacts were called, was a freelance journalist from East Berlin, identified only by his code name "Josef," who had skillfully inveigled his way into the inner circle of the Solidarity trade union after writing a series of articles about the organization. He tried to peddle the articles to a West German magazine, but his letter was intercepted by the Stasi. When confronted by secret police officers, he realized his personal freedom was in danger and he "volunteered" to become an agent. In time, according to Stasi documents, he "performed with enthusiasm."

1. John O. Koehler, *Stasi: The Untold Story of the East German Secret Police* (Westview Press, Boulder, Colorado, 1999).

Virtually nothing happened within Solidarity that was not reported to the Stasi, and, thus, to the Soviets.[2]

The Polish people entered the year 1980 still seething and suffering from the 30 percent general food price increases. Sporadic strikes and protests continued while Soviet forces were conducting threatening maneuvers along the Polish border. In May, Brezhnev traveled to Warsaw for a summit meeting of the Warsaw Pact. The communist bloc military alliance closed its session by criticizing the United States for "trying to destroy détente."

By July 1980, Poland's foreign debt stood at about $20 billion. Another massive increase of about 60 percent in meat prices triggered an eruption of massive confrontations with authorities in nearly all parts of the country. The most critical industrial complexes in the region stopped production. This included aircraft and helicopter plants, chemical factories, steel mills, and coal and mineral mines. Threats of dismissals fell on deaf ears. Worker strike committees were formed at all affected industries and tried to negotiate with government functionaries. Across the board, workers demanded pay increases, free union elections, and guarantees that rebellious workers would not be harmed in any way. Transport and railroad workers walked off their jobs in Lublin, about 150 miles southwest of Warsaw, and within days all of the city's industries were shut down. Bulletins from KOR, the Workers' Defense Committee which was formed in 1976 to fight for the freeing of jailed strikers, were distributed throughout the country reporting on the unrest. While turmoil was raging, Communist Party boss Edward Gierek was vacationing on the Black Sea. His apparatchik for security, Stanislaw Kania, ordered that four army regiments be dispatched to the Gdansk region to try to restore order. In this explosive atmosphere of August 1980, 130 members of the New York Police Department's Pulaski Association

2. Ibid.

deplaned in Warsaw after visiting Rome and meeting with the Polish pope. "As we stood on the tarmac, we were astounded by the large number of soldiers with machine guns that ringed the arrival area," recalled Police Lt. Peter Bartoszek of Pelham, N.Y. "We came from Italy, where everyone was happy and jovial. But here, in the land of our ancestors, the mood was sullen and somber—all businesslike, no smiles or small talk as we went through customs. Even our bus driver was like that. We noticed that most of the butcher shops were ringed with long lines and no meat. People were looking very sad and all dressed similar in dark and gray clothing, no color or life. The only bright spot was our visit to a Catholic church, which was packed to overflowing with individuals and families attending mass. It was truly heart-warming." Lt. Bartoszek said the hotel staff wanted to buy the visitors' jeans and belts and other clothing. "We gave them what we could. After experiencing this visit, we left with heavy hearts and I thanked the Lord for allowing me to live in America."[3]

In their attempt to placate the workers, the government finally relented on wage demands and granted increases of between 10 and 20 percent, but this failed to cool the unrest which began at a major tractor plant of about 10,000 workers at Ursus, a suburb of Warsaw. That strike was led by Zbigniew Bujak, who, hunted by the secret police, was forced to live in hiding for more than four years. Another eruption followed at the Lenin shipyard in the Baltic Sea city of Gdansk, where the first major work stoppage had occurred ten years earlier. This time, 17,000 workers walked out because of food price increases and the firing of an electrician and militant free union activist named Lech Walesa and two other activists, one of whom was a militant welder, Anna Walentynowicz, called "the woman of iron" by her fellow workers. Walesa had climbed over a wall surrounding the yard and in a passionate speech persuaded the workers to strike.

3. Interview with Mr. Bartoszek.

Walesa was elected their leader, the first rung on his journey to fame. He quickly proved himself a demanding and effective spokesman of fellow workers, winning agreements from management on wage increases and nullifying dismissals. Strikers in other areas near Gdansk pleaded with the Lenin shipyard workers to join them in solidarity and continue the stoppage. Walesa agreed. A general strike for the area of Gdansk-Gdynia-Sopot was declared, an event that shook the communist government into action by agreeing to negotiate at the highest level. At that point, at least 350,000 had stopped working. In retaliation, the government cut off Gdansk's telephone service, not only in the city but for the rest of the nation as well.

On August 24, Solidarity Strike Bulletin No. 2 printed this letter from Pope John Paul II to Stefan Cardinal Wyszynski:

> Beloved and Revered Cardinal: I write to assure your Eminence of my closeness to you during these difficult days. I am with my country and countrymen throughout your ordeal, with all my heart and in all my prayers. News concerning Poland occupies the main pages of newspapers, it is constantly seen on the television screen and heard on the radio. I pray that once again, the Episcopate with the Primate at its head and supported by the trust in Her who is the defender of our country, may be able to aid the nation in its struggle for daily bread, social justice and a natural light to its own way of life and achievement. A very profound need impelled me to send you these few lines. I am with you at the feet of Our Lady of Czestochowa with solicitude, prayers and blessing.
>
> With deepest reverence,
John Paul II.[4]

4. *The Polish August: Documents from the Beginnings of the Polish Workers' Rebellion Gdansk—August 1980* (Labor Focus on Eastern Europe, London, England).

There was no public reaction from the Kremlin to this letter. But, judging by prior outbursts over the Polish dilemma, one can easily imagine that Brezhnev and his comrades must have been steaming. Would they not have interpreted this letter as an outright act of "subversion," support of what they would have considered as counterrevolutionary activities by the Vatican? And so prominently displayed, to boot!

The evening prior to the publication of the letter, Walesa's committee met at the Lenin shipyard with a government committee led by Vice Premier Mieczyslaw Jagielski. The British journalist Neal Ascherson wrote that Jagielski, "his face grey with distaste, came striding down a lane of shouting, laughing shipyard workers and hustled his delegation into the conference building."[5] He described how the meeting was held in a room with a glass wall behind which workers chewing green apples and Western photographers stared and made faces at the negotiators. "Worse still," Ascherson wrote, "every word Jagielski spoke was broadcast to a huge hall where the full Inter-Factory Strike Committee (MKS) was listening, and to the thousands of shipyard workers lying on the dusty grass or clustered around loudspeakers outside."

One settled in the negotiating room, Walesa handed Jagielski 21 demands drawn up by strikers from 388 plants. The negotiations were intense. Finally, the government relented and agreed to all demands. Even acceptance of only the first point would have been a momentous victory, as the regime allowed the establishment of free trade unions "independent of the Communist Party and its enterprises." Other important provisions included a guarantee of the right to strike and the security of strikers; compliance with freedom of speech and press as well as independent publishers; availability of the

5. Neal Ascherson, *The Polish August* (Penguin Books Ltd, Harmondsworth, Middlesex, England, 1981).

mass media to representatives of all faiths; and release of all political prisoners. There were also provisions for wage increases; selection for management positions on the basis of qualifications, not party membership; and elimination of special privileges to secret and regular police personnel, such as special stores where the privileged could purchase food and other goods not available to average citizens.[6]

While the agreements ended the Gdansk-area strikes, unrest in other areas continued. It prompted Moscow to intensify pressure. The day after the Polish regime signed the agreement with Solidarity, the Politburo established a commission led by the virulent ideologue Mikhail A. Suslov to deal with the growing Polish problem. The commission was instructed to "pay close attention to the situation unfolding in the PPR (Polish Peoples' Republic) and to keep the Politburo systematically informed about the state of affairs in the PPR and about *possible measures on our part*," an ominous phrase indeed. In the preparation of talking points for discussions with the Polish leadership, the Politburo recommended to Brezhnev, as well as to KGB chief Andropov, that the Poles be told "the agreement extracts a high political and economic price for the 'regulation' it achieves. We, of course, understand the circumstances in which you had to make this onerous decision. The agreement, in essence, signifies the legalization of the anti-socialist [read anticommunist] opposition." It continued: "Because the opposition intends to continue the struggle to achieve its aims, and the healthy forces of the Party and society cannot acquiesce in regressive movements by Polish society, the compromise that has been achieved will be only temporary in nature. One must bear in mind that the opposition is expecting, not without reason, that help will be forthcoming from the outside."[7] The minutes of this session

6. Ibid.
7. Extract from Protocol No. 213, Sept. 3, 1980 session of the Politburo classified top secret, eyes only. Translated by Professor Mark Kramer of the Cold War Intl. History Project, GWU.

reveal the extreme anxiety that engulfed the Soviet leadership. The tenor of the discussions bordered on hysteria. "An organization has emerged that aims to spread its political influence through the entire country. *The complexity of the struggle against it stems from the fact that the members of the opposition disguise themselves as defenders of the working class and as laborers*" [emphasis added]. The foundation of the communist-founded union was being shaken to its core.

One of the orders given to the Polish Communist Party leaders was that they must "launch relentless counterpropaganda against efforts to water down the principle of classless socialist patriotism under the slogan 'All Poles in the world are brothers,' as well as the efforts to idealize the pre-revolutionary past of Poland; and in the political struggle against anti-socialist elements, carry out the appropriate attacks against them, rather than merely going on the defense."[8] And so, the Kremlin's henchmen roamed Poland, pressuring party officials to fall in line with the Soviets' tough stance toward the country's now-independent union, free from communist domination. Edward Gierek, the Party leader, met the same fate as his predecessor Wladyslaw Gomulka ten years earlier: he was sacked and expelled from the Party. Stanislaw Kania, a Moscow faithful and hardliner who had been responsible for internal security (i.e., overseeing the secret police apparatus), was chosen to replace Gierek. But the elevation came not without a public warning from Moscow. The Soviet Communist Party newspaper Pravda said the Polish state existed only at the Kremlin's pleasure and its communist system "is guaranteed by the fraternal unity with the other socialist countries."[9] With this turmoil engulfing the communist hierarchy as well as the Polish people, where did the Church stand in all this? This is what the British journalist Neal Ascherson astutely observed: "In this darkness,

8. Ibid.
9. Arthur Rachwald, *Solidarnosc: In Search of Poland* (Hoover Institution Press, Stanford University, 1990).

the instinct of most people was simply to grope backwards to the last solid object they could remember touching. In most cases, this was the Church. Close to it, and reassuringly firm, were the simple monuments of traditional Polish nationalism. It was here, like fugitives feeling their way out of a smoke-filled building, that Poles came together, sensed their collective strength, and re-grouped." He added that the Catholic Church had not always led the nation from among the ranks of the working people. "It was Cardinal Wyszynski, above all, who had ensured that the Church would never again become identified with its ruling oligarchy," he wrote.[10]

While the Kremlin was stewing over how to handle the rebellious Polish workers, as well as the country's well-nigh rudderless Communist Party, the United States Central Intelligence Agency (CIA) was able to keep the White House up to date with precise information on military preparations not only of the Polish and Soviet forces, but of the communist satellites East Germany, Czechoslovakia, Hungary, and Romania as well. On August 14, 1972, Colonel Ryszard Kuklinski, a high-placed member of the Polish general staff, had volunteered his services to the CIA after becoming dismayed by the plight of his people.[11] Until November 1981, when the colonel, his wife, Hanka, and his young sons, Bogdan and Waldemar, were extricated to the West, he supplied the most secret plans for possible military intervention. As a result, the United States government was able to adjust and readjust its own high-priority counter-action plans. These plans included the implementation of boosting U.S. military forces, both active and reserve, as well as deploying new and highly secret weapons systems in Western Europe. In 1984, the Polish communist regime tried Kuklinski for treason in absentia and sentenced him to

10. Neal Ascherson in *The Polish August.*
11. See Benjamin Weiser, *A Secret Life* (Public Affairs Books, New York, 2004).

death. Some six years after the collapse of the East European communist regimes, this sentence was set aside, especially because of the personal intervention of Zbigniew Brzezinski, national security adviser to President Jimmy Carter.

With Colonel Kuklinski risking his life and the Polish workers still resisting the communist regime despite the August agreement, the Soviet Politburo met again on October 31, 1980. Leonid Brezhnev, increasingly displaying periodic feebleness, was in a more coherent mode as he addressed his 18 comrades after a meeting with Polish Party leader Stanislaw Kania, who assured him that his government would resolve the internal strife "on its own and by its own means."[12] Brezhnev apparently did not take much stock in Kania's assurances. "Events in Poland have deteriorated so far by now that if we let time slip away and do not correct the position of the Polish comrades, we will—before you know it—be faced with a critical situation that will necessitate *extraordinary* [emphasis added] and, one might even say, painful decisions." Brezhnev's meaning was not lost on the comrades. A plan, which no doubt had already been delivered to Kuklinski's CIA handlers, called for a three-pronged move into Poland by Soviet, East German, and Czechoslovakian combat and supply units on December 8, 1980.[13] This was rescinded after Defense Minister Wojciech Jaruzelski pleaded for a postponement, which was granted after Party boss Kania pledged that Poland would remain a socialist country.[14]

The postponement must have markedly increased East German Party leader Erich Honecker's distress, since only 10 days earlier, on November 28, he had written to Brezhnev pleading that there should

12. Document No. 3, CWIHP, Woodrow Wilson Historical Center GWU, Washington, D.C.
13. Vojtech Mastny, Working Paper No. 23, CWIHP, Woodrow Wilson Historical Center. Warsaw Pact Supreme Commander Marshal Victor G. Kulikov, asked Jaruzelsksi to grant permission for the action.
14. Ibid.

be a discussion with Kania "in order to work out collective measures to assist the Polish friends in overcoming the crisis which, as you know, has been intensifying day after day." Honecker made use of the information fed him by the secret police command posts he had established in a number of Polish cities. They reported that riots and strikes were continuing with virtually no intervention by authorities. He told the Soviet leader in a tone that betrayed hysteria, or close to it:

"According to information we have received through various channels, counterrevolutionary forces in the People's Republic of Poland are on the constant offensive, and any delay in taking action against them would mean the demise of socialist Poland. *Yesterday our collective efforts would have perhaps been premature, but today they are absolutely necessary and tomorrow they would already be too late"* [emphasis added].

Honecker also told the Soviet leader that his fellow tyrants, Czechoslovakian and Bulgarian leaders Gustav Husak and Todor Zhivkov, who also saw their socialist workers' Gardens of Eden rapidly withering into oblivion as workers were inspired by government inaction, had also urged a Moscow meeting. "We ask you, Leonid Ilyich, to understand our **'extraordinary fears'** [emphasis added] about the situation in Poland. We know that you also share these fears."[15] The meeting of top officials of the Warsaw Pact was held on December 5, after which a bland press release was issued saying the Polish situation had been discussed and that the turbulent country's leaders understood the gravity of the situation and that Brezhnev's speech was "an inspiration" to the participants.[16] Three days later, Warsaw Pact forces led by the Soviet Union began their intimidating 13-day maneuver called Soyuz (Union) 80.

15. Free University Berlin: SED-Politburo und Polnische Krise 1980/1982.
16. Results of a meeting among leading officials of the Warsaw Pact member-states in Moscow, 5 December 1980. Translation by CWIH, Woodrow Wilson International Center for Scholars, GW University.

This renewed waving of the big stick, threats of an invasion by the Soviet Union and some of its allies, notably East Germany and Czechoslovakia, prompted action over in Washington, D.C. The CIA's precious asset, Colonel Kuklinski, provided the details. On December 3, following the advice of Dr. Brzezinski, the outgoing President Carter sent a blunt warning to Brezhnev over the Washington-Moscow hotline that U.S.-Soviet relations would be "highly negatively affected" if Poland's problems were solved with force. President-elect Ronald Reagan joined in the warning. Washington passed Kuklinski's information on to the Vatican, prompting a letter, on December 16, from Pope John Paul II to Brezhnev. In his acclaimed biography of Pope John Paul II, *Witness to Hope*, the eminent American theologian George Weigel wrote that the Holy Father "in discreet language of diplomacy" implicitly drew a "parallel between any Soviet invasion of Poland in 1980 to the Nazi invasion of Poland of September 1939." Brezhnev ignored the pope. It is unlikely that the letter was meant to rally the West, since it was kept secret. Besides, such a rallying call was not needed, since the pope had been kept informed on the West's contingency plans by Dr. Brzezinski.

While the tormented Polish people, still suffering from food shortages, were wishing each other Wesoly Swiat, a Merry Christmas, and worshipped in overflowing churches, the communist leadership and functionaries were in continuing disarray, as they had been all year. The unrest continued, with sporadic protests until the end of the year.

7 INFAMY!

Catholic pilgrims to the Vatican were enjoying a warm spring afternoon on Wednesday, May 13, 1981. Among them was a group of Poles from the parish in Krakow where Karol Cardinal Wojtyla, now Pope John Paul II, had served as a young priest. Now the brethren of the beleaguered nation came to pay homage to the Polish pope, along with a throng of some 15,000 of many nationalities. At the sound of five bells ringing from atop surrounding churches, the Holy Father arrived at St. Peter's Square standing in an open white oversized jeep which had been dubbed the Popemobile. The crowd cheered and waved papal flags as the Popemobile circled the square once, then started a second round before the car stopped at a spot where the pope was to deliver a speech. It was 5:19 when he picked up a little blond-haired girl and hugged her tenderly. When he put the child down, he reached out to shake hands with another girl. A man standing in the crowd a few yards from Pope raised an arm over the heads of the bystanders, his hand holding a pistol aimed in the direction of the Holy Father. Because he was wedged in, he had no chance to take careful aim. The man fired a series of shots from a 9mm Browning automatic pistol, one bullet smashing through the pope's intestines; another ripped through the ring finger of his left arm, ricocheted, and grazed his right arm. The pope collapsed into the arms of his long-time secretary and confidant Monsignor (now Archbishop) Stanislaw Dziwisz. For moments the crowed stared in disbelief, then broke into load moaning and wailing. The Popemobile raced to the ambulance that was always stationed in the proximity of public papal appearances. Once transferred, the pope was taken to Gemelli Hospital, reputed to be the finest in Rome with a staff of first-rate surgeons. As with the shooting of President Reagan forty-two days earlier, the bullet into his abdomen just barely missed the Holy Father's spine, abdominal aorta, and pancreas. Surgery lasted 5 1/2 hours and he was given nearly six pints of blood.

Two other bullets missed the pope but hit two American women, Ann C. Odre, a 58-year-old devout Catholic and widow from Buffalo, N.Y., and Rose Hall, 21, from Shirley, Mass. Both recovered, though Mrs. Odre suffered the removal of her spleen.

In the confusion and pandemonium that followed the shooting, the assailant tried to escape through the crowd. However, bystanders chased after him and he was caught by Vatican security men, pressed into a police vehicle, and then driven to the Vatican police headquarters, where he was transferred to an armored vehicle and then taken to the central police headquarters. The weapon was recovered. After an interrogation that lasted through the night, the would-be murderer of Pope John Paul II was identified as 23-year-old Mehmet Ali Agca, a Turkish national. Italian investigators checked the "wanted" circulars provided by the Paris-based International Police Organization, Interpol, and found that Agca had escaped from a prison near Istanbul where he had been serving a life sentence for the murder of Abdi Ipekci, the respected editor of the newspaper *Milliyet*. A day after he shot Ipekci, Agca put a letter in a mailbox opposite the newspaper office. It warned that if the pope's visit to Turkey, which was scheduled for three days later, was not called off, "I will definitely shoot the pope." His reason? "Western imperialists, who fear that Turkey may establish a new Political, Military and Economic Force in the Middle East with brotherly Islamic countries, have rushed at a sensitive time to send Crusader Commander John Paul to Turkey under the mask of a religious leader."[1] This prompted Turkish authorities to reinforce security during the pope's visit even after Agca's arrest. The visit proceeded without any incidents.

On May 28, as the Holy Father was recovering from his wounds, his friend Stefan Cardinal Wyszynski died of natural causes. He was 79 years old. With Pope John Paul II in deep mourning, the reaction to this double tragedy from around the world had been overwhelming in heartfelt sympathy, ranging from the average Polish citizen to world leaders. "I pray for him," said President Reagan, who himself was still recuperating from his own assassination attempt. But there was one message that was not only incredibly hypocritical, but a bald-faced lie. It came from a man who had often enough voiced his distain for any religious leader and especially for the Polish pope. Soviet Communist Party leader Leonid Brezhnev's cable read that he was "profoundly indignant at the criminal attempt on your life." Hypocritical because he had tried to organize the shooting of the pope himself!

While hundreds of millions around the world were praying for a swift recovery of Pope John Paul II, Italian police quietly went into overdrive delving into the background of Agca, the would-be assassin. The initial unofficial story that quickly circulated around the world described the shooter as an adherent of the "Gray Wolves,"

---

1. *The Plot to Kill the Pope* by Paul Henze (Charles Scribner's Sons, New York, 1983).

the extreme rightist National Action Party founded by Colonel Alparslan Türkes, an admirer of Adolf Hitler. This was thoroughly debunked by Paul Henze in his book *The Plot to Kill the Pope* and by Claire Sterling in *The Times of the Assassins*. Both writers exhaustively and expertly investigated and reported on the background of Agca and his perplexing travels in the Middle East and Western Europe. Enlisting the aid of the West German Federal Intelligence Service, Bundesnachrichtendienst (BND), and the Federal Criminal Police Agency, Bundeskriminalamt (BKA), Italian authorities established that Agca had visited various cities and towns in West Germany, Austria, and Switzerland, as well as the Bulgarian capital, Sofia. Although born into a poor family, Agca graduated from teacher's training and later attended the universities of Ankara and Istanbul. But he never seemed to have had a steady, well-paying job, which provided Italian investigators with the puzzle of how he had managed to acquire the thousands of dollars that he had deposited in various Turkish banks. He traveled with a passport issued in his own name and at least one other false Turkish travel document. His first appearance in Italy was at the port of Palermo, when he stepped off the ferry from Tunisia on December 13, 1980. Two days later, he was in Milan for a meeting with Musa Serdar Celebi, a rightist running a Turkish nationalist group in West Germany who, Agca told Italian interrogators, had told him that a notorious smuggler, Bekir Celenk, who spent much of his time in Bulgaria, would pay him three million West German marks (then about $1,260,000) if he killed the pope and that a haven in Bulgaria was assured.[2] Basically, this implies that the Bulgarian government would hide him. Arrested by the Italians, Celebi denied the conversation. However, West German authorities had had Celebi under surveillance for some time, probably for his smuggling activities. In fact, a telephone conversation in

2. Ibid.

late April 1981 between Celebi and Agca just months before his attempt to assassinate Pope John Paul II, was intercepted by the Germans. In it, Agca, who was then in Majorca, Spain, confirmed that he had received the money and said "I will now go to Rome and finish the job."[3]

As Agca was being subjected to intensive interrogation, Western journalists had a field day with speculations about the Turk's motive. Agca quickly confessed that he was the shooter. The Italian judiciary chose to ignore the many speculations and rumors, including neo-fascist plot, Islamic terrorism, etc., and ruled that he would be tried attempting to murder the pope as a lone gunman, thus assuring a speedy trial. In the weeks before, as well as during, the trial, Agca changed his story and his behavior many times. During his trial, which began on July 20, his behavior was at times so bizarre that attendants felt he was trying to feign insanity.

Nevertheless, Presiding Judge Severina Santiapichi and a jury of six found Agca guilty. He was sentenced to life imprisonment. The details of the Turk's personal and political background and travels, as well as those of his compatriots and Bulgarian officials, have been published in the two excellent books, *The Plot to Kill the Pope* by Paul Henze and *The Times of the Assassins* by Claire Sterling. Thus, I shall discuss the frenetic attempts to cover up the Bulgarian security service's involvement and the Soviet KGB's surprising connection to Agca.

In less than two months after the shooting, the KGB reported that a spy for the Hungarian secret police had said that "the Secretariat of State, which is investigating the assassination attempt of Pope John Paul II, believes it is not impossible that it was a deliberate action of Moslem circles in order to prevent the spread of Catholicism in the 'Third World'." Therefore, the report speculated, one must count on a

3. Ibid.

cooling in Vatican-Arabic relations. "The first indication for this development is the cancellation of a visit by a Vatican delegation to Egypt." In view of the pope's near-fatal shooting, it was incredible that the KGB thought it important that preparations were being made for "administering the Church without the pope," as what else would they be doing during his recovery? It was not unusual that the KGB indulged from time to time in wishful thinking. To wit: "The influence of the pope's Polish confidants and the West German cardinals is evident in this regard. Thus the pope, following his recovery, must be put under a strong internal control in order to preserve his health."[4] It seemed as if they thought a non-visible pope would result in tension abating in Poland and the other Eastern bloc countries. Pope John Paul II lived another 24 years and traveled throughout the world, including many other trips to Poland.

This aforementioned document was the first of 40 Soviet and Bulgarian reports I found that discussed the assassination attempt. These documents will be discussed chronologically as they were received in East Berlin from high officials of the Bulgarian State Security Service Durzhavna Sigurnost (DS). One cannot dismiss the probability that the missives were part of an elaborate disinformation operation to dupe even the East German allies into believing in Moscow's and Sofia's non-involvement. But if this is what the Soviets and Bulgarians sought to achieve, it is unlikely that it worked, as the requests for help in calming the turmoil in Poland and other Eastern European territories began to sound almost hysterical within months, something the experienced and well-trained East German intelligence experts could not have missed.

As the Bulgarian involvement and speculation of Soviet instigation occupied the news pages and broadcasts, the East German Stasi had

---

4. East German Ministry for State Security (Stasi) top secret document No. 8857/81, dated July 7, 1981, marked translation from the Russian. BSTU No. 000198.

begun its disinformation campaign "Operation Papst," Operation Pope, to draw suspicion off its Bulgarian comrades. It was directed by Markus "Mischa" Wolf, a four-star general who headed the Main Administration for Foreign Intelligence (HVA). On August 31, 1982, he received an encoded telegram from the "Department for Active Measures" of the Bulgarian security service. It read: "Lately the mass media of a number of capitalist states carried tendentious material and lies that said the attempted murder of Pope John Paul II in 1981 had been the work of organs of the KGB and that the Bulgarian security organs closely supported the terrorist Mehmet Ali Agca in that they supplied money and weapons. Obviously, this is a campaign directed by the secret services of the enemy with the aim of discrediting Bulgaria by accusing it of connections with terrorist organizations. The Bulgarian security organs beseech you, in view of the situation that has developed, to speed up the preparation of documents for use in our joint Operation Pabst." A month later, a sealed envelope marked "Operation Pabst," sent by the Bulgarian "Department for Active Measures," was delivered to Wolf. No file regarding its contents was found.

A second telegram pleading for help was received in East Berlin on December 4 by State Security Minister Erich Mielke,[5] who passed it on to General Wolf. This communication read: "The arrest of the member of the Bulgarian Air Line 'BALKAN' office in Rome, Sergei Antonov, is dismaying and the accusation that he participated in the assassination attempt has no basis in fact. Antonov has no connection to our intelligence services nor with Agca and other participants. The aim of this grave provocation is to strengthen the hostile campaign of the American propaganda centers with 'factual material' in order to prove that Agca was trained by our services on orders from the KGB of the USSR." The telegram said that the Italian

5. Telegram No. 1304/82. BSTU No. 000007.

investigative judge Ilario Martella had traveled to the United States in order to study the sources used in a *Reader's Digest* article on the murder attempt written by Claire Sterling. "This visit was to prepare for reinforcement of the hostile campaign. Obviously, this is a broad and intensive active measure of the CIA and the Italian security services in an attempt to strengthen global anticommunist propaganda." The telegram emphasized Ms. Sterling's and Mr. Henze's contacts with the CIA and U.S. Embassy officials in Rome. Such an action, of course, would apply to any competent journalist who would pursue a myriad of sources in their legitimate journalistic endeavors. The telegram closed with another appeal for assistance "to counter the hostile campaign of Western propaganda centers and to supply us with any material you have about Henze and Sterling." Even before the second telegram arrived in East Berlin, Wolf's Department X, responsible for manufacturing disinformation, had already shifted into high gear.

The efforts of Department X spanned over four years, manufacturing phony stories about the CIA "steering" the activities of the extreme right movement "Gray Wolves." It even forged a "confidential" letter which the conservative Minister President of predominantly Catholic Bavaria, Franz Josef Strauss, was supposed to have sent to the head of a Turkish rightwing movement in 1980. In the bogus letter, Strauss made disparaging remarks about the person and politics of Pope John Paul II. The forgery was aimed at creating the impression that Strauss, because of his bogus "intimate contacts" with the head of the rightwing party, had already known that Agca had planned to murder the pope during his visit to Turkey in 1980 and did nothing. Copies of the letter were sent anonymously to Italian, British, and Turkish news organizations.[6]

6. Auftrag Irrefuehrung, Carlsen Verlag, Hamburg 1992. Authors Guenter Bohnsack, HVA Department for Active Measures, and Herbert Brehmer of the HVA Department Western Intelligence Services.

The trial in Rome of Agca and periodic announcements regarding the attempted assassination continued to saturate the newspapers, radio, and television throughout the Western world. Few expressed doubt that the assassination attempt had not been engineered by the Bulgarian secret service, particularly since it had carried out the murder of Georgi Markov, a playwright and novelist revered by his fellow Bulgarians. Markov began to despise the communist regime when it supported Moscow in the 1968 invasion of Czechoslovakia. Markov was granted official permission a year later to leave for the West on the pretext of visiting a brother who lived in Italy. Two years later, he moved to Great Britain and worked as a radio newsman and commentator for Radio Free Europe, the British Broadcasting Corporation, and West Germany's Deutsche Welle, the equivalent to the Voice of America. Markov enjoyed an ever-increasing audience in Bulgaria as he relentlessly chastised the government and the Communist Party, particularly its brutal leader Todor Zhivkov. There were other dissident rumblings in Bulgaria at the time, but Markov was considered to be Zhivkov's worst foe, and an assassination plot on Markov was hatched on Zhivkov's orders. On September 7, 1978, Markov was waiting for a bus in London on his way to work when he was jabbed in the right thigh. He noticed a heavyset man, about 40 years old, picking up an umbrella and hailing a taxi. By evening, Markov developed a high fever and was hospitalized, and four days later he was dead. An autopsy extracted a minute pellet attached to a pin from the wound. A top-level team of forensic experts examined the pellet, into which a tiny hole had been expertly drilled using laser technology. A coroner's inquest eventually established that Markov had died from the poison Ricin, for which no antidote exists. After the collapse of communism, two former top KGB officers admitted KGB collaboration with Bulgarian State Security and that the umbrella used as the murder weapon had been purchased in the

United States by a KGB operative and sent to the Soviet Union, where a laboratory handled the conversion.[7]

Why dwell on the Markov case? Because every high-level Bulgarian intelligence and security official also participated in pressuring the East German Ministry for State Security, and members of the Politburo, to manufacture disinformation and propaganda in an effort to lift suspicion off Sofia and, of course, Moscow, as to their involvement in the assassination attempt of Pope John Paul II. Regrettably, no KGB documents to cement this connection could be found. Most likely these were destroyed, since they were likely held by General Wolf's HVA where the shredders were whirring round the clock when the Stasi was disintegrating in 1990. However, the late Colonel Rainer Wiegand, who held a top-level position in the counterespionage directorate, told me that often the most sensitive matters were handled orally by KGB liaison officers with Stasi counterparts so as not to leave a paper trail.[8] But there is enough material available regarding the attempt that points in the direction of Bulgaria and the Soviet Union.

Bulgarian judicial authorities announced in March 1991 that the former chief of intelligence, General Vladimir Todorov, had destroyed the Markov dossier. To escape arrest, he and his family fled to Moscow, but they returned to the Bulgarian capital when the government protested and requested his extradition. He was tried in June 1992 and sentenced to 16 months in prison.

General Stoyan Savov, Todorov's second in command, was also indicted, but he put a bullet into his head rather than stand trial. A

---

7. The admissions were made by KGB Colonel Oleg Gordievsky in his book *KGB: The Inside Story* (HarperCollins, New York, 1990), and more extensively and in greater detail by former KGB Maj. Gen. Oleg Kalugin in *The First Directorate: My 32 years in intelligence and espionage against the West* (St. Martin's Press, New York, 1994).
8. In 1992, I interviewed Wiegand, who had defected to the West before East Germany's collapse. He was an important source for my book *Stasi: The Untold Story of the East German Secret Police.*

Bulgarian journalist, Hristo Hristov, wrote a series of articles on the Markov case published by the Sofia newspaper *Dnevnik* in June 2005. He revealed that another member of the DS, Vasil Kotsev, who allegedly commanded the Markov operation, died "mysteriously" in an auto accident in 1991. Both the Savov and Kotsev names appear as signatories on the Sofia letters and telegrams begging the East Germans for help in drawing off suspicion of complicity in the attempted murder of Pope John Paul II. It reminds one starkly of the adages "Methinks he doth protest too much" or "Where there's smoke, there's fire." Were they the prime movers in the department of "wet affairs," or mokrij delja as the KGB and its predecessors named their murder squads? Both Savov and Kotsev had been lieutenant generals: the former was deputy interior minister overseeing state security; the latter was chief of foreign intelligence.

The similarity between the Markov murder and the attempt on the pope also extends to the type of persons who carried out the "jobs." Both were former criminals. Agca was convicted of murder in Turkey. He managed to escape from prison and fled to Bulgaria, where he was recruited and trained by the DS. The Markov killer was identified as Francesco Gullino, an Italian born in Bari in 1946. Bulgarian border police caught him smuggling narcotics and in illegal currency transactions. Obviously given a choice "work for us or go to prison," he was recruited as an agent by DS in 1970. He roamed through Europe in a small truck, according to files discovered by the investigative newsman Hristo Hristov. Gullino was dealing in antiques and eventually settled in Copenhagen, where he bought a house and opened a picture-framing business. When Gullino's name was revealed as the suspected Markov killer, Danish police and Scotland Yard detectives, acting on a tip, located him in February 1993.[9] He had become a Danish citizen. Denying any involvement in the killing

---

9. The (London) Sunday Times on Line, June 5, 2005.

of the Bulgarian writer, he confessed to committing espionage. Fingerprints and handwriting samples were taken; but because the Danes had no evidence against him, he was released. Nevertheless, the Danish Ministry of Justice contacted the new Bulgarian government for information on Gullino, but they received no response. Subsequent attempts by the British government requesting cooperation were also ignored, and the case died.[10] How does one say in Bulgarian: "Let sleeping dogs die"? After all, the government was trying to make a new start as a democratic one, and the Bulgarian members of the wet affairs squad, as well as the man who gave the order to kill Markov, Todor Zhivkov, were already long dead. Gullino sold his Copenhagen house about a month after his police questioning and left the country for an unknown destination. Efforts to locate him hit a blank wall, as is not unusual in such cases.

As for Mehmet Ali Agca, on December 27, 1983, Pope John Paul II went to Rome's Rebibbia prison to meet with his attacker. The two spent 21 minutes alone in a dingy one-man cell. The pope prayed for him, called him "my brother," and gave him a silver rosary.[11]

The Vatican has never revealed details of this conversation between the pontiff and Agca. There was speculation that the Turk may have confessed and revealed details he had withheld during his trial. Evidently, this is what the Bulgarians feared. On February 10, 1984, Erich Mielke, the Stasi chief, received a letter from Bulgarian Minister of the Interior Dmitri Stojanov. "The pope's visit with Agca is for us inconvenient as it is also being exploited by the enemy for his propagandistic aims," the minister wrote. "This is one of the reasons that we must continue our combined efforts in combating the campaign of the West until we have completely exposed the lies and stopped them." He also expressed great concern about the arrest and pending

10. Ibid.
11. Zenet news service, Rome, June 14, 2000.

trial of Sergei Antonov of Balkan Airline's Rome office. Stojanov asserted that the Italian investigative judge Martella "is resorting to methods aimed at subjecting Antonov to a new psychological shock in order to achieve his total physical destruction." The pope's meeting with Agca and the pontiff forgiving the "sins" of Agca, the Bulgarian Minister said, was also being used to influence the Antonov case. "Thus we must take measures which would distract the enemy's attention from the 'Antonov Case'." Stojanov closed his plea by expressing his "deeply felt appreciation for the brotherly help you have given us until now and for your essential contributions in the battle to expose and prevent the hostile Western campaign against our socialist community." It was obvious that Stojanov and his secret police compatriots considered Antonov a key player in the attempt to kill the pope; and disinformation efforts, conveyed to him by his attorneys, seem to have worked. Antonov steadfastly maintained his innocence, and after three years in investigative detention he was released and immediately left Italy for his homeland. In June 1997, reporters of the German newspaper *Bild* tracked Antonov down in Sofia, living in a dilapidated apartment building with his mother. "The man is a wreck—absent-minded and his eyes twitching behind thick glasses," they wrote. His mother was quoted as saying: "He doesn't even speak with me and at night he talks loudly with himself. In the first two or three years after his release from jail, he was normal. Then his illness became worse, and now he doesn't want to see anybody and speak to anyone."[12] Antonov died in February 2007. He was 59 years old. As for Agca, the Italian government pardoned him on June 13, 2000, at the behest of the Vatican, and deported him to Turkey to serve 10 years in prison for the 1979 murder of the newspaper editor.

After the collapse of the East German communist regime, Magistrate Rosario Priore, who led the extensive probe into the pope

12. *Bild Zeitung*, June 19, 1997.

shooting from its beginning, received the Stasi documents mentioned in this chapter. In the course of his investigation, Alexandre de Marenches, former head of French Foreign Intelligence and Counter Espionage Service (SDECE), was questioned and confirmed that he had informed the pope in 1980 that his service had learned of a Soviet decision, made at "the highest level," to eliminate the pope. Although he did not know the details, de Marenches said he found the information credible. Dr. Priore requested details of the visit from the Vatican but received no response.[13] He said the Vatican rejected many of his requests, on the basis that these were internal matters.[14]

In May 1991, at the request of the magistrate, Italian Premier Guilio Andreotti requested from Mikhail Gorbachev any information that might be in the KGB archives that could shed light on the attack. The Soviet ambassador in Rome responded that there was nothing in the archives that showed that the Soviets were behind the attack.

Relentlessly pursuing the case, Dr. Priore asked German authorities to interview Stasi Minister Erich Mielke, foreign intelligence chief Markus Wolf, and Günther Bohnsack, who collaborated with the Bulgarians in the disinformation and propaganda effort. Neither Mielke nor Wolf cooperated. Bohnsack was interviewed, and this is what the magistrate's report said:

"Bohnsack said he was surprised that the request for assistance from the Bulgarians had been dealt with 'so high up,' at the level of the Politburo, something which was considered unusual. He said the mission of his department was to prepare a lead that would point to the CIA and accompany all this with rumors and other 'evidence.' The

13. Tribunale di Roma. Ufficio Instruzione—Secione 1a. N. 9031/85A P.M. section 3.2.1, pages 211-216.
14. Interview with the author, July 22, 1999.

rumors were spread through agents, contacts, and trusted persons. Even the East German embassy in Rome collaborated in spreading these rumors.

"Bohnsack revealed that another key point was the case of Antonov, the representative of Balkan Air and, evidently, a man of the Bulgarian secret services. The Bulgarians feared that in prison he could talk about things that were not to be revealed. In describing the HVA [Ed.: East German foreign intelligence service], he said it was similar to the Soviet one and second in importance among those of East bloc countries, only to the KGB.

"With regards to the election of the pope, Bohnsack said that from the 1970s it had already been determined that Poland was a problem, a weak political link in the East bloc, a situation that was often discussed. 'We considered Poland an enemy country. We feared that Poland could interrupt strategic flows between East Germany and the Soviet Union. The election of the pope was, from our point of view, particularly disquieting. We feared the Pope of Rome could carry out policies against socialist countries. But there was a disparity of opinions. Some even thought it was positive, but among those who thought it was a disaster, they would have had nothing against the pope's disappearance.

"Bohnsack said the Bulgarians admitted that Antonov was one of their men, but they did not confirm that he had something to do with the attack. 'However, Antonov was aware of many things, and if he had collapsed and started to talk, he could have caused significant harm to Bulgaria.'"

Finally, Bohnsack was quoted saying that relations with the Soviet KGB had been "intense," and that it "is inconceivable that, if the pope's attack had been carried out by an East bloc country, that the KGB was not informed and had given its approval. That remark reminded of a popular saying in Bulgaria that 'when it rains in Moscow we open the umbrellas.' He emphasized that 'we never believed that the CIA responsible in the plot to kill the pope. It was a pure invention . . . an attempt to deflect attention'."[15]

Dr. Priore said the assassination attempt was not the deed of a single person and anyone saying this "derides the Italian public and judiciary," adding that Agca was "the person who was given the task, but behind him was a complex organization with several levels." He pointed out that within days of his arrest in 1981, Agca implicated Bulgarian officials, starting with their offer of safe haven post successful assassination, and then retracted it on his first days of the trial.[16]

At least part of the order of November 13, 1979 (mentioned in chapter 4) issued by the Secretariat of the Soviet Communist Party's Central Committee, directing the KGB to use all possibilities to "prevent the new course of policies initiated by the Polish Pope; **if necessary with additional measures beyond disinformation and discreditation** [emphasis added]," was also leaked to an Italian newspaper. On January 20, 2000, *Il Tempo* published an interview with former Soviet president Mikhail Gorbachev, one of the signatories of the order. The writer, Stefano Mannucci, asked Gorbachev to comment on the order. Answer: "It was the Cold War . . . we had to discredit the actions of the pope. Do not forget that, in 1979, the Cold War was at its peak and that ruled the logic of our action. And in this light, the activity of the pope, geared toward fighting totalitarian regimes, could only be perceived as dangerous and hostile by the Soviet government. The document you are mentioning reflects this very thing. They talked about political actions and propaganda. As far as 'ulterior actions,' there are no details about them in these documents. There are talks of initiatives similar to the political measures and propaganda. Nothing was ordered against the pope as a

15. Tribunale di Roma. Ufficio Instruzione—Secione 1a. N. 9031/85A P.M. section 4.6.7/8.; pp. 356–358.
16. Interview with Germany's *Focus* magazine No. 25, 2000.

person, and it could not be otherwise. At that time, similar action had been eliminated and forbidden from the KGB's arsenal."

Following the timeline of the events leading up to the shooting produces a convincing trail of guilt. Although the future Pope John Paul II was a known anticommunist, the decisive battle truly began with the 1979 visit to Poland, less than a year after he was elected pope. Brezhnev virulently objected to the visit, and lost. The reaction of the Polish people, the burgeoning growth of the communist opposition movement, and Walesa's 1981 visit with the pope, made the masters of the Kremlin react with a consternation the West had not seen since the peoples' revolts that led to the invasions of Hungary and Czechoslovakia. The shooting and the Western world's reaction, the ties to the Bulgarian secret police, and their desperate attempts with the East Germans to manufacture a giant coverup strengthened the belief of a communist plot. And the statements by former East German Stasi Colonel Günther Bohnsack cement it: the Kremlin engineered the plot to kill the Polish pope. Of course, there will still be those who say it's *only* based on circumstantial evidence, which Black's Law Dictionary defines thusly: "Circumstantial evidence is testimony or evidence which is not based on actual or personal knowledge or observation of the facts in controversy, but of other facts from which deductions are drawn, showing indirectly the facts sought to be proved."

In March 2006, an Italian Parliamentary Commission under Paolo Guzzanti released its report on the assassination attempt. It came to the "categorical conclusion" that it was the Soviet military intelligence service Glavnoe Razvedyvatelnoe Upravlenie (GRU) which masterminded the plot, rather than the KGB. A top American expert on the GRU, who wished to remain anonymous, said the GRU was better established in field operations. For example, the head of the Bulgarian Airline office in Rome who was implicated, Sergei Antonov, unquestionably had his contacts with the GRU, since airlines were under military intelligence jurisdiction. The American expert stressed, however, that KGB chief Andropov was in charge overall of the assassination operation. The Italian commission said it had incontrovertible evidence that Antonov had been standing close to Agca at the time of the shooting. Senator Guzzanti said the evidence is based on two computer analyses of the photograph that showed the Bulgarian sporting a thick moustache and large eyeglasses. Stripped of the adornments, the face was that of Antonov, who had been aquitted at his trial for lack of evidence. How to explain the original suspicion that the KGB was responsible, and the references to it in the East German Stasi documents? The KGB was better equipped to carry out disinformation operations and was entrenched with the Stasi experts, while the GRU concerned itself almost exclusively with military espionage.

Addendum

The following interview in September 2005, conducted by the author with Paul B. Henze, the author of *The Plot to Kill the Pope*, has been added to illuminate Mr. Henze's efforts to discern the position of the Vatican regarding the assassination attempt and especially that of the pope regarding his enemies.

Q: Did you contact or visit the Vatican in the course of your researches into this subject?

A: I was advised by my good friend Jan Nowak-Jezioranski not to contact the Vatican directly but to depend on his contacts, which he had maintained for many years. He was personally acquainted with Karol Wojtyla, having known him from his earlier activities in Poland. Cardinal Wojtyla also knew of Jan Nowak as the director of Radio Free Europe's Voice of Free

Poland, of which he was a listener. After Wojtyla's election as Pope John Paul II, Nowak's contacts deepened and became more frequent.

During my visit to Rome in September 1981, I visited the Vatican, walked through St. Peter's Square, and retraced all the moves Agca was known to have made, as well as visiting the places where he had stayed and been observed. I also, as an ordinary tourist, visited all the areas in the Vatican open to the public, including the Vatican library, but I had no official contact with Vatican officials.

Q: Did the pope himself know of the researches you were undertaking at the initiative of the *Reader's Digest*?

A: Jan Nowak assured me that he had briefed the pope's private secretary, Monsignor Stanislaw Dziwisz,[17] on my research plans and of the fact that Claire Sterling had also been asked by the magazine to work on this situation. I met with Claire Sterling in Rome in September 1981. We agreed on coordinating and dividing our efforts, with her concentrating on Italy and me concentrating on Turkey, while keeping each other informed on what we found. In the fall of 1981, I did a preliminary report on what I had learned for the *Digest* and gave a copy to Jan Nowak. He told me that he had passed it on to the Vatican and had reason to believe that the pope had read it.

17. Promoted to bishop in 1998, to archbishop, 2003, and after the death of Pope John Paul II in April 2005 Dziwisz was chosen by Pope Benedict XVI as Archbishop of Krakow, the seat Karol Wojtyla had held before his election as pope.

Q: What about your subsequent work, which led to the publication of your book in 1983, such as your research and interviews in Turkey?

A: I kept Jan Nowak informed of each stage of this research and made the first and subsequent drafts of my book available to him. We often discussed the pope's attitude toward the plot. Nowak assured me that the Holy Father had no doubt about the fact that the KGB had mounted the plot. He did not believe that it had been a manifestation of Turkish anti-Christian feeling. Nor did he see any reasons for Bulgarian enmity against him. He regarded Mehmet Ali Agca and his associates as the hired tools of forces they did not understand. When he went to visit Agca in prison he made this clear to him and found that Agca had no enmity against him.

Q: Why did the pope not directly accuse the Soviet KGB of having targeted him? Why did he at least not instruct Vatican spokesmen to express this suspicion?

A: I discussed these questions with Jan Nowak on several occasions. His explanation was that the Holy Father concluded that if he accused the Soviets directly of trying to eliminate him, they would merely deny that they had done so and would generate a barrage of pseudo-evidence that they were innocent—perhaps toward the end of blaming the plot on the Bulgarians or alleged Turkish fanatics, the elements that had been most prominently exposed in the complex framework the KGB had created to implement the scheme.

The pope felt that no matter how strong the accusations he might make would be, they would not necessarily be accepted widely in the West (he had no doubt about attitudes in Poland itself), and his accusations would sever all meaningful contact between the Church and Soviet and East European communist authorities. On the other hand, he concluded he would be in a stronger position vis-à-vis the old men in the Kremlin if he refrained from making open accusations—or letting such accusations be made by his closest associates—letting suspicion grow and evidence of Soviet complicity accumulate. He would thus hold over the heads of the Soviet hierarchy the possibility that he he might eventually accuse them with solid evidence. Under such circumstances, they would have no excuse to deny him contact with believers under communist domination and would be constrained to behave more cautiously toward the Church and toward developing movements in Poland to spring free from Soviet domination. The pope wished to have as much open access as possible not only to Polish Church authorities, but also to all Church authorities in East Europe, including Orthodox Church elements in the Soviet Union itself. He was convinced that his reaction to the attempt to kill him—from which he had been miraculously spared—could be exploited against the men who had instigated it.

Q: Did Nowak give your book to the Vatican? Did the pope read it?

A: Jan Nowak told me that he had seen that the book was delivered to the Vatican secretariat. He believed that the pope had read it. He was sure that the pope's closest confidant, Monsignor Dziwisz, had read it.

Q: Did you ever question or criticize the pope's approach to dealing with the plot by refraining from accusing the KGB?

A: No, never. I understood his position and considered it a measure of his skilled statesmanship. His reasoning was logical and proved accurate. The Soviets were never able to wipe off the suspicion and resorted to all sorts of wild stories to deflect attention from their role—as I detailed in my book. John Paul served his basic purpose well. The Soviets were unable to stem his influence, which actually grew steadily through the years that followed.

8 THE SPYING PRELATE

The discovery of communist secret-police dossiers could be seen as the proverbial water hose used to flush destructive moles from their holes. In this instance, the hose was used to flush out the Catholic Church, especially in the Vatican, where the moles—the communist spies—did their dirty work. As previously pointed out, many files were destroyed when the Soviet Union collapsed. But enough were found, particularly in the archives of the East German Ministry for State Security (MfS, Stasi), to expose this treachery. I shall deal with a number of cases. One of the most complete dossiers is that of Monsignor Paul Dissemond. It is three inches thick and covers the cleric's contacts with the Stasi starting in 1974, when he was 54 years old. He was a member of the cardinal's staff and secretary general of the Berlin Bishop's Conference, a position in which he had close contacts with the highest-ranking officials of the Church not only in East Germany, but in the Vatican as well. When his assignment at the Bishop's Conference ended in May 1987, Dissemond was replaced as the Church's official MfS contact by another prelate. The Stasi removed him from its registry as an IM—or unofficial collaborator, as the agents were called—on December 12, 1989, one month after the Berlin Wall fell and ten days after East Germany's attorney general began criminal proceedings against Stasi chief Erich Mielke.[1]

Dissemond is a fascinating case, in that his first contacts with the secret police were made at the behest of Alfred Cardinal Bengsch, the Archbishop of Berlin. Catholic Church authorities had assigned priests as liaison with government officials, including Stasi officers.[2] Their mission was to obtain strictly controlled building permits to erect or repair churches and, especially after the construction of the Berlin Wall that turned the country into a prison, to seek permission for East Germans to visit the western part of their country to attend to fatally ill immediate blood relatives—children, mothers, fathers, sisters, brothers—or their funerals. Permits for construction of church facilities were the easiest to obtain, since building expenses needed to be paid in West German deutsche marks—or in any other "hard," or convertible, currency that was sorely needed to prop up the ailing and mismanaged communist economy in the East. Getting exit permits most often meant hard bargaining sessions, during which Stasi officers would demand "something of interest." This, at the beginning of the contacts, would seem innocuous. One such request to the monsignor was made shortly after he assumed the liaison assignment, and before

1. Mielke was suspected of various crimes, including high treason. After the total collapse of East Germany and reunification of the country, Mielke was tried and found guilty of the 1931 murder of two Berlin police officers during communist-inspired clashes. At the age of 86, he was sentenced to six years in prison. The full story can be found in my book: *Stasi: The Untold Story of the East German Secret Police*.
2. Prior to Dissemond's assignment, the liaison was handled by Msgr. Otto Gross from 1967 until his death in 1974. His IM code name was "Otto."

he was even registered as an agent. However, he had already been assigned the code name "Peter." In a Stasi report covering the meeting with Dissemond in November 1974, he was listed as a "candidate" and not yet as an IM.

Dissemond was asked to comment on the reaction of Cardinal Bengsch to his meeting with the regime's "watch dog" over religious activity, the Stalinist Hans Seigewasser. The meeting had been called after the secret police obtained "unofficially" a copy of an internal Hirtenbrief, a pastoral letter, sent by Cardinal Bengsch to all East German bishops. The letter dealt with complaints and grievances voiced by parents and young persons over continuing discrimination of Christians by the communists in matters of education. Since the early 1960s, the government had intensified its "measures to create a socialist personality," which translates into turning young people away from Christian teaching toward communist dogma. "After the meeting, the cardinal met with a small group at his office to evaluate his meeting," Dissemond was quoted as telling his interlocutor, Major Helmut Wegener, known to the monsignor only by "Herr Lorenz," his Stasi alias. He was chief of Department 4, responsible for surveillance of the Catholic Church.[3] "On the whole, the cardinal was satisfied with the meeting, which he said took place in an atmosphere of objectivity. Basically, he had been afraid that it could have come to severe disputes and seriously worsened the relations between the Church and the State," the monsignor told the major and continued: "The state secretary asked outright if this had been the intention of the pastoral letter, and the cardinal denied this. But he pointed out that the bishops maintain that the Christian upbringing is an inalienable responsibility of Catholic parents and the Church as a whole, and they are united in agreeing with the basic

3. Dept. 4 was part of Chief Directorate XX, which oversaw the government apparatus, church activities, the arts, and underground activities.

tenets of Vatican II, which have been accepted by the majority of all nations."[4] Cardinal Bengsch told the state secretary, according to Dissemond, that the Church was in no way interested in a deterioration of relations between state and church. "As to the questions raised at the meeting, the cardinal made it clear that there could be no agreement, but since we all must live together in one state, reaching a modus vivendi should continue to be possible."

Dissemond did not limit his report to the cardinal's meeting with the government church overseer. He told the Stasi officer that in the talk with his staff, the cardinal revealed that the "Vatican and the bishops of the DDR were in agreement that the example of Archbishop Casaroli's negotiations in Poland, which gave rise to many misunderstandings, is not to be followed in the DDR. Should negotiations become necessary, these should be conducted only on a political level between a Vatican commission and the government of the DDR and no other bodies." This was an obvious reference to quieting East German fears of Church negotiations not only with government or Communist Party officials, but also with restive labor organizations or religious dissidents, as had happened in Poland.

On the basis of his talk with Dissemond, Maj. Wegener recommended that the reaction of Cardinal Bengsch to the meeting with the state secretary be confidentially relayed to the state secretary for religious affairs. Maj. Wegener remarked that the "Treff," Stasi jargon for a clandestine meeting, was held without any special "Vorkommnisse," or occurrences. "The candidate impressed me with his open-mindedness." This appeared to have been the monsignor's only "Treff." A month later, Wegener suddenly died, a fact withheld from Dissemond, who was told that Herr Lorenz had been assigned to other duties. Wegener was replaced by Captain

4. This obviously was a reference to the Council addressing believers and unbelievers, as it expressed its respect for the integrity and freedom of humany and its repudiation of coercion as a means for bringing people to faith.

Hans Baethge, alias Herr Ebert. By now, Dissemond, code-named "Peter," was no longer a candidate but had become an IMB, an unofficial collaborator with enemy contacts.

Reports on Dissemond's meetings with the Stasi in November 1974 and in April 1975 were destroyed or partially shredded. One which survived undamaged, dated April 1, 1975, dealt with the intention of Archbishop Casaroli to visit Berlin in June. The monsignor told his Stasi interlocutor that Casaroli, then secretary of the Council for Public Affairs, had written to Cardinal Bengsch that the Vatican had reached the point at which an approach to the East German government was going to be made to prepare for negotiations over diocese borders. Arrangements for the visit would be made through East Germany's Rome embassy. "The archbishop requested the cardinal kindly to understand that he, as representative of the Vatican, will be the official guest of the government and any meeting with the leading clerics would merely be as a visitor." In other words, the visit should not be construed as a clerical event. Making this information available to the government obviously gave officials a leg up. The report ended with a caution: "The intentions of Caseroli are known only to a small internal circle of Cardinal Bengsch. Therefore, this information must be handled on a strictly confidential basis."[5] Monsignor Dissemond's new case officer Baethge wrote that "Peter" would travel to the Vatican to deliver transcripts from a pastoral synod. "During our talks 'Peter' agreed to my request that he would ferret out details about Casaroli's planned meetings with East German government officials."[6] Such a request is termed by U.S. intelligence officers as an "EEI," or essential elements of information, and is made to covert agents.

After his return from Rome, Dissemond was debriefed on May 5

5. Report by the religious affairs department of the MfS dated April 1, 1975. BSTU No. 000012.
6. Report of April 25, 1975. BSTU No 000019-21.

by the chief of the entire religious affairs division of the Stasi, Colonel Hans Ludwig, again signifying the importance of this "Treff," and the newly promoted Major Baethge. The monsignor's report covered the preparations for the Casaroli meeting and the fears voiced by the West German government and West Berlin's Senate over the Vatican surrendering to communist demands for re-drafting the episcopate borders, as well as creating a separate episco-pate for West Berlin. The West Germans obviously were mindful of the pursuit of Ostpolitik by Pope Paul VI, with Casaroli being the intermediary. "During conversations in Rome, Casaroli emphasized that the Pope (Paul VI) believes that communism will be around for a long time and that therefore one needs to come to accommoda-tions with the communists, and that this should govern the negotia-tions," Dissemond revealed. This kind of information on the Vatican's thinking would have certainly encouraged the East German regime's belief that at some point the Vatican would knuckle under to the pressures for total control. In this respect, a passage on Ost-politik in George Weigel's superb biography of Pope John Paul II is noteworthy. Weigel's conversation with Archbishop Casaroli specifi-cally centered on Poland. But the political climate in other East Euro-pean communist satellites was not dissimilar. Adopting a strategy of "tactical concessions" would provide "breathing space," the arch-bishop was quoted as saying.[7]

Casaroli's negotiations with East German foreign minister Oskar Fischer were reported on June 12, 1975. The report had sections torn from it so that it was not possible to describe details of the talks. However, by examining certain words and sentences that sur-vived, one could deduce that the talks involved increasing pressures by the regime to have the Vatican change the borders of the various dioceses, districts under a bishop's jurisdiction established in 1933

7. George Weigel, *Witness to Hope* (New York, HarperCollins, 1999), p. 229.

by a concordat between the Vatican and the newly elected Hitler regime.[8] Since part of the diocese extended beyond communist East Germany into the democratic western part of the country, the communist regime had been pressing for change so as to better control the activities of the Church and eliminate the influence of a West German bishop over a number of churches and their activities in the East. This was a subject which would "plague" the tyrannical regime until its demise.

The introduction of that report remained intact and showed that the monsignor was no longer a "candidate" but a full-fledged IMV. Thus, he was not "just" an Inoffizieller Mitarbeiter, an unofficial collaborator, but the additional "V," according to the Stasi manual on abbreviations, meant he had been registered as an "unofficial collaborator who maintained confidential relations to persons under investigation or surveillance." The importance of this "Treff" was made evident by the fact that Major Baethge was again accompanied by Colonel Hans Ludwig.

With each report that survived destruction, it became apparent that Dissemond was being drawn closer and closer into the Stasi's web, passing along more and more information of confidential character, though not necessarily vital to the survival of the Church in the East. Stasi Major Baethge wrote a five-page recapitulation of four "Treffs" with "Peter" between February and April. These dealt mainly with a series of closed conferences of bishops in which, according to the monsignor, "the problematic questions on Christian education and that the leading clerics decided to continue their reticence on

8. The borders were established in a July 1933 agreement called the Reichskonkordat consisting of 32 articles. The new Hitler government pledged to uphold freedom of religion, including the practice of Catholic religious instruction classes in public schools. Although the Nazis later reneged on some provisions, the borders remained unchanged. After the founding of the Federal Republic of (West) Germany, its Federal Constitutional Court in 1957 upheld the validity of the Reichskonkordat. It is the only still valid foreign policy agreement of the Nazi era.

dealing with political or social questions." The latter was an assurance that the regime needed not worry that the East German Catholic priests would stir up trouble as their counterparts did, in Poland, which had fomented for nearly a decade.

In a three-hour meeting in November 1975, Dissemond provided the Stasi details of a private discussion he had had with Cardinal Bengsch on Archbishop Casaroli's talks in the West German capital, Bonn, with Chancellor Helmut Schmidt and Foreign Minister Hans-Dietrich Genscher. Both officials reportedly not only insisted on staying informed on any Vatican contacts with the East Germans on the border issue, but that they must be consulted beforehand. "Peter also revealed that Cardinal Bengsch told him confidentially that, with the Vatican's concurrence, Julius Cardinal Doepfner had decided to remain chairman of both the Berlin Conference of Bishops as well as the Bishops Conference of Fulda," according to the Stasi report. The location of an important institution of Catholic Church leadership in Fulda, a town in the heart of "capitalist" West Germany, had long been a thorn in the side of the East Germans, who could not quite gain complete control of the diocese as a result.

During the IX Congress of the Socialist Unity Party, East Germany's Communist Party, in the spring of 1976, a number of functionaries demanded that greater ideological influence be exerted in schools and institutions of higher learning. This was another initiative to weed out Christian/Catholic teachings in East German schools. At a Stasi meeting in June, Dissemond was asked to report on the Church hierarchy's reaction. "Cardinal Bengsch declared that the Catholic Church saw no reason to comment officially on the expected new pressures. However, the bishops agreed with the cardinal that, at the diocese level, greater emphasis be given to religious instructions on questions of faith," the monsignor revealed. "Instructions will be provided in writing to priests and religious teachers, particularly dealing with examples of discrimination against Catholic grade school pupils and students seeking permission for admission to universities. The priests and teachers were instructed on how to address these problems with government officials." Needless to say, this information provided the regime with ample time to prepare for any confrontations, to avoid clashes that had become nearly daily occurrences in neighboring Poland. Other meetings throughout 1976 continued to deal chiefly with the regime's pressure regarding diocese borders.

When Dissemond traveled on church business to Rome in April 1977, the Stasi tasked him to report on a number of subjects, including the Vatican's position on the follow-up session of the Conference on Security and Cooperation in Europe (CSCE) in Belgrade, as well as on the planned Moscow Conference of Religious Peace Movements in Moscow.[9] As usual, the monsignor complied. The Vatican would continue to work with the CSCE and participate in all future sessions. "The Vatican views the conference as a continuation of efforts toward reconciliation as was initiated in Helsinki and will avoid any actions which would run counter to that," the agent in cassock reported. He added that the Holy See urged that all participants work diligently toward removing remaining obstacles on the road to reconciliation. Thus, despite the turmoil in Poland, in which the Church played a role, the CSCE members from communist countries were assured that they would not be confronted with unpleasant surprises. Regarding the Church's participation in the Moscow peace meeting, Dissemond revealed that "a group around Casaroli is in favor, but another is strictly against it and, therefore, the pope decided to send only an observer delegation." He added that the Catholic Church of Poland and East Germany "will strictly adhere to the Vatican position and not attend." Clearly, the Vatican was pointedly signifying that, in view of the Polish situation, it would not provide any fodder with which the Kremlin might try to burnish its already brutal image.

9. April 4, 1977, MfS HA XX/4 report No. 1528. BSTU No. 000091-97.

At this same clandestine Stasi rendezvous, the monsignor volunteered to inform on a private meeting between the departing head of the liaison office for government relations of the German Bishop's Conference in the West German capital, Bonn. Prelate Wilhelm Woeste had been transferred to the position of Suffragan Bishop of Muenster and had had a farewell meeting with federal Chancellor Helmut Schmidt, during which, according to the monsignor, Schmidt said he worried about West German relations with the United States. The gist of the talk was passed on in a report to the Bishop's Conference, where Dissemond obtained access to it. "Schmidt said his government could not yet precisely evaluate how the policies of the USA will develop and the position of the new President of the USA, Carter, does not at this point allow conclusions on the character of future relations and subsequent consequences," the monsignor told the Stasi. "Because all important personnel were replaced, Schmidt said it deprived the Bonn government of much-needed consultation and rebuilding trustworthy contacts will take some time." This information was certainly not of special value to East German intelligence analysts, since the West German government was dominated by the Social Democratic Party and was saturated with their own spies.[10] However, Dissemond's report on the Woeste meeting with the head of the Bonn government was of value to his handlers, as this allowed them to evaluate the reliability of other internal information he provided.

A memorandum dated July 15 and found in the monsignor's dossier said IMV "Peter" was suddenly hospitalized with an undisclosed ailment and noted that he was expected not to be "available" for some time. However, three days after Christmas 1977, another brief note said, Colonel Ludwig and Major Baethge had a "Treff" with

---

10. John O. Koehler, *Stasi: The Untold Story of the East German Secret Police* (West View Press, Boulder, CO, 1999), chapter 5.

IMV "Peter" at a Stasi safe house, or secret location, code-named "Wassermann." No details were given except that the meeting "served to solidify mutual confidence and his commitment to the MfS."

Throughout 1978, a series of "Treffs" were held, all dealing with conferences held by Cardinal Bengsch and a number of bishops to deal with the continuing government pressure to realign the diocese borders. These discussions included Alois Mertes, a Catholic member of the conservative Christian Democratic Party (CDU) delegation of the West German Parliament who wanted to be informed on what action the Church intended to undertake. As already reported, the Bonn government was opposed to the Church in East Germany becoming "independent" and, thus, subject to closer scrutiny by the state. The Stasi instructed the monsignor to furnish "**concrete**" [emphasis added] details on the discussions.[11] Although Pope Paul VI had been ailing, the communist regime had counted on his approval of the border configurations. What they obviously had not expected was the pope's death on August 6, 1978, and the election of the Polish Archbishop of Krakow Karol Wojtyla, as Pope John Paul II on October 16.

The conferences were stalled while Cardinal Bengsch was in Rome for the funeral of Pope Paul VI and the election conclave. Within days of the new pope's election, Bengsch consulted with Cardinal Giovanni Benelli. This, likely based on Dissemond's revelations on that meeting, became the basis for a top-secret Stasi analysis prepared for Erich Honecker, the Communist Party boss and head of state, as well as the Politburo and the state security hierarchy. "Cardinal Benelli is an opponent of attempts to normalize relations between the DDR and the Catholic Church," the analysis said. It emphasized that Benelli was a "close confidant" of leading West German Christian Democratic Party politicians, all of whom were also in staunch opposition.

11. Reports of MfS unit XX/4/II. BSTU No. 000107-000118.

Although, as previously mentioned, Pope Paul VI was willing to lean in favor of the communist demands, the Polish pope created a new situation. "According to the first reports on the position of the Vatican," the analysis said, "one can not expect that the newly elected pope will devote any time to this complicated problem." But there was an expression of hope for the future. "Pope John Paul II has privately said on several occasions that as pastor he strives toward supporting the Catholics in the socialist countries and that he intends to continue negotiations with socialist states speedily in order to reach binding results," according to the analysis, "and he voiced his interest in negotiations with the DDR."[12] It astonishes one how badly the analysts misread this new pope, who surely must have had more on his mind—the brutal oppression of his Polish brethren as the most dire example—than the political desires of East Berlin.

No matter how the East German government leaned on the new Catholic hierarchy to fall in line with their demands, nothing worked. They tried to have the recently elected Pope John Paul II visit East Berlin. Their foreign minister visited the Vatican, only to return empty-handed. Party chief Honecker himself angled in vain for an invitation from the pope. Pope John Paul II remained firm; and by the time the Berlin Wall crumbled, the diocese borders remained as they had been drawn up more than 50 years earlier, integrated with the West.

On August 3, 1999, I interviewed Monsignor Dissemond in his spacious and well-appointed East Berlin apartment. As a witness, I asked retired U.S. Air Force Lt. Colonel E. F. "Fritz" von Marbod to accompany me. A German speaker, he had been my superior when I served in a USAF counterintelligence unit. When I telephoned Dissemond and requested an appointment, he accepted readily. He acknowledged contacts with the Stasi for more than a decade at the

12. MfS Analysis and Information report No. 625/78, dated October 25, 1978, marked top secret and titled "Opinion of Vatican dignitaries about the relations Vatican-DDR as well as a number of internal problems." BSTU No. 000001-6.

behest of his superiors. "All of my contacts and discussions were fully approved by Cardinal Bengsch and always centered on humanitarian matters such as exit permits for hardship cases like family deaths." He denied ever having revealed any internal and confidential information without the approval of his superior or that he was ever asked to furnish certain information. Despite his Stasi handlers' reports, the monsignor claimed all of his dealings were of a benign character, insisting that only humanitarian matters were discussed. Why did the Church feel it necessary to deal with the secret police on these matters, rather than the government's department of religious affairs? "I don't know; it started a long time before I was given the job," Dissemond said. When asked if this equated to dealing with the Gestapo during the Nazi years, he did not respond and merely shrugged his shoulders.

It was obvious that the monsignor felt he was on safe ground, since his handler Hans Baethge most likely had assured him that pertinent dossiers had been destroyed. Those that survived from 1974 to 1979 gave no hint that he had ever provided information on persons that could have led to prosecution for anti-state activities.

After an hour of questioning, I agreed with Colonel von Marbod that we were wasting our time. Throughout the interview, Monsignor Dissemond was friendly and seemed calm and composed. His demeanor, von Marbod and I agreed, was what the Germans called "Scheinheilig," which translates into "feigned innocence."

After the interview, we revisited the archive where the Stasi files were stored. As luck would have it, Mr. Ruediger Stang, the archivist, had just found another file with material concerning Dissemond. It put the lie to the monsignor's contention that he had done nothing to aid the tyrannical regime in maintaining its grip on an already-restive population. This file consisted entirely of awards, medals, and gifts presented to Dissemond.

In November, 1976, he was awarded with a "present" of 500 marks (about $250). The recommendation by Major Baethge read: "Collaboration with IMV 'Peter' has so far produced valuable information for the Party and State leadership. Based on strengthening the relationship of personal trust to the MfS, it was possible, with his help, to influence positively the leading clerics in the DDR on a number of important matters. The award serves to promote mutual confidence and a trustful collaboration with the IM." Two years later, in "celebration of the 30th anniversary of the founding of the DDR," the informer received another 500 marks. The recommendation by Lt. Colonel Joachim Wiegand, head of the Catholic Church section XX/4: "The IM has always carried out his assignments reliably and with a sense of responsibility. The collaboration developed continuously and was aimed at avoiding confrontations between the State and the Church. In this respect, the IM has performed his assigned tasks well." In "honor" of the 31st anniversary of the totalitarian regime, the monsignor was awarded with an unspecified present valued at 500 marks. The citation, written by Lt. Colonel Wiegand, read: "IMV 'Peter' is a leading personality with responsibility in an area that allowed him to obtain valuable information for the MfS. Furthermore, because of his direct support, measures could be taken to prevent negative activities in connection with larger public assemblies. The IM, in his leading position, is always acting to further a good relationship with the State, and the present is intended to continue the strengthening of his confidential relations to the MfS."

On October 28, 1983, the 34th anniversary of the MfS founding, Monsignor Dissemond was awarded another 500 marks because "the collaboration of the IM with the MfS resulted in obtaining valuable information about an operational matter, enabling the HA [Ed.: Main Department for religious affairs] to take appropriate action." Specifically, wrote Lt. Colonel Wiegand, he provided suggestions and recommendations regarding a group of eminent persons whose "politically negative activities could, therefore, be prevented." This sentence can have only one meaning: he informed on opponents to the communist regime, as 1983 was the year during which the political opposition, chiefly embedded in the Catholic and Lutheran churches and bubbling underground, began to emerge into the open, undoubtedly encouraged by the events in Poland and the steadfastness of the anticommunist Polish Pope John Paul II. In expressing his praise for Dissemond, Lt. Col. Wiegand wrote: "In past years, the IM has proven his honesty and reliability by providing written material and oral reports of a strictly confidential character." Ah, yes, the monsignor consulted with the Stasi on such humanitarian problems! Unfortunately, no documents could be found pointing to arrests and imprisonments resulting from Monsignor Dissemond's "honesty and reliability," as his Stasi superiors lauded him.

Finally, IMB "Peter"—IMV had been changed to IMB—received the communist regime's greatest honor, the Medal of Merit of the DDR. This is the citation in full:

> The IMB "Peter" has worked on an unofficial basis with the MfS for 10 years. In the past years, IM "Peter," who is active in a position of responsibility, has proven himself by his great reliability, honesty, and initiative in carrying out his assigned tasks. Thus, because of his collaboration, much information valuable to the Party and State leadership in carrying out certain operations was obtained. Above all, because of strengthening the mutual trust with the MfS, his help made it possible to prevent confrontations between the State and the Church. The award of the Medal of Merit of the DDR on the occasion of the 35th anniversary of the MfS is intended as a special recognition of the single-mindedness of IMB "Peter" with which he supported actively and with prudence the policies of the Party in church matters.

In between receiving his medal and the 500-Mark "awards," the Stasi showed its appreciation for the trusted informer with numerous gifts valued at 4,434 marks (about $2,217), including such birthday presents as a grill, deck chair, chinaware, expensive liquor, a chess set, and, of course, flowers. The secret police also showered Dissemond with table lamps, a clock, expensive beer mugs, and books. Clearly, the German adage "Eine Hand Waescht die Andere," one hand washes the other, fits the Dissemond case perfectly.

Of course, a valuable informer such as the Secretary General of the Berlin Bishop's Conference needed to be feted with lavish breakfasts, lunches, and "Kaffee und Kuchen," the German equivalent of afternoon teatime. But his Stasi handlers couldn't take him to just any restaurant, which would have violated the rules on maintaining the conspiracy. Thus, the Objekt Wendenschloss was chosen as most appropriate for such an exalted Catholic official. This was a villa on the western outskirts of East Berlin with idyllic surroundings near the River Spree. The Stasi shared the place with the Soviet KGB for its secret meetings with clandestine agents. The place was apparently in big demand, as users needed to make reservations using special Stasi forms. The feasts with Dissemond never lasted fewer than six hours. Some examples: December 28, 1982, 12:30pm–18:00. Lunch: roast goose, wine, champagne, afternoon coffee and cake. For a meatless lunch on Friday, March 1, 1985, the request said: "For lunch, please, if possible, we would like trout, but please, no carp." Wine and champagne were served with each meal. One must wonder whether the communist secret police officers tolerated the monsignor, before eating, folding his hands and ironically asking for God's blessing of the tainted food.

Although his formal assignment as the Stasi contact and informer ended in 1987, he continued his dastardly contacts as a "freelance informer" until the fall of the Berlin Wall. A note by Major Baethge on September 23, 1989, following a meeting: "The Treff was used at the same time to thank the IM for his collaboration with the MfS. Even after the functional changes in 1987, the IM assured us that he will use all opportunities, including influencing the leading clergy to continue activities in the spirit of his hitherto collaboration. Since he has already been offered other missions within the Berlin diocese, his connections with leading Catholic clerics continue to be assured." Was the esteemed Monsignor Dissemond a spy until the Stasi's bitter end?

Monsignor Dissemond was exposed as a Stasi informer in February 1992 by the newspaper *Berliner Zeitung*. The newspaper proposed him as the Catholic counterpart to Manfred Stolpe, the president of the Consistory of the Evangelical Church, who had met regularly in secret with the Stasi for years. The newspaper wrote that in contrast with Stolpe, Dissemond said he "never met conspiratorially in dubious Stasi locations." I have already shown that this assertion was not true. In an interview with the newspaper, the monsignor said that the meetings merely dealt with humanitarian questions. "When priests were imprisoned, I negotiated with them over their release," he told the newspaper, which was almost verbatim what he said to me in the 1999 interview. The problem with the latter assertion is that no priests were jailed after 1961.[13] In June 1993, the Berlin newspaper *Tagesspiegel* carried a lengthy report on Dissemond's connections with the Stasi, saying that Georg Cardinal Sterzinsky confirmed that the Church had investigated them. Although Dissemond had given the Stasi internal Church information, it was decided that he had not "jeopardized the freedom of any person." No action was taken against the monsignor, and he was allowed to retire. He died in 2006 after a brief illness.

---

13. Interview with Dr. Bernd Schaefer, one of Germany's foremost experts on the Church in East Germany, author of *Staat und katholische Kirche in der DDR* (Boehlau Verlag, Koeln, 1998).

9 A POTPOURRI OF SPIES

s previously explained, Monsignor Dissemond was handled by Stasi Department XX/4, charged with surveillance of the Catholic Church in the DDR, because his clergy posting was in East Berlin and not in the Vatican. But there were two even more important German agents who were run by the foreign intelligence department Hauptverwaltung Aufklaerung (HVA). The HVA, headed by Lieutenant General Markus Wolf,[1] was the communist bloc's most formidable espionage service next to the Soviet KGB, having

1. Wolf, at age 11, was taken to Moscow in 1934 by his German communist parents. While attending the German Karl-Liebknecht Schule, a middle school for children of German communist exiles, he allegedly became a secret police informer during Stalin's murderous purges in 1936-1938 and denounced a number of his teachers who disappeared in labor camps. Wolf and his parents were among very few German communist intellectuals who survived the purges. He became a Soviet citizen in 1942 and a member of the Soviet Communist Party, and trained in a secret school in espionage and sabotage assignment. The school was closed when the war turned in favor of the Red Army. Wolf turned up in Berlin two weeks after the war ended. He served on a Moscow diplomatic assignment. He became one of the first members of a clandestine espionage group which eventually became part of the Stasi. (See John O. Koehler, *Stasi: The Untold Story of the East German Secret Police* [Westview Press, Boulder, CO, 1999].)

jurisdiction over operations outside East Germany, including the Vatican. In contrast to all other Stasi departments, Wolf's officers destroyed virtually all case files when it became clear that the regime was about to collapse. When the MfS headquarters was stormed on January 15, 1990, by tens of thousands of Berliners, the HVA shredders had already been working around the clock for days. Thus, it seemed that agents working abroad might never have been unmasked. But Wolf would be disappointed. His obsessive "deutsche Gruendlichkeit," German thoroughness, was bested by his Western enemies.

What the "Man without a Face," as Wolf liked to call himself, had overlooked was the resourcefulness of operatives of the United States Central Intelligence Agency and the hundreds of magnetic tapes bearing important details on sources that had been stored outside Berlin. CIA officers were able to obtain microfilms bearing index cards with the personal data of about 280,000 persons who had collaborated with the HVA between the early 1950s and 1988. The CIA operation was code-named "Rosewood." Needless to say, the Agency will not reveal how it got its hands on the microfilms. One version had it that a Stasi officer had sold them during a clandestine meeting on a Mediterranean island for $3 million; another said instead of taking the films to Moscow for safekeeping, a KGB colonel sold them to the Americans. The German government had tried for 13 years to get at least copies of the films, going even so far as having officers of the Bundesnachrichtendiest (BND), the Federal Intelligence Service, practically camping outside CIA headquarters in Langley, Virginia, unsuccessfully seeking access. Finally, the CIA transferred the information onto 381 CD-ROMs and handed them to the Germans in June 2003.

Magnetic tapes, named SIRA,[2] were stored in a concrete bunker at

---

2. Abbreviation of "System zur Informationsrecherche der Aufklaerung" or System for Information and Research of Intelligence, which the Stasi's foreign intelligence department established in 1969 with computers obtained in West Germany from the high-tech Siemens Company specializing in communications.

an East German People's Army military base. They were discovered shortly after Germany was reunified in 1990. But experts working with the newly created Federal Archive for Documents of the Ministry for State Security (BSTU) were unsuccessful in decoding the material. Finally, a former security expert of the East German Army broke the code in 1998. Now authorities learned that Wolf had two ace spies in the Vatican, though it would take another five years until they could be identified through the CIA "Rosewood" files. One had already died at age 72 in 1987, after decades of diligent work for the communists. He was Brother Eugen Brammertz, a Benedictine monk who was first registered by the HVA as an agent on November 13, 1953, while serving at the St. Matthias Abbey in Trier, a city near the Luxembourg border. His code name was "Lichtblick" (Enlightened View), registration number 8560/65, both of which were active until his death. The other agent was Alfons Waschbuesch, who was a student at the University of Munich when he was recruited on August 8, 1965, at age 21. His code name was Antonius, registration number XV/205/68.

As both cases are related (they were handled over the years by the same case officers), I will first deal with Brother Brammertz, who had a most interesting background. Born in 1915 into a Catholic family at Aachen, a city near the Dutch/Belgian border where he graduated from high school, Brammertz entered St. Matthias Abbey in 1934, was accepted as a monk in 1935, and a year later began his university studies, majoring in philosophy and theology. He was ordained a priest in 1939. Drafted into the Luftwaffe during World War II, he served as a medic. At war's end, Brammertz was held in a Soviet field hospital.[3] One source has said that while in captivity, he came in contact with the Soviet secret police, the NKVD. Details are unavailable.

---

3. Personal background was published in an obituary of Brammertz, March 13, 1987, provided by the secretariat of St. Matthias Abbey, Trier, Germany.

However, while most German prisoners were held many years after the war, Brammertz was released quickly and wound up in Berlin, where he is said to have renewed contact with the Soviets. Former Colonel Karl Grossmann, who served as deputy chief of HVA foreign counterintelligence, said in an interview that in the early 1950s, "the MVD (later KGB) Residentura [Ed.: local MVD office] in Berlin had a serious problem, but I don't remember the details. Anyway, they transferred some of their agents to the HVA and it is highly possible that Brother Brammertz was among them." Grossmann's memory seemed to be correct. The HVA personnel index card returned to the Germans by the CIA showed that a Karl Brammertz was registered in 1953. It also showed a first name Eugen, but that was stricken and substituted with Karl, which had been his given name. He had adopted Eugen after his ordination as a priest and assignment as a monk to the St. Matthias Abbey. His occupation was listed as "Pater" (Father), with a Ph.D. and membership in the Benedictine Order.

According to a top German researcher on communism and the Catholic Church, Brammertz was sent "nolens volens," or willy-nilly, by his abbey to Rome in 1975, where he worked as a writer and translator for the German edition of the Vatican newspaper *Osservatore Romano*.[4] The "willy-nilly" aspect of his transfer is questionable. It is more likely that Brother Brammertz requested his transfer, probably at the behest of the HVA, and it was approved by the Order because of his scholarly background and abilities. In an interview with the Rome newspaper *l'Espresso* in October 1999, HVA chief Markus Wolf described Brammertz as "one of the most brilliant monks, member of a Scientific Commission and very close to Cardinal Agostino Casaroli." Wolf said his department communicated with the wayward monk through "Instrukteure," instructors who

4. "Endgueltig Entarnt—Spione im Katholischen Kirchendienst," March 2000 article by Dr. Bernd Schaefer, scientific associate at the Hannah-Arendt-Institute for Research on Totalitarianism, Technical University, Dresden, Germany.

relayed requests for specific information, and "Kuriere," couriers whose job was to pick up the agent's reports for transmission to Berlin. Both were stationed in the East German embassy in Rome under diplomatic cover.

Any counterespionage expert sifting through Brother Brammertz's background—the NKVD/MVD contacts, the highly probable transfer from the Soviets to their East German cohorts in 1953 after he finished his formal education—would conclude that he might well have been a "sleeper" agent. The Soviet had a long history in preparing sleepers which were activated after years of dormancy. For many years, the HVA also had used sleepers, or long-range agents, which Wolf's officers called "Perspectivagenten."[5] In an April 2005 interview with the Italian newspaper *La Repubblica*, Wolf touched on the recruitment of sleeper agents: "I loved to recruit young agents and then wait until they had grown older."

The SIRA tapes contained 219 pages covering espionage summaries of reports provided by Brammertz starting in 1974, but he became more and more active in the early 1980s and remained prolific until his death. Each report classified him as "A," the code for "Reliable," and the value of information he provided ranged from III, medium, to I, very valuable. The summaries also indicate that a great number of reports were also transmitted to "Service Unit 5030," the code for the Soviet service, the KGB. In this connection, it is worth noting that many times the information for the East Germans was valued as III, but when it was handed to the Soviet it became a II, indication that it was of greater value to Moscow. Nearly all reports on the tapes were shared with the KGB.

Though, as already pointed out, the comprehensive reports had been destroyed, the SIRA entries contain terse one- or two-sentence

---

5. John O. Koehler, *Stasi: The Untold Story of the East German Secret Police* (Westview Press, Boulder, CO, 1999), p. 199.

summaries of the information the monk conveyed. On November 21, 1974, Brammertz reported on the "Vatican foreign policy development apropos Ostpolitik. Relations with socialist countries—Hungary, Poland, and DDR—entitled steps toward clarification of the relationship with the DDR and Poland." Nearly a year later, Father Brammertz handed the Stasi a secret Vatican paper on ideological diversion in connection with Ostpolitik which provided "information on personnel composition of Vatican Orders and Collegiums dealing with Ostpolitik." This report certainly would have been valuable to the Soviets as well as the Polish secret police in dealing with the Polish unrest, as well as maintaining a vigil over the Catholic Church authorities in the other "socialist countries." A report of great value was supplied by the monk on April 20, 1976: it dealt with "the activities in the East of Abbey St. Matthias in Trier and its connection to the CIA." How unfortunate that we do not have the full report! In that same year, 1976, he provided at least another 12 reports, all rated by the HVA as valuable. These included "tactics, strategy of, and collaboration with West European Catholic authorities in the East."

Following the election of Pope John Paul II and his first visit to his homeland as pope in 1979, Brammertz, most likely acting on instructions from his HVA "Instrukteur," concentrated more and more on the Vatican's activities regarding the worsening situation in Poland. In mid-1980, he supplied information on "the influence of Polish clericals on the Vatican" and an analysis of the pope's pilgrimage to West Germany in November 1980, concentrating on the Bonn government's "assessment of the situation in Poland." On account of dozens of reports, all of which were shared with Moscow, the monk undoubtedly was tasked to pay special attention to the Vatican's relations with Western intelligence services such as the CIA and the West German Federal Intelligence Service (BND) on matters involving the Polish crisis. He also reported on Catholic organizations such as Opus Dei and the Order of Malta and their alleged contacts with the

CIA. In September 1984, Brammertz delivered a lengthy report on "the new position of Opus Dei in connection with the Polish pope," which apparently was the basis for a nine-page summary on the "secret society with about 75,000 members located in 87 countries." The summary, which described Opus Dei as fiercely anticommunist, said: "Since the election of Pope John Paul II, the Societas Sacerdotalis Sancta Crucis et Opus Dei has enjoyed an enhancement in its status which even experts and 'insiders' of the Catholic Church find astounding." It pointed out that predecessors of John Paul II, such as John XXIII and Paul VI, either viewed Opus Dei with "disapproval or skepticism." The East Germans naturally were highly alarmed that "this secret society can be attractive and insidious to young people who may already be opposed to socialist society," especially in Poland and Hungary. The summary may well have been prepared for anti-Catholic propaganda measures, since it accused Opus Dei of fostering "economic criminality of the highest order, and engaging in weapons and narcotics smuggling". It was a vitriolic and vicious attack on this conservative organization. No documents were found pointing to arrests of Opus Dei members on the basis of information provided by Brammertz. Neither could the monk provide any evidence that the organization was engaging in what the layman would consider criminal activities.

During the last year of his life, Father Brammertz was as busy a spy as ever. His reports continued to zero in on the anti-government activities in Poland, the Vatican's personnel policies, papal travel plans, and the financial scandal involving the Vatican Bank. His last report before his death from a stroke in March 1987 was received in East Berlin on February 18 and dealt with the pope's visit to West Germany and plans for a trip to communist East Germany. As much as he had been valued by the Stasi intelligence officers, he was equally esteemed by fellow monks. The obituary published by his abbey praised the monk's devotion to his Church and his literary accomplishments, which were also cited when the West German government awarded him the Federal Cross of Merit. It is astounding how he was able to operate as a spy for such a long period without raising any suspicions.[6] Because his complete Stasi dossier had been shredded, it could not be established whether and how Brammertz was remunerated for his service, or if he was recruited on an ideological basis. Although the Stasi had used blackmail to coerce priests living in East Germany to become informers, no indication could be found that it was applied in the case of the monk.

The Spying Monk's Protégé

Alfons Waschbuesch, the other ace spy in the Vatican for the East German communists, lived in the town of Konz, about five miles west of Father Brammertz's abbey at Trier. The monk taught religion in two high schools in Trier from 1953 until 1973. Waschbuesch attended one of the schools and came to the attention of the teacher, who passed his name on to the Stasi as a potential agent. He was a perfect candidate for a sleeper assignment. As General Wolf had said, he liked recruiting them when they were young and impressionable, and activating them as they had become older and moved higher up in their respective fields. After he graduated, Waschbuesch enrolled at the University of Munich in 1965 to study philosophy, the classics, and archeology. It was on August 17, 1965, shortly after his first year, when he was registered as an inactive agent, a sleeper. A top-secret extract from statistics of the HVA listed 1967 as the actual recruitment on "ideological basis" and assigned the code name "Antonius." After graduating with a Ph.D., Waschbuesch joined the Katholische Nachrichten Agentur (KNA), which was formed in 1952. The KNA, or Catholic News Agency, reports on Church events within and outside Germany

6. While in Rome, Father Brammertz lived at the beautiful Pontifical Benedictine College of St. Anselmo, which sits on a hill overlooking the dome of St. Peter's Cathedral. He died there and was buried in its cemetery of the monks.

for daily newspapers, Catholic periodicals, and radio and television outlets. Being conversant in Italian and English, besides his native German, Waschbuesch was posted in Rome, where he was as prolific a Stasi spy as Brother Brammertz. The SIRA tapes yielded 214 pages of summarized reports produced by agent "Antonius." Like the monk, Herr Doktor Waschbuesch was also rated as "A," or reliable.

The first report that could be found arrived in East Berlin on May 26, 1976, and covered "Vatican foreign policy, its policy toward the East and relations with socialist countries."[7] The following December, Waschbuesch provided comprehensive information on the political activities of the Vatican vis-à-vis East Germany and the socialist camp. He concentrated on the Vatican's Ostpolitik in Poland and Hungary. Virtually all of his reports during 1977 dealt with the Vatican's policy and activities in Poland as well as with future plans for intensifying Ostpolitik. With each successive year, Waschbuesch boosted his production: 13 reports in 1979 and 15 a year later, most dealing with Church activities in Eastern Europe, Vatican personnel problems, and papal travel plans. Like those of Father Brammertz, the reports furnished by Waschbuesch, except ones dealing only with German Catholic Church affairs, were relayed to the Soviet KGB.

Toward the end of 1981, Waschbuesch delivered to the East German communists an in-depth analysis on the position of Pope John Paul II and the Vatican with regard to the tumultuous events in Poland, as well as the Vatican's evaluation of international political questions. Unfortunately the complete reports were destroyed, but their details certainly must have been welcome in Moscow, considering that the Soviet leadership was now facing greater issues than a tough Polish pope, including a staunch and vocal anticommunist U.S. president, Ronald Reagan. Since Waschbuesch's communication with the Stasi increasingly concerned the Vatican's apprehensions

7. All Waschbuesch ("Antonius") reports were obtained from SIRA Teildatenbank 12, Druckauftrag Nr.: 1799—gedruckt von BStU. November 22, 1999.

about events in Poland and stirrings in other communist countries, including East Germany, his case officer, or "Instrukteur," most likely tasked him to concentrate on those areas. He paid special attention to "the political motivations" in the pope's travel plans and the Holy Father's "ideological intentions" in selecting countries for his pilgrimages. But "Antonius" found time to also report on internal matters of his employer, the Catholic News Agency (KNA), such as political positions and personnel structure. Waschbuesch's last report from the Vatican again covered the foreign policy and the pope's policy vis-à-vis East Germany was handed to the Stasi in July 1983, before he returned to West Germany.

Waschbuesch was promoted to chief editor of KNA's office in Wiesbaden, which was responsible for coverage of several dioceses. The transfer did not end his service as a communist spy. In July 1985, he delivered a six-page report on "anticommunist activities" of his employer, the Catholic News Agency. The last reports by "Antonius" were recorded in October 1987. One described the reactions of the Catholic Church leadership to the visit to West Germany by East German Communist Party leader and head of state Erich Honecker; the other outlined welfare activities of Church groups to assist priests in communist countries. Even though Waschbuesch's reporting seemed to have ended, a top-secret personnel data summary dated December 14, 1988 was found among the "Rosewood" material returned by the CIA. His code name "Antonius," as well as HVA registration number XV/205/68, was still active, and he was described as married and the owner of a house in the city of Mainz and an automobile.

I contacted Waschbuesch by telephone at his office in Koblenz, but he refused to answer any questions about his involvement with the HVA. He said his superiors told him not to speak about his past, and that I should speak to them instead. When I asked for a name, he would not reveal one. I later learned it was Hans Casel, director for public relations for the Trier Episcopate, whom I sent an e-mail and politely asked these questions:

1. Has Waschbuesch ever told you why he betrayed his Church?
2. His HVA registration card notes that he was recruited on the "basis of ideology." Do you know about that?
3. Has he ever openly, or at least to you, regretted that he had been a spy for the archenemy of the Catholic Church?
4. Do you know how Herr Waschbuesch was paid by the Stasi for his service?
5. When was Herr Waschbuesch hired for the Koblenz diocese?
6. I understand that Herr W. is married. Has he any children?

It took Mr. Casel a month to reply, in a manner that was less than forthcoming. "When Dr. Waschbuesch was hired, we were informed about his entanglements. We had detailed conversations with him. Beyond that, we intensively informed ourselves through contacts with Church and government authorities. That we hired Dr. Waschbuesch is based on the Catholic Church's dogma that it not only demands forgiveness of others, but that it is also obliged to forgive others. In order to put the events in the proper perspective, it would perhaps be helpful to know that we informed the chief editors of the secular media with which Dr. Waschbuesch, as the press officer, is in regular contact. They have all accepted our decision and dealt with it with appropriate discretion. At this point I do not wish to furnish further answers, since publication of the aspects we mentioned does not appear to us to be helpful." Obviously, for Catholic traitors in the former East Germany, the Church had a more severe

treatment—such as defrocking or excommunication—than was practiced in the Western part of the country.

I did not receive an answer from the management of the Catholic
News Agency to my question as to whether Waschbuesch was fired
after he was exposed as a spy for those who for nearly a century used
murder, torture, and brutal imprisonment to destroy his religion.

Dr. Bernd Schaefer, one of Germany's top experts on the East
German communist regime's campaign against the Catholic Church,
expressed consternation over the different treatment of clerics and lay
persons who had been Stasi informers in East Germany, and West
German spies such as Waschbuesch. "In Eastern Germany, great
efforts were made to uncover clerics, lay persons and employees of
the Catholic Church who collaborated with the secret police. In a
number of cases, this led to sanctions and loss of careers. While the
Benedictine Order had at least an interest in uncovering the activities
of 'Lichtblick,' in the case of Waschbuesch the highest authorities of
the German Bishop's Conference quietly selected another route—
change of job, promotion, and, especially, silence. Contrary to its
interest in the East German Church officials who were IM, the KNA
also did not report anything about its own agents." Asked about the
Waschbuesch case, Ruediger Stang, a department head at the former
communist Ministry for State Security archive in Berlin, chuckled and
replied: "The Church has forgiven him." How to explain the West
German silence versus the East? Maybe they were just too embar-
rassed to make a big "scene" of exposing the spies.

Judas

Less than a year after the election of Karol Cardinal Wojtyla as Pope
John Paul II, the Polish Bishop's Conference needed a priest with
journalistic experience in the Vatican to prepare position papers and
press releases. Prelate Stefan Cardinal Wyszynski chose Father Konrad
Stanislaw Hejmo, a slender six-foot-tall 43-year-old Dominican with

a sonorous voice, who had befriended Cardinal Wojtyla while attending university lectures of the latter. He edited the Catholic monthly *W drodze* after graduating with degrees in theology and social sciences. In Rome, Father Hejmo also cared for Polish pilgrims whose travel to the eternal city had increased markedly since Cardinal Wojtyla had slipped the fisherman's ring onto his finger. Despite the continuing, and often violent, anticommunist agitation, the government did nothing to stop the faithful from leaving the country on pilgrimage. The government leadership obviously feared a travel ban would aggravate the unrest even more. The Polish ecclesiastical hierarchy recognized Father Hejmo's diligence and concern over the pilgrims' welfare by naming him, in 1984, director of the Polish pilgrim center Corda Cordi. He spared nothing to make his brethrens' visit a memorable experience, arranging audiences with the Holy Father and organizing tours of the eternal city's holy places. His work was highly valued and recognized by the Vatican. Besides having been accepted as a confidant by Pope John Paul II, he was also close to the pope's assistant and confidant, Archbishop Stanislaw Dziwisz. And thus, Father Hejmo was privy to the pope's strategies on dealing with his besieged homeland. He once told the Polish Catholic news service KAI that his favorite pastime was "attentively following the life and teachings of the Holy Father John Paul II and the life of the Church."

As Pope John Paul II was on his deathbed during the last days of March 2005, Father Hejmo was accorded nearly unlimited access to the pope's assistant and the attending physicians and nuns caring for the Holy Father. Gathering information on the pope's battle for life and the atmosphere within the Vatican, Father Hejmo kept the Polish people informed over Vatican Radio, which lifted him to nationwide fame. When the pope died on April 2, the priest organized the estimated one million Polish pilgrims who had flocked to Rome for the funeral. Three weeks later, on Sunday,

April 24, Father Hejmo led several hundred of his pilgrims to Saint Peter's Square to join royalty and state and government chiefs from throughout the world to celebrate the installation of Joseph Cardinal Ratzinger as Pope Benedict XVI.

Three days after the solemn ceremony, the 69-year-old Father Hejmo suddenly left Rome and flew to Warsaw. His world had been torn asunder. The Dominican priest had learned that he was about to be exposed as having spied for communist Poland's secret police.

Officials of the Polish Instytut Pamieci Narodowej (IPN), the Institute of National Remembrance, which had seized and researched secret police files, obviously waited until after the pope's death and the election of a new pontiff before going public with Father Hejmo's misdeeds, realizing it would become a huge national disgrace. IPN president Leon Kieres, a professor of jurisprudence, announced that his Institute had found a dossier of about 700 pages pointing to Hejmo's collaboration with Sluzba Bezpieczenstwa (SB), the State Security Service.[8] Prof. Kieres said the SB had assigned father Hejmo the code names "Dominik" and "Hejnal." The dossier also contained tape recordings of Hejmo's meetings with his secret police case officer. Pawel Machcewicz, a historian with IPN, said that since 1975 Father Hejmo had "regular meetings with Waclaw Glowacki, his SB case officer, to whom he reported on conflicts within the Polish episcopate and denounced clerics from the opposition (i.e: anticommunist)."[9] The initial contacts were approved by the superiors of Father Hejmo, who was in charge of publishing a monthly periodical for Catholic youth. Since the press was rigidly controlled by the communist regime, which determined the amount of newsprint allocated to publications, the Ministry of Information steered Father Hejmo to secret police officer Glowacki for assistance. Apparently, an increase

8. Warsaw press conference, April 27, 2005.
9. 3sat telecast, June 8, 2005.

in newsprint was granted in small increments, and the secret police got the information they wanted from the talkative priest. According to an entry in the priest's dossier a year after the first meeting, the secret police officer wrote an assessment in which he said Father Hejmo had "qualified himself as a Candidate." Wrote Glowacki: "He is privy to interesting information, is talkative, and, should he be sent to Rome, he would be of interest to the foreign intelligence service." As to method of recruitment, he wrote: "Step by Step." And when he was assigned to Rome, the internal security service, (SB) transferred him to the foreign intelligence department.

A year after he arrived in Rome, he was contacted by a Pole who lived in West Germany. The man, who called himself "Lakar," claimed to be an adviser to the West German episcopate in Cologne, where he had a home. The two became friends, and Hejmo would make periodic visits to the city on the Rhine where he informed "Lakar" on activities within the office of the pope. Polish journalist Krzysztof Tomaszewski,[10] who had extensive access to the secret police files, told me: "He also passed information on how Polish primates receive sensitive information from the Holy Father, and he named bishops who took secret messages from the Vatican to Poland. Once he also brought a letter addressed to the pope from a member of the Polish anticommunist opposition." During questioning after his exposure, Hejmo told Mr. Tomaszewski that "the envelope was open so I copied the letter." Eventually, Lakar was identified as Andrzej Madejczyk, an operative of the Polish secret police and, authorities believe, for the East German Stasi as well. Tomaszewski said the man paid Hejmo as much as 500 deutsche marks (about U.S. $200) at each meeting, for a total of 20,000 West German marks (about U.S. $7,800). He admitted to Italian reporters that he had received money from Lakar. "I came to Rome without

10. Pseudonym.

money. There were kindhearted priests who gave me money. I was a poor student. That agent also gave me money, but through priests." He apparently had forgotten that he signed receipts whenever he was paid, even before he came to Rome. The receipts said the payments were honorariums "for information regarding the Vatican."

In the first days after his exposure, the Dominican was besieged by the press, clamoring for interviews. On April 29, he met with reporters of Rome's newspaper *La Repubblica*. "I have never been a spy. Call me an idiot, or naïve, but not a spy." He told Milan's *Corriere della Sera* that reports he had written about the papacy for the Polish Bishops' Conference were being used by the communist secret police. "I once spoke about it to the Holy Father," he told the newspaper. "We were having lunch with other priests, and all of us said we had 'guardian angels,' meaning controllers working for the government. Even the pope knew he was being spied on."

The reaction of the Church hierarchy in Poland was one of disbelief, even outrage, that one of their fine servants was being so slandered. Cardinal Andrzej Maria Deskur termed the charges "absurd, inexplicable."[11] Cardinal Deskur, who was close to Pope John Paul II throughout his pontificate, thought the accusation against Father Hejmo was an attempt to besmirch the late pope. Father Maciej Zieba, head of the Dominican Order in Poland, reacted harshly toward the IPN, charging that the accusation was "made out of context." Father Zieba flew to Rome to question his subordinate. Apparently, the Dominican superior was not satisfied with Father Hejmo's answers.

When he returned to Warsaw, Father Zieba was confronted with a statement to the press by IPN historian Machcewicz. "His [Hejmo's] position was an ideal spot from which to observe the field around the pope. He transmitted to the security service information on

11. Interview with *la Repubblica*, May 1, 2005.

pilgrimages of the pope, whether or not the pope met with Lech Walesa during a visit to Poland, and details of planned meetings. Hejmo informed on the Vatican's preparations for a visit of General Jaruzelski. It was valuable information not only for the state security service, but also for the state and party leadership who, as a result, were able to better plan strategy, as an example, for talks with representatives of the Vatican." The still-skeptical Father Zieba was allowed access to Hejmo's dossier, after which he told the press that what he had seen was "convincing and shocking." Father Hejmo kept insisting that "except for a certain naïveté and talkativeness, my conscience is clear."[12] To this, his superior, Father Zieba, responded: "He had accepted money for his services, signed receipts, visited his case officer in Cologne. That is not naïve or talkative: it is a breach of trust."[13] Father Ziebo relieved Hejmo of his Rome position and sent him to a cloister "to think about what he had done." However, a year later, journalist Tomaszewski told me he was astonished to learn that not only was the spying priest "at least defrocked," but that he was back in Rome running the pilgrim center despite having seriously violated rules established in 1973. Then Cardinal Wojtyla, the future pope, and Cardinal Wyszinski decreed that all contacts with the secret police had to be reported to the curia. Obviously, the curia decided to let forgiveness reign.

More Spies

After Soviet KGB chairman Yuri Vladimirovich Andropov ordered increased espionage operations in the Vatican in 1969, the services of Eastern European satellites became even more active than they had been. KGB officials in the Ukraine, a heavily Catholic Soviet republic, were searching high schools and universities for intelligent

12. Interview with *Saechsische Zeitung*, July 1, 2005.
13. Ibid.

young men with foreign-language talent. By the beginning of 1980, a half dozen young university graduates, who had been recruited some years earlier, had graduated from KGB training facilities and were commissioned as officers. Then they were told of their top-secret assignments: approach Catholic Church officials and seek assistance in enrolling in a seminar in Rome to prepare for priest-hood. The prospective sleeper agents arrived in the Holy City in the mid-1980s or early 1990. But within months they were on their way back home. Andropov's operators had not counted on Father Robert A. Graham, the Jesuit from San Francisco who had become the Vat-ican's unofficial spy-catcher. ANSCA, a Rome news agency special-izing in Catholic affairs, said in a 1982 article that Father Graham was the "Vatican espionage specialist."[14] Father Graham, who had been concerned with spies in the Vatican going back to when the Nazis tried it, had become an expert in counterintelligence. He quickly unmasked the group, and they were sent back to the Ukraine. Obviously to satisfy repeated inquiries from the press about "rumors" of the Ukrainian infiltration, a news conference was held in May 1993, at which Achille Cardinal Silvestrini said the "claims" would be investigated. The cardinal, who was the prefect of the Con-gregation of Oriental Churches, said Father Graham was appointed to supervise the probe. Accompanying the cardinal was Father Jakov Kulic, secretary of the Congregation. Father Kulic said a bishop of Ukraine's Greco-Catholic Church had been under investigation in connection with the KGB infiltration. He did not name the bishop, but said "at least" three bogus seminarians had been unmasked

---

14. This was told to the author in July 1999 by a high-ranking official of Italy's security service who wished to remain anonymous. ASCA, the Rome news agency concentrating on Catholic affairs, said Father Graham "has for more than 30 years searched for spies that have operated in church circles and the Holy See." Father Graham was associate editor of the Jesuit weekly publication *America*. He was a prolific writer for a number of Catholic publication; among the books he authored was *The Vatican and Communism during World War II*.

"before the collapse of communism in Eastern Europe." The results of Father Graham's investigation were never officially revealed.

Interestingly, Father Graham, co-author with Dr. David Alvarez of *Nothing Sacred: Nazi Espionage Against the Vatican*, wrote about a similar attempt by the Nazis in 1943 involving men from occupied Soviet Georgia who were sent to Rome to establish a bogus seminary. They, too, were unmasked and sent back to Georgia. Dr. Alvarez told me that Father Graham, who died in 1997 at the age of 84, never mentioned the Ukrainian operation to him. My Rome source said he was not surprised, because Father Graham was obliged to keep many situations under wraps. This might well explain why the Vatican secretary of state ordered that Father Graham's private archive consisting of 55 boxes, which had been sent to the archive of the California Province, Society of Jesus, be returned to Rome. Officials at the California Province were told that the secretary of state wanted to have the material vetted before it could be publicly accessed. At this writing, the Graham papers are stored in the basement of the secretary of state's office, though the California curie was told they would eventually be returned. Not surprisingly, the Vatican is extremely sensitive about espionage cases not only within the walls of the Holy City but within the ranks of its clerics in general. For example, in September 1999, I met in the Vatican with Archbishop John P. Foley, head of the Pontifical Council for Social Communications, to discuss my book project. I assured the archbishop, a genial man from Pennsylvania whom I had known since 1985, that the book would in no way denigrate or besmirch the Church. Instead, it would show that the communists had gone to any length and spared no expense in their quest to destroy the Church. I handed the archbishop copies of documents that originated in the pope's secretariat and wound up in the hands of Polish and Soviet intelligence. The Most Reverend Foley was shocked. "They are the real thing," he said in a tone of voice that expressed dismay. The following day, a Vatican courier arrived in my hotel with a letter from Archbishop Foley thanking me for the "documentation you brought on what the Eastern European secret services knew about the Vatican." He said he had "not only forwarded all the documentation, but your request for a meeting with someone in the Secretariat of State." Two days later, another courier brought a note from Archbishop Foley with a copy of a letter sent him by Secretary of State Cardinal Angelo Sodano. "I gratefully acknowledge your diligent courtesy in bringing the matter to my attention," Cardinal Sodano wrote. "At the same time, I would appreciate it if you were to express my thanks to Mr. Koehler. At the present time, in fact, it is not necessary to disturb him further."[15]

In an article published in 1969 in *Columbia*, the monthly magazine of the Knights of Columbus, Father Graham wrote about electronic eavesdropping in the Vatican by the news media and communist intelligence services. "Newspaper 'espionage' may be harmless or at the most a minor evil," he wrote. "This is not the case of espionage by governments hostile to the Church. The security problem is one of the abiding concerns of papal aides. Some Vatican officials still have a vivid recollection of foreign clandestine intrusion." Father Graham wrote about tapped Vatican telephones; that confidential messages by radio or telegraph were intercepted and decoded, files rifled, and the Holy See's representatives surrounded by informers. Vatican officials "had to cope with hidden radio transmitters, fake students planted in Roman seminaries, traitorous workers in its offices, and agents sent from the world's capitals to

15. Frankly, I had not expected much cooperation. I totally understood this reluctance to confide in writers not intimately known to the Vatican hierarchy after publication of a number of books falsely and slanderously accusing Pope Pius XII of having been a handmaiden to the Nazis and not interceding in the persecution of Jews. The writers knew full well that the opposite was true. In 1943, the *New York Times* depicted Pope Pius XII as a "lonely voice crying out of the silence of a continent." On his death in 1958, Israeli prime minister Golda Meir wrote in a condolence letter: "During the years of Nazi terror, when the Jewish people went through the horrors of martyrdom, the pope raised his voice to condemn the perpetrators and to commiserate with the victims."

gather classified information. Father Graham acknowledged the reluctance of Vatican officials to reveal the spying within the walls of the Holy City. "Spy scares are not in the style of the Vatican, but experience is a good teacher," he wrote. "There are no illusions in the Vatican offices about either the will or the ability of enemies of the Church to probe secretly into the Church's life and movements."

Communist Czechoslovakia's regime was as brutal in oppressing the Catholic Church as all the other Eastern European governments. Priests had to be licensed by the government to tend to their flocks. Prison terms for recalcitrant clerics were par for the course. The most prominent of the persecuted was Josef Cardinal Beran, who first was locked in a Nazi concentration camp for three years. Then, as the Archbishop of Prague, he was arrested by the communists and imprisoned from 1949 to 1963, when he was released but forbidden from exercising his ministry. Finally, in 1965, he was expelled from his homeland; he settled in Rome, where Pope Paul VI elevated him to cardinal. The new cardinal devoted much of his time to caring for refugees from Czechoslovakia, including a number of priests who had fled to the West to escape imprisonment. These priests were housed in the Collegio Pontificio Nepomuceno. Among them was Father Frantisek Kuncik, who had escaped to West Germany at age 17 and then went to Rome to enter a seminary for studies in theology and philosophy. Ordained in 1965, he was assigned to a parish in the small town of Tisoi in the foothills of the Dolomite Mountains of northern Italy. There he became sexually involved with an Italian woman, who followed him to Rome when he was re-assigned. He apparently was successful in hiding his transgression from his Church superiors. But Czech intelligence, which had the refugees, especially clerics, under close surveillance, became aware of Kuncik's sins and blackmailed him into spying for the Czech State Security and Intelligence Service (StB). His assignment was to spy on Cardinal Beran, who also lived at the Collegio. Kuncik eventually managed to ingratiate himself with the cardinal so well that he became his chauffeur. He often was invited to dinners his boss hosted for high church officials and important Czech priests, where he was privy to highly sensitive discussions about the Church's work in Czechoslo-vakia.[16] Cardinal Beran died in May 1967. In 1970, Father Kuncik suddenly left Rome for Prague without first informing his superiors. Italian security officials believed that he and his paramour had con-tacted Czech embassy officials, most probably StB agents, who arranged his secret departure.[17] In Prague, he took off his priestly collar, was married, and worked for the government producing anti-Church propaganda.

Jaroslav Fojtl, another Czechoslovakian priest living at the Czech Collegio Pontificio Nepomuceno, also departed Rome suddenly for Prague without notifying his superiors. It was not known whether this was coordinated with those who assisted Father Kuncik. Father Fojtl, too, had been unmasked as a spy for the communists. Italian security officials believed both Kuncik and Fojtl had been "advised" by Vatican officials to go home.[18] Fojtl was 35 years old when he escaped to Austria in the late 1950s. After living in a refugee camp for two years, he went to the West German city of Munich, where he began his studies for the priesthood. Exiled Czechoslovakian priests whom he had befriended advised him to move to Rome and enter a seminary to finish his studies. Fojtl stayed only for a year and returned to Czechoslovakia, where he was said to have fallen in love with a cousin. As in the case of Father Kuncik, the Czech StB took advantage of Father Fojtl's moral turpitude and blackmailed him into becoming a spy. Once more the new spy returned to the Holy City. Although he was able to report on the activities of Czech exiles,

16. Conversation in 1999 with a highly placed Italian government official who wished to remain anonymous.
17. Ibid.
18. Ibid.

which had increased in numbers after the 1968 Soviet and East German invasion of Czechoslovakia to prevent the country's break with the Warsaw Pact, he was not an effective spy.[19] Apparently, the Italian security service SISMI had him under surveillance after it received information from the West German Bundesamt für Verfassungsschutz (BfV), the Office for the Protection of the Constitution charged with domestic counterespionage. The BfV had observed Fojtl photographing attendees of the Ostakademie, a Catholic institution in Königstein, a town near Frankfurt in West Germany. The Ostakademie, formed at the height of the Cold War in 1958, dealt with problems of the Church in communist countries, including persecution of believers and refugee problems.

The Spy Who Wasn't

One of the most sensational "espionage penetrations" was that of Colonel Alois Estermann, commandant of the Papal Swiss Guards, who, along with his wife, was murdered on May 4, 1998. The murderer, Vice-Corporal Cedric Tornay, shot both of them with his 9mm service pistol and then killed himself. A nun, who heard the shots, investigated and found the dead in the Estermanns' Vatican City apartment. Within days, the news media, especially newspapers in Germany, were speculating that the 43-year-old Estermann had been an agent for the East German Stasi's foreign intelligence service since 1979 and that his code name was "Werder." The *Berliner Zeitung* wrote that there had been a spy who delivered sensitive information on Vatican affairs between 1979 and 1988. Officials at the archive of the former Stasi acknowledged they knew of an agent with that code name, but could not confirm that it was Estermann. The news media was so fixated on Estermann "the alleged spy" that they totally ignored the 23-year-old shooter who, as it turned out, was in a rage

19. Ibid.

after the newly appointed head of the Swiss Guard informed him that he had been turned down for the commendation medal "Benemerentis."[20] When Tornay's room was searched, authorities found in a desk drawer butts of hand-rolled cigarettes in which, according to a toxicological examination, were traces of cannabis (marijuana).[21] This would explain reports by superiors and fellow Swiss Guard companions of Tornay that he often displayed periodic "irresponsible behavior and lack of respect."[22]

The news media, however, was bent on making Colonel Estermann the Stasi's ace spy in the Vatican. The Polish newspaper *Super Express* reported that Markus Wolf, who was chief of the Stasi foreign intelligence department, said in an interview: "We were very proud when we successfully recruited Esterman in 1979 as a spy. This man had unhindered access to the Vatican and, through him, we as well."[23] However, in another interview with Swiss Television, Wolf said he never mentioned the name Estermann but said merely that he had had a "good source." As it turned out, Wolf was speaking about Eugen Brammertz, the treacherous German monk who once briefly carried the code name "Werder," and whom I discussed earlier in this chapter. And so the story of "super spy" Estermann, the chief of the pope's Swiss Guard who never was privy to Vatican secrets of interest to the communists, was put to rest as a badly—yea, amateurishly— media-manufactured canard.

---

20. Investigation Report of the Assassination of Colonel Estermann by the investigative judge of the Vatican Court Attorney Gianluigi Marrone, 1999.
21. Ibid.
22. Ibid.
23. *Berlin Kurier*, May 10, 1998.

10 SPYING CONTINUES, TO NO AVAIL

C
ommunist case officers tasked their Vatican spies to concentrate on gathering information on the activities of the Holy See in supporting the Polish opposition to the communist regime. Despite the government agreement in August 1980 that recognized Solidarity as an independent workers' union, strikes continued as the economic problems mounted, sharply cutting into food supplies. The people's discontent with their government was steadily intensifying. This was the setting when the Soviet KGB disseminated, in early 1981, a four-page top-secret assessment titled "Trends in the policies of the Vatican vis-à-vis the socialist states" to the "fraternal" services.[1] Its tone was one of desperation to an extent I had not previously noticed in KGB reports on the Polish crisis. "The

1. Archive of the former East German Ministry for State Security (MfS or Stasi) Nr. 1083/81 BSTU Nr. 000008. Translated from the Russian.

chief foreign policy task of the Vatican consists at present to strengthen the role of the Catholic Church within the social and political life of the socialist states and to transform it into a realistic power for influencing the domestic and foreign policy of these states," the assessment said. "In order to solve this task, the Vatican, recognizing the specific circumstances of each socialist state, must adjust the methods used by the Church in influencing the public in its relations to the government."

Although the document does not reveal the source of its information, it is clear that the spy was close to the papal office of the secretary of state, which, according to the assessment, "places the highest value on the activities of the Polish Catholic Church which, since the Pontificate of Wojtyla as pope, has strengthened its position considerably. This has become evident in that she has become a sort of mediator between the organs of the state and the opposition." The KGB lamented that within a year, the number of Church attendees had increased and that the "influence of the Church in the mass media has strengthened as well." It assigns "considerable credit" to Pope John Paul II with the "achievements of the Polish Episcopate by his decision to strengthen step-by-step its influence on the masses by taking advantage of the dissatisfaction of the people with the social-economic policy of the government, while at the same time avoiding an open confrontation with organs of the state for making political demands." These tactics "deprive the political leadership of a lever for repressive measures against the Church." According to the assessment, the Vatican told Polish Catholic Church leaders to continue a policy of "quiet diplomacy," but at the same time cement activities designed to "broaden infiltration of radio, television and the press because the Vatican views this as a basic element in strengthening the Church's influence over the population." The pope, according to the assessment, had sent a letter to the leadership of the Polish Church saying that "work in this direction must be performed step-by-step since it is of foremost importance to secure what has already been attained in the process of liberalization." The Vatican, the Soviet espionage service said, had "urged its episcopates in communist countries to take advantage of and stir up discord between state organs and the various social and ethnic groups in socialist countries, and then make an attempt to take on the role of peacemaker and mediator."

In closing, the KGB assessment betrayed its deep concern over the influence of Poland's unrest on other East European communist countries and requested its security service to answer these questions: 1. In order of importance to the Vatican, list the various socialist countries in which assigned tasks are to be solved. Which methods are being employed? 2. What concrete possibilities does the Vatican see in strengthening its position and that of the Church in the socialist states? Which are the most important domestic political factors the Vatican can exploit? 3. How does the Vatican evaluate the current relations between Church and government in the socialist states? 4. Which facts point toward the Vatican's success in solving, to some extent, its tasks? Unfortunately, a document with answers to these questions could not be found.

"The role of Zionism and the Catholic Church in the Activities of Solidarity" was the heading of a June 12 report by a spy for the Hungarian intelligence service which was shared with the KGB as well as with the East German Stasi.[2] The report said Church circles in Rome were worried about the development of events in Poland. "The Roman Catholic Church supported from the beginning the demands of Solidarity, but has cautioned against excessive political actions. Political circles in the West and the Church now battle for greater influence over Solidarity," the spy told his handler. "The most dangerous is KOR

2. Stasi document HA XX/4-8751, marked top secret. Translation from the Russian. BSTU Nr. 000197.

[Ed.: the Committee for Defense Against Repression]. With its help, Walesa wants to express his political demands.

"The KOR, which includes a great number of intellectuals, has far-reaching connections in Western Europe and in the USA. However, the KOR has the closest connection with international Zionism. Thus, the KOR representative in Rome has established very good contacts with Italian Jews," the report said, adding: "Competent representatives of the Vatican, including the pope, are convinced that instructions which reach Poland originate with Zionists. The USA and Israel, as well as Polish emigrants in Western Europe, play an important role in their delivery." In closing, the report emphasized that the Polish leadership of the Church had assumed the role of the go-between [Ed.: between government and Solidarity] "because they are of the view that political mistakes could damage what has been so far achieved." In closing, the report pointed out that the death of Stefan Cardinal Wyszynski a month earlier "cannot change anything on what has been achieved so far, since the Church is also interested in stabilization."

A few months earlier, on October 17, 1980, the East German Stasi distributed a highly sensitive top-secret assessment based on reports of its Vatican spies which, as always, was shared with the KGB to be passed on to the Soviet leadership. "High dignitaries of the Vatican maintain that the pope, who comes from the People's Republic of Poland and who has great influence there, is one of the chief reasons for the present situation," the assessment declared. "Obviously, his idea about a 'common Christian Europe' plays a decisive role. Although this idea rests mainly in the area of morals and ethics, it nevertheless has also practical effects over the methods of the forms of government and methods of governing as viewed by the pope," adding that the pope found confirmation of the possible realization of his ideas in Western Europe during his visits to Ireland and France and his residence in Italy. "To also realize this idea in Eastern Europe, the pope views the People's Republic of Poland where, after all, he maintains the best of all contacts." The assessment pointed out that Pope John Paul II continually added to his detailed knowledge about the actual situation in Poland by the many visits from cardinals, bishops, and priests, as well as the many Polish civilians, numbering from 300 to 1,000, who attended his weekly general audiences at St. Peter's Square.

Since the unrest in Poland began, according to the East Germans, the influence of the pope "can be noted not only by the display of his portraits throughout the country, but also by the many demands of the workers and the methods employed in the disputes that have the imprint of the 'moralistic basics' of the pope, just as he had already displayed in the People's Republic of Poland as Cardinal Wojtyla." A number of members of the Curia said that they could not "comprehend" how the pope could send a message to the Poles contradicting that of the country's primate, Cardinal Wyszynski, who, for example, called upon striking workers to return to their jobs while the pope "highly emphasized the right to strike." Judging by the oft-displayed brilliance of the two men and their anticommunist backgrounds, one can easily assume that the contradictions were based on a clever tactic allowing the cardinal to appear as a mediating force in order to maintain some relations with the regime, while the pope addressed the desires of the people. This may well have been a tactic to create confusion and apprehension within Moscow's leadership, particularly when one reads the KGB's comment on the "primary attention" paid in the Vatican's newspaper *L'Osservatore Romano* and in the newscasts of Vatican Radio. The assessment said:

> Many individual talks with Vatican officials also dealt in great detail with those events, and one came to the realization that in this connection, the pope for the first time openly voiced his true position toward the socialist countries. At the same time, this proved that the pope is under the influence of the USA.

East Berlin's spies also reported that many Polish exiles "of Catholic as well as Jewish faith" who resided especially in France and the United States had "asserted considerable influence" over the events in Poland. Both countries had a large and staunchly anticommunist population of Polish descent, influential civic organizations, and Polish-language newspapers. "At the same time, the question of providing financial aid to the striking workers—including also from Israel—is viewed as an attempt by these circles to again strengthen their influence in the Vatican. Polish exiles in the USA are strongly supporting the pope's policies regarding the People's Republic of Poland with financial aid. They also provided considerable sums for missionary activities of Polish priests. That has made Poland the European country that sends the most missionaries to the Third World."

A number of meetings of the Soviet Communist Party's Politburo, at the time the KGB assessment was circulating around the East Bloc intelligence services, were chiefly concerned with the Polish situation, which was also influencing anticommunist movements at first in East Germany and Czechoslovakia and later in Hungary and Romania as well. The most vehement pressure on Moscow for military intervention came from Erich Honecker, the East German Communist Party boss, and from his Czechoslovakian counterpart Gustav Husak. Both men had good reason to sweat. Both men probably would have spent time in prison had it not been for the brutal put-down of the 1953 workers' revolt in East Germany by Soviet forces and the Soviet, East German, and Polish military invasion of Husak's land in 1968. On April 24, 1981, a top secret "Special Dossier," prepared by seven Politburo members including KGB chief Yuri Andropov, Foreign Minister Andrei Gromyko, and Defense Minister Dmitri Ustinov, dealt with the Polish situation and what steps the Soviet Union should take to assuage the problem. The dossier said the PZPR (Polish Communist Party) "has lost control of the processes under way in society," adding that "Solidarity has been transformed into an organized political force which is able to paralyze the activity of the party and state organs and take de facto power into its own hands. If the opposition has not yet done that, it is primarily due to its fear that Soviet troops would be introduced and because of its hope that it can achieve its aims without bloodshed and by means of creeping counterrevolution." Considering the massing for "maneuvers" of three Soviet mechanized infantry and armored armies of 150,000 men as well as East German and Czechoslovakian divisions close to the Polish border, the apprehension of the Poles was understandable. A two-page, single-spaced document resembled more hand-wringing and expressions of disgust with "inept" Polish Communist Party leaders such as Kania and Jaruzelski. However, it did repeat a suggestion to, as a "deterrent to counterrevolution, maximally exploit the fears of internal reactionaries and international imperialism that the Soviet Union might send its troops into Poland."

An undated KGB directive apparently sent to East Bloc security services at the height of the unrest in 1980/81 devoted five pages to operational instructions for the Polish secret police.[3] Copies were sent to the security services of other Warsaw Pact countries, whose functionaries must have scratched their heads and wondered why it was necessary to point to "a few problems of the subversive activity of the Roman Catholic Church against Socialism." After all, the Soviets had been dealing with these "problems" for more than 60 years by resorting to mass murder and imprisonment in concentration camps. One wondered what the authors of the document had been smoking when one read: "Lately, the Vatican of the Roman Catholic Church has more and more become an element of international politics in that it can not advance her own solutions and is in no position to find

---

3. MfS document HA XX/4-233, BSTU Nr. 000058, marked secret—translated from the Russian.

prophylactic measures with which to neutralize the enthusiasm for Marxism. The Vatican's diplomacy knows that the Roman Catholic Church will suffer great losses if she only has relations with the capitalist world. In the eyes of Catholics, the Church's prestige and significance in general has declined." And this was written *after* the world—and hundreds of communist spies—witnessed the euphoria and jubilation of the Polish people during the visit of Pope John Paul II in 1979. "The Episcopate is attempting to create a psychosis of persecution and threats to the Church by the state. The state security service knows all prognoses and plans developed by the Church for action until 1983." This, then, is part of the KGB directive, slightly edited to spare the reader some of its bureaucratic gobbledygook:

"The state security service will conduct operational measures, in line with the policies of the Party and government, to limit the reactionary activities of the Polish Catholic Church in an effort to win over some of the priests to loyalty vis-à-vis the state. The operational efforts must concentrate mainly on infiltrating the Church with unofficial collaborators [Ed.: informers] in order to uncover the political line of the Episcopate. *The state security service will react decisively and effectively against all indications of political activity of the Catholic Church and to all attempts to disturb public order and safety by resorting to juridical and administrative measures*" [emphasis added]. In other words, if priests, or nuns for that matter, speak out against the government or the Communist Party or aid rebellious workers in any way, it would be off to prison or house arrest.

The unrest in Poland dated back to at least 1956 and was entirely caused by extreme discontent of the working class with little influence of the Church until the mid 1970s. In fact, some Church officials tried repeatedly to mediate the disputes. The new KGB concern over Church influence of anticommunist activities no doubt stemmed directly from the election of a Polish pope who had never concealed his abhorrence of communism. But why would the security officials continue to ponder the Church's activities when Moscow had already decided that the only way to put down the unrest was with armed force?

On February 9, 1981, the East German Stasi's Hauptverwaltung für Aufklaerung (HVA), the foreign intelligence service, issued a seven-page super-secret report of which only six copies were distributed and which had to be returned in three days to the HVA.[4] It was titled: "The views of Vatican dignitaries on the situation in Poland and other internal problems." Parts of the report read almost entirely as if it had been written by a newspaper gossip columnist. It dealt almost exclusively with the factions within the Curia that differed with the pope's handling of the Polish crisis. One faction was led by Archbishop Pangrazio of the Curia and Archbishop Silvestrini, secretary of the Council for Public Affairs (Foreign Minister) in the State Secretariat. "These and others agree that the serious economic difficulties can only be solved in close cooperation between the state and the Church. In the Curia, the opinion prevails that only with tight cooperation between the Polish state and the Polish Bishop's Conference can the workers be brought back to their jobs. Jointly one could also go against the anarchist groups within the unions. *Solving the problems by the Poles alone would also serve the circles in the Vatican which, in contrast to the pope, are not ready to agree to 'certain tendencies of USA policies'*" [emphasis added].

That there was dissention in the Vatican on policy matters was long known. However, the East German spy report reveals the amazing naïveté of Archbishop Pangrazio about Poland's dire economic problems and how to solve them. "First, the government must assure that the workers work more and better. And second, prevent the forming of a union of farmers, because a further weakening of

4. MfS document 74/81, BSTU No. 001185. Because of the notation "this information is only for personal use so as not to endanger the source," the information was likely provided by the German Benedictine monk Eugen Brammertz (see chapter 8).

Poland's agriculture would lead to a 'final catastrophe.' Both questions make cooperation between state and church urgently necessary." Had the archbishop buried his head in the sand during all the years in which government mismanagement and corruption steadily led to the severe food shortages that plagued the country for at least a decade, that led to the people's revolt?

Many bishops of the Curia posed the question as to why the pope agreed to meet with Lech Walesa, since his visit to Rome had been organized by the major Italian trade unions with which, until that time, the Vatican had an "unsatisfactory" relationship, the report said. "Below the threshold, one can detect among Vatican dignitaries disagreement with the pope in many respects." Some Curia members "emphasized that the mass media is making Walesa into a public persona, but as a person he is a nobody." There were other disparaging remarks that bordered on snobbishness, such as "Walesa is not a cultured person and lacks an education." One can only wonder how the millions of Walesa followers and the communist functionaries plagued by the Solidarity leader would have reacted toward the Church had they known about these assessments.

The report left little doubt that Pope John Paul II was running a tight ship and was more engaged in managing Vatican affairs than was his predecessor Pope Paul VI, especially in carrying out an effective Ostpolitik to communism's detriment. "The overemphasis of the Polish problems by the pope could lead to an impediment of Ostpolitik." In other words, some of the Curia members favored continuing to deal with the Polish government in a firm but friendly manner. But the Polish pope, who had been toe-to-toe with communist oppression of the Polish people and his Church for decades, was not to be persuaded by the "traditionalists." The East German intelligence quoted its Vatican spy as reporting that the existence of two main factions had become clear. "First, there are the old traditionalists who are bent on securing present achievements. Second, those who follow the pope no matter what. He [the pope] has, in 1980, attacked his own aides. In private conversations with various bishops, he was said to have gone so far as to speak of loafers and idlers who are not able to write clear reports and commentaries. The pope has been criticized for his predilection for Polish affairs, which has created insecurity among even some high-ranking officials. Only the influence of Cardinal Casaroli and some others has prevented it from coming to an open dispute."

A Major Crisis Looms

Inside the Vatican throughout the 1980s, the spies were as busy as ever, now chiefly concerned with the Polish situation. It would not have been lost on them that President Ronald Reagan's director of the Central Intelligence Agency, William Casey, had visited the Vatican in the spring of 1981, shortly before the assassination attempt on Pope John Paul II.[5] A source in Rome, speaking on condition of anonymity, said that in his meeting with the Holy Father, Mr. Casey asked if the Church could help in secretly transporting printing presses and radio equipment to the Polish resistance. Apparently the meeting was successful, since Solidarity and other resistance groups eventually made use of the equipment, although the Polish secret police managed to uncover and confiscate some of it, though not enough to hinder dissemination of leaflets and the airing of clandestine broadcasts. On June 26, 1981, the KGB distributed a lengthy top-secret report it had received from the Hungarian intelligence service, which obtained the information from its agent in the Vatican. In studying the information, it is not unreasonable to deduce that the spy was spoon-fed by Vatican officials who were acting on suggestions by Mr. Casey to impress Moscow that the United States would not be an inactive bystander to a Soviet invasion of Poland. By this time, Washington had already ordered the

5. Interview with Richard Allen, President Reagan's first national security adviser.

deployment of four AWACS aircraft to Ramstein Air Force Base in West Germany. They were part of "Exercise Sentry Creek" tasked with NATO ground-based radar to monitor East European air activity.[6] To illustrate its importance, below is the KGB report[7] in full:

"The American government has developed a plan for the event that the Soviet Union, i.e. the Warsaw Pact, decides to intercede militarily in Poland. This plan includes a number of diplomatic, economic, and other sanctions.

"The government of the USA views a military intervention as the most aggressive move of the Soviet Union since the end of World War II. Such a move would result in serious and unforeseen consequences for international relations for the USSR and for the other socialist countries.

"According to the American assessment, a military intervention in Poland would unleash massive resistance in which a significant portion of the Polish army would join. The USA would furnish appropriate help to the Polish rebels by sea and over Western land routes.

"The American assessment says further that the leading elements of the Soviet Union's leadership are split over the method to be employed in solving the crisis and their consequences. So far, no officials representing various views have accepted the risk of military meddling.

"American government circles are interested in learning whether representatives of other socialist countries have received directions in case of military action in Poland; and, if so, what are they?

"According to the assessment of the Vatican Curia, the Soviet Union will be forced to intervene with armed forces in the events in Poland in

6. General Vernon Walters was one of several U.S. administration troubleshooters and a former Deputy CIA Director. He visited on numerous occasions between 1981 and 1988 with Pope John Paul II to brief the Holy Father on U.S. moves to counter Soviet threats to Poland. During the visits, General Walters, a devout Catholic who spoke 16 languages, also showed the pope reconnaissance and satellite photos of East bloc military activities adjacent to Poland. The general died in January 2002.
7. MfS document 8718/81, Department X, June 26, 1981, BSTU Nr. 000018.

order to secure the railway and motor transit routes. For ideological and political reasons, the USSR will remove the members of the [Polish] Central Committee and the Politburo of the PVAP, the Polish Communist Party, and with the help of a new leadership re-establish the old political relations. If the Poles resist, than this resistance will be broken with military force. If, however, there is no resistance, the Soviet Union would magnanimously support the new system.

"In contrast to the Curia's assessment, the pope, however, is of the opinion that a slower development in Poland could prevent military action. In order to avoid an intervention, the pope, without considering the opposition of the Curia, is said to have written a letter to the Soviet head of state in which he informed him that prior to a second surgery, he would travel to Poland and would appeal to the Poles to practice moderation. In selecting a new Primate of Poland [Ed.: Cardinal Wyszynski had died on May 28, 1981], the pope let it be known that he would be guided by the same consideration. (At present the possible candidates for Primate of Poland are the Bishop of Krakow, although he is viewed as a weak personality, and a professor of ethics and social science of a Catholic university where the classes are conducted in the German language.)

"If despite all (the pope's appeal) military intervention takes place, the pope has the intention to use a Polish diplomatic passport for travel to his home land in order to call on the people to resort to civil (not military) resistance."

In closing, the KGB report said: "The Vatican Curia is against the pope's excessive 'Polish activities,' but it is not able to do anything about it."

Open resistance to the Polish communist regime continued unabated. The severe food shortages had increased and fueled neverending work stoppages. Although the Soviet Union had aided Poland with more than $4 billion, it was not nearly sufficient. Thus, Deputy Prime Minister Mieczyslaw Jagielski traveled to Washington, where he met with Vice President George Bush and Secretary of State Alexander Haig to request aid. The United States agreed to supply dairy products worth $650 million. While the aid prevented starvation, it did nothing to assuage the people's anger. The unrest continued unchecked, nearly becoming violent. Robert Gates, who headed the Central Intelligence Agency's section for surveillance of the East bloc before becoming the CIA director, wrote in his book *From the Shadows* of a dangerous escalation of resistance in Poland. The agency's officers reported that in April, "extremists" were preparing to use Molotov cocktails against Polish police and militia in attempts to take over government buildings and Communist Party offices throughout the country. Needless to say, Mr. Gates was privy to extremely sensitive information furnished by the agency's most valuable asset in Poland, Colonel Ryszard Kuklinski, assigned to the Defense Ministry as liaison officer to the Soviet Army. On the evening of September 15, 1981, the colonel sent a 500-word message—he called it a "telegram"—to his agency case officer.[8] He described his presence two days earlier at a top-secret meeting of the National Defense Committee (KOK) which for the first time had been attended by the Communist Party's first secretary Stanislaw Kania. "The imposition of martial law was discussed without coming to a decision," the colonel wrote. "Almost all of the participants supported it." Although Kania did not question the imposition of martial law, according to Kuklinski, he told the meeting that a "confrontation with the class enemy is unavoidable." This would first involve a "struggle using political means, but if that should fail, repression may be adopted." One of the generals present said that Solidarity already knew details of the operation which had been code named "Wiosna," meaning "Spring." The CIA's asset wrote that a counterespionage officer had assumed command of planning to "prevent

8. Virtual Archive, Cold War International History Project, Woodrow Wilson International Center.

further leaks." Here is how Colonel Kuklinski described some of the operational details:

"Martial law will be introduced at night, either between Friday and a work-free Saturday, or between Saturday and Sunday, when industrial plants will be closed. Arrests will begin around midnight, six hours before an announcement of martial law is broadcast over the radio and television. Roughly 600 people will be arrested in Warsaw, which will require the use of around 1,000 police in unmarked cars. The same night, the army will seal off the most important areas of Warsaw and other major cities. Initially only the MSW's [Ed.: Ministry of Interior] forces will be used. A separate political decision will be made about 'improving the deployment of armies,' that is, redeploying entire divisions to major cities. This will be done only if reports come in about larger pockets of unrest. One cannot rule out, however, that redeployments of divisions based far away from the areas of future operations will commence with the introduction of martial law or even earlier. For example, it would take roughly 54 hours to redeploy the 4th Mechanized Division to the vicinity of Warsaw.

"Because the investigation [Ed.: into the leaks] is proceeding, I will have to forgo my daily reports about current developments. Please treat with caution the information I am conveying to you, since it appears that my mission is coming to an end. The nature of the information makes it quite easy to detect the source. I do not object to, and indeed welcome, having the information I have conveyed serve those who fight for the freedom of Poland with their heads raised high. I am prepared to make the ultimate sacrifice. But the best way to achieve something is with our actions, not with our sacrifices. Long live free Poland! Long live Solidarity, which brings freedom to all oppressed nations!" Colonel Kuklinski signed the message with his pseudonym "Jack Strong."[9]

9. Colonel Kuklinski and his family were exfiltrated from Poland through East Germany and arrived in the U.S. appropriately, on Veterans' Day, November 11, 1981.

One month following the KOK meeting, Kania was stripped of his position and General Jaruzelski, who had become prime minister in February while retaining his position as defense minister, also took over as head of the Party. But changes in the leadership did nothing to stop the sinking of the economy. Food shipments from the United States helped, but not enough to adequately feed the people. Textile workers continued striking to protest the shortages. Major investments had virtually halted, and construction projects which had started in the cities had been abandoned. Those Poles lucky enough to receive hard currency from relatives or friends in the West were able to purchase Western foodstuffs in the Pewex shops, the foreign currency shops which were prevalent in all communist countries.

As the Polish government was preparing for the imposition of martial law as a resolute, brutal instrument to eradicate any opposition, the Solidarity union met from September 26 to October 7 for the second convention round, elected Lech Walesa, and adopted a social program. A month later, when some 400,000 workers were on wildcat strikes, Solidarity's National Commission (KK) resolved that there was a need for negotiations on a national agreement with the communist government on appointment of a Social Council for the Economy to establish guidelines for economic reform. Indeed, it was a fluid situation for Solidarity, as its National Commission Presidium approved a 24-hour protest strike if the Parliament voted to grant the government special powers, and a nationwide general work stoppage if these powers were exercised. By this time, word had reached the opposition forces that the government had decided for massive repressive action by employing the military and special police units. In a last-ditch attempt to solve the unrest peacefully, the Solidarity leadership on December 3 declared that it would be ready to talk to the government, but only on condition that the latter renounce its plans to apply force against the people. The gesture seeking a peaceful solution was in vain.

The Soviet Central Committee, chaired by Brezhnev, met again on December 10, 1981, for discussions of the Polish situation that had occupied the leadership for more than a year and was gaining in intensity. Much of the discussion dealt with the severe food crisis in Poland which the Soviets could help but, as Foreign Minister Andrei Gromyko put it, "the nature of the Soviet-Polish economic, political, and other relations will depend on the way things shape up in Poland."[10] In other words: Jaruzelski, you will get aid, but not until you wipe out Solidarity. It had been clear that Moscow was not going to risk a unilateral military invasion. However, the discussions concluded that, "due to the international attention," the Soviet Union would provide military support "only if Poland cannot deal with the situations on its own and requests help."

Martial Law and its Aftermath

At ten minutes before midnight on December 12, 1981, all telephone and telegraph connections went dead. Just after midnight, television and radio broadcasts stopped. Martial law was in effect for Poland, declared by General Jaruzelski under the Soviet threat "do it or else." At 6 A.M., television returned to the air, and an announcer in the uniform of a colonel introduced Jaruzelski for his public declaration of martial law. Six hours earlier, the Council of State had resolved to authorize martial law, and formal authority was assumed by the Military Council for National Salvation (WRON).

Anna Niedzialkowska, a girl barely 10 years old, lived with her mother in Brudnowo, a small town about 18 miles southeast of the city of Bydgoszcz, the scene of many major strikes and a particularly brutal incident in March 1981. Several Solidarity strike organizers were beaten by riot police. Lech Walesa was called to the scene and

10. Top-secret working notes of the December 19, 1981, session of the CPSU CC Politburo. Virtual Archive, Cold War International History Project.

was able to restore order, though the tension, which remained high throughout the year, affected a wide area around Bydgoszcz. Here is how Anna remembered the morning of December 13:

"It was early morning on Sunday when I was awakened by someone pounding on our door. My mom opened up, and there was our neighbor who lived on the floor below ours in the apartment block. He was very upset, screaming 'war, war,' and ran to another apartment door. Nobody knew at the beginning what was happening. As every Sunday, we went to church, which was completely filled. I also remember that there was no normal programming on TV, just Jaruzelski. Our phone did not work, as well those of all of our neighbors. It was a day I will never forget."

Thomasz Pompowski, who lived with his parents in the city of Wroclaw, was an eight-year-old who went on to become a journalist. He remembers:

"It was early on Sunday, the Third Advent. The church bells rang as always. That day, December 13, 1981, the winter was very severe. Temperatures were well below freezing. Poland was covered by a thick layer of snow. My mom removed snow from our small Fiat. My father drove us to church over the streets we always used every day, and they were nearly empty and quiet. We attended a mass to pray for my brother who only a few days before had had a serious operation. My father went on to the hospital to be with my brother. Only after we left the church did we hear that Jaruzelski had announced a state of war. When we got home, Mom turned on the TV and we heard Jaruzelski saying: 'Rada Panstwas wprowadszilla stan wojenny.' In the Polish language, it was the expression for 'state of war.' I remember my mom saying 'he declared war against his own nation.' Only in the afternoon, when my mom took us for 'Gorzkie zale,' the traditional religious service honoring a suffering Christ in Lent, did we see military vehicles and tanks in front of the Wroclaw railroad station. On the way back home, we passed more military and police vehicles and a tank. Then police stopped us and checked Mom's papers. To frighten the people and to show the power of the Communist Party, columns of military and police vehicles drove through the city with their emergency signals blaring and blue lights flashing. I admit that I was scared when they passed our apartment building. After that, they did this every weekend. From Radio Free Europe, which was the only station my father Jan would listen to, we knew that the Soviet Army [Ed.: There were 54,000 troops still stationed in Poland] was somewhere on the streets and on alert in their barracks. In our city, we had a special district where they lived. Moreover, in the city of Legnica, about 60 miles to the west, several thousand Soviet troops were stationed there, including units with tactical nuclear weapons. We also heard that America had suspended economic assistance to Poland."

What neither Anna or Thomasz knew that Sunday morning was that at least 1,755 leaders and prominent members of Solidarity and other resistance groups had already been rousted from their beds in the cities of Warsaw, Radom, and Gdansk by agents of the state security service backed up by heavily armed squads of ZOMO, the paramilitary riot police. It was a precision performance based on a Ministry of Justice order signed just hours earlier.[11] Lech Walesa, who two months earlier had been elected national chairman of Solidarity, was hauled from his home in Gdansk and taken by plane to a government safe house in Warsaw. He was later transferred to a remote hunting lodge. During the next months, 9,736 Polish citizens—8,728 men and 1,008 women—were arrested and sent to 36 "isolation centers" which were dispersed throughout Poland, from the Soviet border in the East, to central Poland, and to the western border with communist East Germany.[12]

11. Order Nr. 50/81/CZZK, Minister of Justice, of December 13, 1981.
12. Forum o Internowanych w czasie Stanu Woynnego. Attachment to "Daily Information" dated 14.12.1981. Results of activities undertaken by the Ministry of Justice in connection with martial law.

As the world's democracies watched in consternation the unfolding of another brutal chapter of communist disregard for a people's longing for freedom and independence, President Ronald Reagan telephoned the Polish pope on December 14 to express the American people's—and his own—shock. "Your Holiness, I want you to know how deeply we feel about the situation in your homeland," the president said.

"Our sympathies are with the people, not the government. Our country was inspired when you visited Poland, and to see the people's commitment to religion and belief in God. It was an inspiration to the whole world to watch on television. All of us were very thrilled," the president told the pope, adding that "I look forward to the time when we can meet in person."

Within 48 hours after the declaration of martial law, large military forces, including tanks, surrounded the Lenin shipyard in Gdansk, where the first anti-government strike had erupted under the leadership of Lech Walesa. A day later, the first shots were fired at the coal mine Manifest Lipcowy in southern Poland near Katowice, where striking miners decided to resist the ZOMO unit which opened fire without warning. Four miners were wounded. The next day would become one of the bloodiest. Striking miners of the nearby Wujek mine were gathered within its walls. Outside, the crowd included women and children. The riot police dispersed them with water canon and tear gas. The action incensed the miners, who responded with crowbars and slingshots. A ZOMO unit, supported by a tank that had smashed through a wall, opened fire. Result: six miners died on the spot, three died later, 22 suffered serious wounds, and dozens had less-serious injuries. The next days saw protests and street fighting in the North at Gdansk, where one man was shot dead and two others were wounded. Over the next week, the remaining strikes in other parts of the country were broken. For the Polish people, it had been the worst Christmas since World War II. To help ease the food shortages,

President Ronald Reagan ordered that foodstuffs be sent to Austria for shipment to Poland and to help feed Polish refugees in Austria.

An espionage report from the Vatican classified "top secret" was distributed by the KGB three days after Christmas.[13] It said that "the declaration of martial law in Poland has created much anxiety among Vatican officials. They fear that it may be the beginning of a civil war that would cause enormous loss of life. This would lead to interference by forces of the Warsaw Pact. Vatican circles believe that the Soviet Union might also participate 'indirectly' with Soviet soldiers in 'disguise.' At this juncture, Pope John Paul II is exercising great caution in evaluating the events, since he does not want to enhance the internal tension," the spy reported. In "interest to protect the source," the report urged extreme caution in handling this information. Considering that the unrest in Poland in general, and the martial law specifically, had been reported almost daily in the non-communist press world-wide, one must conclude that even the spymasters must have viewed their activities as exercises in futility. That would explain why, as opposed to earlier years, the number of espionage reports from the Vatican had been reduced to a dribble. Also, it must be noted that I could find no reports on the meetings of CIA Director Casey and the president's emissary, General Walters, with the pope. The Vatican spy-catchers seemed to have done a yeoman's job.

The Polish government and Communist Party, and of course Moscow as well, were reeling from another serious blow. Two of their most seasoned and prominent diplomats defected and sought asylum, with their families: Romuald Spasowski, the ambassador to the United States, and Zdzislaw Rurarz, the envoy to Japan. Both settled in the United States. The defection of Ambassador Spasowski was an especially serious loss. It had been his second posting to the U.S.

13. Stasi document Nr. 9480 dated December 28, 1981, "Information from the Security Organs of UVR (Hungarian Peoples Republic)"—translated from the Russian.

and he had previously held the post of deputy foreign minister. His daughter and son-in-law had defected several months earlier. The day after his defection, Ambassador Spasowski spoke on Radio Free Europe and told the Polish people and the rest of the world that he had defected to show his support for Lech Walesa and Solidarity. "The cruel night of darkness and silence was spread over my country," he said. One can be certain that both diplomats were a godsend for U.S. intelligence in evaluating the situation within the Polish government. Ambassador Spasowski and his wife, Wanda, met with President Reagan in the White House Oval Office on December 22. Of the ambassador, the president said: "I'm very proud that he's here in this office. I think we're in the presence of a very courageous man and woman who have acted on the highest principle. And I think the people of Poland are probably very proud of them also." In retaliation, the communist government confiscated the family's property, branded him a traitor, and sentenced him to death in absentia. There had been a number of other defections, including 16 sailors who jumped ship in Canada and six others in Alaska.

The day after his meeting with Ambassador Spasowski, the president delivered his Christmas address to the nation, devoting most of it to Poland. "As I speak to you tonight, the fate of a proud and ancient nation hangs in the balance," he said. "For a thousand years, Christmas has been celebrated in Poland, a land of deep religious faith, but this Christmas brings little joy to the courageous Polish people. They have been betrayed by their own government." The president accused the Polish government and "their totalitarian allies" of countering the "stirrings of liberty with brute force, killings, mass arrests, and the setting up of concentration camps." He reminded his listeners that the events in Poland, occurring almost two years to the day after the Soviet invasion of Afghanistan, "have been precipitated by public and secret pressure from the Soviet Union." He pointed out that it was no coincidence that Soviet Marshal Viktor G. Kulikov, chief of the Warsaw Pact forces, and other senior Red Army officers were in Poland while "these outrages occurred," and that the martial-law proclamations had been printed in the Soviet Union in the fall.

The speech was his toughest speech against the Soviet Union to date. "I want to state tonight that if the outrages in Poland do not cease, we cannot conduct 'business as usual' with the perpetrators and those who aid and abet them. Make no mistake, their crime will cost them dearly in their future dealings with America and free peoples everywhere. I do not make this statement lightly or without serious reflection." He reiterated that Moscow, "through its threats and pressures, deserves the major share of blame for the development in Poland." He said he had sent a letter to Brezhnev urging him to permit restoration of the basic human rights in Poland provided for in the Helsinki Final Act. "I informed him that if this repression continues, the United States will have no choice but to take further concrete political and economic measures affecting our relationship." The Soviet leader never replied to the president's letter.

Tensions throughout the land continued unabated as the stormiest year in post-World War II Polish history came to an end with an announcement from Solidarity that the union planned to continue its resistance.

In Rome, Pope John Paul II greeted 1982 with a speech from the famous window overlooking St. Peter's Square. After a general blessing, the Holy Father said: "I especially want to say a blessing, in this liturgy of today, with some thoughts for my country, of which I am a son: May the Lord give you peace." He spoke of "the Mother of Jasna Gora," the Black Madonna. "For the last 600 years this mother has been present on the Polish land through her image at Jasna Gora. Before her, I repeat: May the Lord spare my country of violence, the state of siege, may he grant you peace." The pope thanked all who were praying for Poland and for those who carried the many signs and banners supporting the Polish people with the word "Solidarnosc." "I see another inscription, 'Committee Friends of Poland,' and they are Italian. At this time, my compatriots can come to Rome only with great difficulty. Therefore, as I find myself here on St. Peter's Square, in Italy, in this land that welcomed me as one of her own, as once she welcomed St. Peter, I want to turn to that topic Solidarnosc, about solidarity, about my country. The word is the expression of one great effort that workers have made in my country in order to ensure that workers have true dignity. In fact, the workers have the right to establish independent unions, whose role is to take care of their social rights, family rights, and individual rights. I thank you for this welcome, for this solidarity that goes beyond my own person." In closing, he wished all a Happy New Year and "that the Lord may bless you and give peace and justice in the world."

Long Road to Freedom Getting Shorter

The first East German intelligence report issued after the declaration of martial law was based on information supplied by a spy who apparently had the confidence of highly placed Vatican officials as well as Franz Cardinal Koenig of Vienna, one of the Church's top experts on religious activities behind the Iron Curtain.[14] As to martial law, according to the spy, the action had been "expected" by the hierarchy "where the talk centered on a so-called 'Argentine Solution' (a military government veiled in nationalism) as the last chance to prevent national bankruptcy."[15] In other words, the Vatican reportedly viewed the crackdown by Jaruzelski as a lesser evil, saying he was "basically not Moscow's man, a moderate nationalist but only a

---

14. Ministry for State Security document Nr. 001326, classified top secret—return after reading—four copies only, January, 1982. BSTU Nr. 000001.

15. The "Argentine Solution" refers to a 1976 coup by a military junta to topple a inept government led by Eva Peron. The junta maintained its power by systematically and ruthlessly suppressing domestic subversives, including communists. Civilian rule was reestablished in 1983 when the military was sapped of its power by losing the Falkland War to the British.

A smoke bomb explodes between protesters and riot police in Warsaw on July, 1989 during a demonstration against the candidacy of Communist Party Leader Wojcjech Jaruzelski. Even as protesters confronted police, Jaruzelski told the party's Central Committee that he would not run. *Associated Press*

Polish President Lech Walesa kisses the hand of Pope John Paul II on June 8, 1981, in Warsaw. A born fighter, Walesa lead the revolution that culminated in the Soviet collapse and became an internationally recognized symbol of Poland's return to self-determination. *Associated Press*

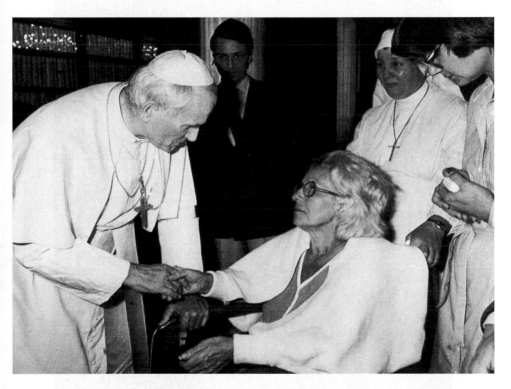

Pope John Paul II visits with Ann Odre of Buffalo, N.Y. who was wounded during the assassination attempt of the Pope on May 13, 1981. *Associated Press*

Cardnial Wielgus, the newly appointed archbishop of Warsaw at a mass at Warsaw Cathedral on January 7, 2007. Wielgus resigned in 2009 after admitting he had spied on the Church for Poland's communist-era secret police. *Associated Press*

Former Soviet President Mikhail Gorbachev, who was a member of the Polit-buro group that decreed drastic measures against the policies of the new Polish Pope John Paul II in November 1979, which eventually lead to the assassination attempt of the Holy Father. *Associated Press*

British Prime Minister Margaret Thatcher on November 3, 1988, lays a wreath on the grave of pro-Solidarity priest, the Rev. Jerzy Popieluuszko, who drowned at the hands of the secret police four years earlier. In the background are the supporters of the anticommunists Solidarity Union. *Associated Press, Martin Cleaver*

Polish Rev. Konrad Stanislaw Heimo, a Dominican Monk who was accused of collaborating with the communist secret police during the 1980s. *Associated Press*

President Ronald Reagan discussing the Polish uprising against communism
in a private meeting with Vatican Secretary of State Cardinal Agostino
Casaroli at the White House on December 15, 1981. The President had earlier voiced his desire to help the Polish people. His meeting also touched on
the President's planned trip to meet with Pope John Paul II at the Vatican in
June, 1982. *White House Photo*

communist with great reservations." This evaluation was based on "many half-measures" employed as martial law began to be enforced. Examples of what constituted "unnatural" half-measures for a military government included "the kid-gloved treatment of obvious provocateurs and the gentle handling of interned functionaries of Solidarnosc who should be the real enemy of this military government." Considering the harsh treatments, including severe beatings, of the thousands who were arrested, one must wonder if the spy had not fallen for a clever psychological-warfare ploy. The Vatican's evaluation of a "soft" Jaruzelski martial law most certainly would have caused consternation within the East German leadership. Fearing that the unrest might spill across the border, Communist Party leader and head of state Erich Honecker had consistently urged Moscow to use Warsaw Pact military forces for strangling the Polish rebellion, a la East Germany 1953, Hungary 1956, and Czechoslovakia 1968.

The conclusion of the Stasi report more than anything reinforced my belief that Pope John Paul II, advised by his own experts, as well as by U.S. General Walters, had been resorting to psychological warfare to create uncertainty within the already shaky communist bloc. "Vatican dignitaries see Poland's future as continually needing to be propped up economically while the country is a constant ideological thorn within the RGW (Warsaw Pact) and a constant 'source of infection' for the other socialist states. No one spoke seriously about Poland becoming at some time a state under a purely Western type government. Rather, her 'ideological thorn and source of infection function' is in the long run for the West more valuable since such a Poland serves continually as a vulnerable state which forces other socialist countries to continually make economic sacrifices," the Vatican spy reported. The identity of this traitor has never been revealed, but he was most likely on the staff of the pope's secretariat.

While Achille Cardinal Silvestrini was preparing his speech to the Conference on Security and Cooperation in Europe, also known as the Helsinki Conference, an agent reporting to Hungarian intelligence was busy trying to determine the tenor of the address the pope had approved.[16] The cardinal was the head of the Vatican Council for General Church Affairs and known for his tough stance toward communism, which equaled that of the Holy Father. This brief spy report, written at the beginning of 1982, was classified top secret and, as usual, shared with the Soviet KGB—which, in turn, handed a copy to the East German Stasi. "He [Silvestrini] will assume a hard and disapproving position toward the Polish military leadership and the Soviet Union," the report said. It is not difficult to imagine how it evoked a guffaw from Soviet Party chief Brezhnev, who had demonstrated in abundance the meaninglessness of international accords unless they suited his communist ideals and expansionism. He was a signatory to the 1975 Helsinki Final Act which recognized postwar borders in Central and Eastern Europe. This, in fact, legitimized Moscow's hegemony over the communist countries in the region. As a quid pro quo, the Soviet Union agreed to "respect human rights and fundamental freedoms, including of thought, religion or belief, conscience, for all without distinction as to race, sex, language, or religion."

Since the Soviet leadership had no intention of honoring the provisions of the treaty, the KGB may not have even shown the report to Brezhnev. It certainly was not discussed at the January 14, 1982 session of the Politburo, where once again communism's Polish dilemma was the sole subject of the agenda.[17] Leonid Brezhnev dominated the discussions, which opened with a review of Polish Foreign Minister Josef Czyrek's visit to Moscow for discussions with hardliner Mikhail Suslov and Forein Minister Andrei Gromyko. "The discussions were useful," Brezhnev said. "Western officials, especially the Americans, are exerting enormous pressure on Poland. In such circumstances, it is

16. Copy of Hungarian and Soviet top secret espionage agent report originating in the Vatican. Stasi Archive Nr. 8208/82, BSTU Nr. 000044.
17. Politburo session transcript (excerpt), January 14, 1982. (http://cwihp.org)

important to offer constant political support for our friends and bolster their spirits. One cannot permit their spirits to sag or to allow them to relinquish what they have achieved with such difficulty." Commenting that martial law was already a month old, the Soviet leader quoted General Jaruzelski as proclaiming "the counterrevolution is now crushed." Brezhnev, who, as mentioned before, was in ill health and would suffer a debilitating stroke two months later, made a rambling assessment of the Polish situation. "In general, one gets the impression that the general as a political actor is very strong and is able, on most occasions, to find proper solutions. Sometimes it seems that he is too cautious and acts more often than necessary with an eye to the West and to the Church." Brezhnev then added "But in the current situation, such gestures will only ruin things." He did not explain, and he then turned to the dire economic situation and Jaruzelski's plea for additional aid, and said agreed deliveries would be made. The "esteemed, dearest Leonid," as Jaruzelski always addressed him in letters, then added almost as an afterthought: "Incidentally, the food situation if Poland is not so bad. There is plenty of bread in the country." The Soviet leader might as well have said "Oh, well, there is no meat or butter, so let our Polish comrades live by bread alone." There were no responses from the other members, all except one of whom were well over 70 years old. The only "youngster," Mikhail Gorbachev, was 54. Needless to say, the meeting solved nothing that would have helped the lot of the Polish people.

A month after this meeting, the KGB received another top-secret Hungarian spy message[18] that might have lifted Brezhnev's spirits a bit, assuming he was still sufficiently compos mentis. Scores of spy reports have dealt with dissention within the hierarchy, probably sensing this would please their masters and lift their spirits at a time when good news within the communist bloc was hard to come by.

18. Stasi/KGB report 8182/82. BSTU Nr. 000041.

Frankly, as I had surmised previously, it was likely that a well-organized disinformation campaign had been launched with U.S. expert guidance after Vatican spy-catchers had put agents out of business, or had "turned" them to become double agents as a possible road toward redemption or being defrocked. The next sentence would point in this direction. "According to leading circles of the Vatican, the Italian and the West German Episcopate do not agree with the position of Pope John Paul II on Poland. They accuse him of acting not according to the interests of the Vatican, but from a nationalistic position." The succeeding sentence is a puzzler. "They [the Episcopates] demand that, with reference to human rights, he act more decisively against the takeover of power by the military and to call upon the Catholic churches the world over to join him." Earlier reports, just prior to martial law, portrayed high Vatican officials as reproaching the Holy Father for being too tough on the communists. Now this report had him as a softie, completely reversing his image. As the Soviet active measures people used to say in such cases: "Oni pilitj piloy—they're sawing our head," a Russian expression for sowing confusion. And confusion must have reigned in the Kremlin. While Moscow was digesting the news about the "softie," the Holy Father spoke in Rome on January 10 and condemned martial law and denounced violations of human rights by the military regime.

Another top-secret report from the Hungarian source on January 15 commented again on "differences of opinion among Church leadership in Poland which Pope John Paul II attributes to the tactics of the Polish government."[19] "In the pope's opinion, the Polish government, while negotiating with Cardinal Glemp to assuage mutual problems, is at the same time doing everything possible to liquidate laic committees who work with the bishops in order to lessen the effects of their work with the people. Whenever leaders of the Polish

19. Stasi/KGB report 1022/82. BSTU No. 000043.

Church visit Rome, the pope summoned those representing positions differing with his to become unified and pursue joint actions toward preventing the government's 'Policy of Division.' "

When the Polish primate, Archbishop Josef Glemp, was in Rome for his promotion to cardinal in July 1982, a servant of Hungary's secret police reported on a lengthy meeting of Pope John Paul II and his new cardinal.[20] "During the discussions between the pope and Primate Glemp, total agreement was reached that the Polish Church must continue its unyielding position [vis-à-vis the government]. A mouthpiece of the Vatican press, *La Civilta Cattolica*, will shortly publish a malicious anti-Soviet article about the situation in Poland. Because of the restrained position of Cardinal Agostino Caseroli [Ed.: Secretary of State], the newspaper, the articles of which are regularly reviewed before publication by the Vatican State Secretariat, has not published any abusive anti-Soviet articles. With the publication of the article, one can assume that Casaroli was forced to submit to the hard line of the pope." Vatican disinformation specialists seemed to be busy.

Though Solidarity's public activities were effectively silenced by the gun-toting enforcers of martial law and the arrests of thousands of members and supporters, three important leaders managed to evade their hunters. They were vice chairman Miroslaw Krupinski, Warsaw leader Zbigniew Bujak, and Wladyslaw Frasyniuk, the leader of the Wroclaw branch. These men restructured the union into an underground movement, a risky undertaking that forced the men to change their location almost daily. They were encouraged in their dangerous efforts by the defection of 800,000 members of the Communist Party[21]—and, of course, by the financial assistance they received clandestinely from the West, especially from the United States AFL-CIO

20. Stasi/KGB report 1323/82. BSTU Nr. 000045.
21. At the Roots of Polish Transformation. Lecture by Prof. Wojciech Roszkowski, former director of the Institute of Political Studies, Polish Academy of Sciences, Warsaw, at University of Virginia, March 2001.

labor union, though the Vatican's financial aid was never publicly revealed. However, the communist oppressors knew about it. The Hungarian intelligence service forwarded a report from its Vatican spy to the KGB that the "labor union 'Solidarnosc,' while still a legal organization, was granted financial help in the amount of $25 million." The top-secret message said the "information originates from diplomatic circles in the Vatican."[22]

As Vatican officials met in March 1982 for discussions of a possible papal visit to Poland later in the year, the communist spy was listening.[23] The Hungarian intelligence report to the KGB said "intense" discussions had "erupted" between various groupings in the Vatican. "Casaroli and a great part of the Italian bishops of the Curia are against the planned visit of the pope to Poland because in their opinion until now the policy of the Vatican vis-à-vis Eastern Europe would be put into question which can aggravate the situation of the Church as well as the believers in socialist countries," the report claimed. "The said group also offered the argument that the Vatican cannot continue the Doppelpolitik [Ed.: twin or double policy] after the pope, while in Africa, warned the Church there against pursuing such a policy, he cannot now inspire them to do the opposite." In other words, the pope was allegedly being advised not to preach to the Church in Africa that it should stay out of politics and do the opposite when it came to Poland. "For the time being, the pope supports the plan for the Poland visit. The group also agrees with the plan which runs counter to Casaroli's Ostpolitik [Ed.: who allegedly favored a more conciliatory stance toward the regime]. According to the group's opinion, the visit can bring help to the Polish people and contribute significantly to activate the resistance movement." In closing, the spy reported that a "great part of the members of the

22. Stasi/KGB report 9073/82 BSTU 000147, dated July 9, 1982.
23. Stasi/KGB top secret report 1973/8404/82, dated March 25, 1982. BSTU Nr. 000051.

Polish episcopate would rather see to it that the visit be delayed, and the group supporting Casaroli hope that Poland will politely reject the visit."

This is exactly what happened. General Jaruzelski, in a five-page letter that can easily stand as a perfect example of utter hypocrisy, told Cardinal Glemp that he agreed that the visit "must bring positive results that would foster unity and rapprochement in favor of the Poles and that would be beneficial to the state." Jaruzelski, pointing to the state of martial law, wrote that "although its many rules and manifestations have considerably eased, the situation is not yet normal, and massive assemblies of people who want to greet the pope could encourage incidents." Thus, the visit must take place when the pope "can be accorded the proper dignity." He suggested that the Church make plans for a papal visit some time in the future.[24] A copy of the letter was attached to the East German Stasi's weekly assessment of July 12, 1982, which said its Vatican spy reported that the pope had planned to give a $10 million credit to the Polish government and that the pilgrimage would most likely take place in 1983. Intelligence officers of the Stasi stationed at Polish secret police offices and the East German embassy and consulates also were reporting that "Solidarity functionaries are passing out a 'Strategy of Underground Leadership of Solidarity' which is closely coordinated with the planned papal visit." The intention of Solidarity, according to the assessment, was to "create an illegal 'Opposition State' and an 'Underground Population.' "It provided no details, saying only that a visit by the pope, even a short one, could "again fire up the mood of the people." It added that "it is expected that the authorities will not be able to control masses of pilgrims in all parts of the country so that it will come to 'excesses in the streets.' In

24. Weekly Stasi intelligence assessment of Zentrale Auswertungs-und Informations-gruppe (ZAIG) Nr. 13321 of July 12, 1982. BSTU Nr.000001.

closing, the Stasi assessment said "the leadership of the underground is convinced that this situation could lead to a decisive confrontation with the authorities of the People's Republic of Poland." The information undoubtedly came from a freelance East German journalist, identified only by his code name "Josef," who had infiltrated Solidarity in 1980.[25]

Another Stasi assessment one week later revealed serious political-ideological differences within the Polish Communist Party, something that had been whispered about but was never seen by this writer in a communist secret police document.[26] "Because of the political-ideological dispute within the PVAP [Polish United Workers Party], the Catholic conception of 'social agreement' has so far not been publicly branded and rejected as an anti-socialist platform." What the term "social agreement" meant was that the Church has let it be known that it agreed with some of the Party's ideas pertaining to the social welfare of the people, but not with its communist ideology of oppression of "anders denkende," those who think otherwise. The assessment again dealt largely with the proposed visit by Pope John Paul II and that Polish authorities confirmed that it would not take place "this year." Leaders within the underground movement looked at a papal visit as an "instrument to achieve their hostile goals," it said, to wit: "Extremists are planning protest actions against the planned liquidation of Solidarity as well as a general strike as a decisive test of power with the government. This goal was decided upon on the basis of the activation of hostile activities, especially among the working class." On the other hand, the assessment said "Moderate representatives of Solidarity see in the visit of the pope a possibility to bargain 'with peaceful means' for the re-activation of

25. John O. Koehler, *Stasi: The Untold Story of the East German Secret Police* (Westview Press, Boulder, CO, 1999).
26. Weekly Stasi intelligence assessment of Zentrale Auswertungs-und Informationsgruppe (ZAIG) Nr.13322 of July 19, 1982. BSTU Nr. 000016.

Solidarity and the release of all internees." In closing, the Stasi report said diplomats from NATO states "expect[ed]" that the pope's visit would increase the people's "spirit of resistance that it will be difficult to control *emotional* eruptions among the people."

There can be no dispute that the open support of the Vatican and the clandestine aid of the United States kept alive the spirit of Solidarnosc and the people's disdain for the brutal communist rule. Nearly every month until the year's end, strikes and protest marches were reported throughout the country. In May, more than 60,000 participated in a protest march in Gdansk without interference from the militia, probably because of the large number of demonstrators. The military dispersed smaller protests in other towns. Also in May, more massive demonstrations erupted in Gdansk and Gdynia, where battles with the militia lasted until deep into the night, leaving four persons dead and 11 injured. A fifth was beaten to death in Wroclaw.[27]

After months of discussions within the Communist Party and Parliament, the regime passed a law banning all labor unions which had been active prior to the enactment of martial law on December 13, 1981. In defiance, strikes continued, prompting the Jaruzelski regime to militarize the major Polish shipyards and to order that workers be punished with heavy fines for refusing to work.[28] With Solidarnosc now banned, the authorities, in the obvious hope of ameliorating the tension, released Lech Walesa from his 11-month internment a month before Christmas. The year ended in continued food shortages and curtailment of personal liberty.

---

27. Polska Agencia Prascova SA, 2005, 25th Anniversary of Solidarnosc.
28. Ibid.

11 ARDOR FOR FREEDOM NO MATCH FOR SPIES

ech Walesa, now newly released from communist confinement, showed up for work at the Lenin Shipyard in Gdansk, only to be denied entry by the military guards, who claimed his pass had expired. Walesa insisted that he be allowed to return to his job as a welder or he would file a complaint with the labor court. Since the authorities knew of a papal visit in the summer, they were disinclined to roil the waters further by harassing a friend of the pope. And so, the Solidarity leader who had fanned the first major anti-government strikes in the 1970s was given his old job back.

But Walesa seemed farthest from the minds of secret police functionaries, especially those of East Germany whose government had been jittery ever since the unrest in Poland had erupted years earlier, fearing that the "infection" could well move westward. Now they were concerned over a second papal pilgrimage, which a top-secret Stasi memorandum for the Communist Party leadership characterized as a "problem."[1] "Plans of the Church for this year's papal visit call for achieving a number of goals, the most important of which are: 1. Continue to strengthen the position of the Roman Catholic Church within the society vis-à-vis the powers of the state. 2. Broaden the possibilities to influence the different groups of society, mainly the workers, farmers, youth, and the art circles. 3. Further popularize the persona of Pope John Paul II among Catholics and the entire society. The state has these goals in connection with the pope's visit: 1. Strengthen Poland's authority in the international arena and seek changes in the position of the West vis-à-vis the People's Republic of Poland. 2. Deepen the credibility of government's policy vis-à-vis the believers aimed at influencing more positively the stabilization of the socio-political situation in the country as well as the process of isolating extremist elements and their initiatives. 3. Support in a more positive direction the activities of the Catholic Church with the aim of creating conditions for further modification of the religious-political dogma versus the state." Last, but definitely not least, there were concerned "operational-political measures" to be applied during the visit and aimed at the following: "1. Control the dimension of the visit and its effect on the society. 2. Support the decisions and initiatives of the government as to the political restrictions of the visit. 3. Countermeasures and elimination of politically unfavorable activities and manifestations while preparing for and during papal visit." In an attached document, the East German secret police wrote: "In connection with the travelers to Poland, unofficial collaborators [Ed.: informers] will be used to assure that East German participants in the event will be deterred from committing hostile or negative activities. Consultation with

1. Stasi Hauptabteilung XX/4 document Nr. 1057/83 dated April 6, 1983. BSTU Nr. 000665-000668.

Polish security organs found that there is no interest in limiting the entry of foreigners into Poland so long as the number of requests for travel permits remain low, and so long as none are made by hostile persons." In other words, procedures were to be in line with those employed during the 1979 visit by Pope John Paul II, when between 200 and 300 Stasi agents were used to keep an eye on foreign pilgrims.

While trials of dissidents and sporadic strikes continued in Poland, espionage reports from the Vatican were reaching the Soviet KGB, as well its East European allies, with greater frequency. Dated May 6, 1983, the top-secret communication said: "Polish religious emigrants, settled in Rome, maintain through Church members regular contacts with members of the underground Solidarity movement. The underground wishes that this time the pope will again pursue the course he began in 1979." The agent, who collaborated with the Hungarian secret police, reported that the Polish opposition "is not counting on a re-emergence of Solidarity and will therefore content itself with using aid from the West, such as food and clothing etc., to sustain their movement against the government." The report added that the aid was being organized by the Vatican. "The pope's closest Polish compatriots are pushing for the papal visit with the intention of stirring up the psychological war to maintain the tensions in Poland."[2]

One week before the pope's arrival, an apprehensive East German secret police began distributing top-secret situation reports to the leadership in Moscow. It was critical for the Polish regime to change its mind and lift its ban on a meeting between the pope and Lech Walesa. "Had they insisted on preventing this meeting, the authorities fear the pope would have publicly supported Solidarity, which could have caused even greater political damage," the report said.[3] It criticized Polish authorities for its "inconsequent position (giving in

2. Stasi/KBG document 3636/86 dated May 9, 1983. BSTU Nr. 000089.
3. MfS Zentrale Auswertungs-und Informationsgruppe report Nr. 13371 dated Jun 14–20, 1983. BSTU Nr. 000001-7.

to the demand for a pope-Walesa meeting) which could only serve to create further difficulties, and this is exactly what happened. There were extremely large public assemblies by clerics. These went way beyond previously reached agreements and were exploited by hostile groups by distributing anti-socialist slogans and mass distribution of badges with counterrevolutionary symbols." After extensive consultation with their Polish counterparts, the East German secret police expressed weariness about large-scale hostile activities and the fear that the participation in public events alone "is to prove that the opposition continues to exist in all its strength." Part of the report mirrored the usual incendiary language of the East German secret police—as specified, there were no "extremely large" public assemblies by the clerics before the pope's arrival.

The East German communists were right in expecting the pope to enunciate a "hard line." After deplaning at Warsaw's Okecie airport, he sank to his knees and greeted his homeland by kissing the ground—which, he said, was like "placing a kiss on the hands of a mother, for our homeland is our mother." A chorus of young Poles sang an old hymn, "Hail Mother of Poland." Pope John Paul II was welcomed by President Henryk Jablonski, who spoke of "conciliation, normalizing relations, cooperation on important questions such as inner peace." While the Polish president guaranteed his regime's continuation of the democratization and reform process, the pope seemed doubtful, to say the least. In his response, the Holy Father ignored the words that the Polish leader had hoped would create a friendly atmosphere. "I consider it my duty to be in solidarity with my compatriots in this sublime and difficult moment." Obviously, the Holy Father was aware that the authorities had restricted access to the arrival area to an infinitely smaller crowd than the one that had greeted him on his first visit as pope in 1979. It was remarkable that the Stasi reporting was so accurate that one had to wonder if the functionaries were stuffing themselves with anti-acid pills when they read: "The pope made direct and indirect *attacks* against the Party and the government, such as condemnation of martial law, condemnation of the 'violation of human dignity,' display of solidarity with imprisonment of hostile persons, with those who have been humiliated, and those who are suffering from injustice, stand firmly for true freedom."

The Stasi report lamented that the 300,000 people along the pope's eight-mile route to the capital responded with ovations to "these and other provocative slogans." The evening before the pope's arrival, a clandestine radio broadcast broke in on a regular Polish government station to tell the pope that "from your words, we shall draw strength for further work."

More than 200,000 faithful had gathered in the evening at St. John's Cathedral in Warsaw's Old Town to greet John Paul II as he arrived to hold a mass for the repose of the soul of the venerable Stefan Cardinal Wyszynski, the Polish primate who had been imprisoned and then under house arrest at two monasteries for three years by the communists, and who had died in 1981. After praying at the cardinal's crypt, he reiterated in his homily what he had said at the airport, that along "with all my compatriots, particularly those who are most acutely tasting the bitterness of disappointment, humiliation, suffering of being deprived of their freedom, of being wronged, of having their dignity trampled upon, I stand beneath the cross of Christ." The congregation inside responded with deafening applause. "Those outside," as the Stasi spies duly reported to their East Berlin masters, "chanted 'Solidarnosc' as a manifestation of sympathy for Walesa, displayed anti-socialist banners, and raised their hands with fingers shaped in V signs." Leaving the cathedral, the pope joked with the parishioners and, obviously referring to the authorities who had urged him to tone down his rhetoric, he quipped: "This is God's logic: let them be more merciful to me so that I can be more merciful to them." Also that evening, some 50,000 persons, including some priests, assembled in Warsaw for a two-hour "anti-socialist demonstration."

Banners were aimed at inciting "anti-socialist hatred and threats of murder," the Stasi wrote. It noted that law enforcement did not interfere and chided the government for "playing down the extent of the protest and remarked sarcastically that it involved 'only a *small group*'." It failed to report the texts of two other banners which read: "Welcome, messenger of hope" and "I came, I saw, God conquered." Victor Simpson, who covered all of Pope John Paul's pilgrimages to Poland for the Associated Press, wrote that the demonstrations in support of the banned Solidarity labor movement were the biggest unofficial gatherings since martial law was imposed. "They were staged in defiance of the warnings from authorities, but security forces in plain sight made little effort to intervene."

Because of their unusually accurate reporting and their emphasis on anti-state activities, I will cite the Stasi reports, some in full, so that the readers may judge themselves as to the acuteness of the apprehension besetting the East Berlin regime.

The pope's homecoming began at Belvedere Palace, where he met with General Jaruzelski for nearly three hours, during which, according to the Stasi report, the pope continued his tough course of meddling in the internal affairs of Poland and attacks against the Party and government. "Accordingly, the pope:

- Renewed criticism of the declaration of martial law.
- Demanded that agreements of August 1980 legalizing Solidarity be honored.
- Demanded repeatedly that a meeting with Walesa be permitted.

"The remarks revealed his efforts to save the existence of opposition activities and structures, establish conditions for achieving legalization and reactivation of anti-socialist elements, and create conditions for establishing political pluralism in order to achieve a division of power. These positions were sharply rejected by Comrade Jaruzelski in a tough debate with the pope." In written criticism by the East Germans of a communist "brother," heretofore never seen by this writer, the Stasi said: "Contrary to the facts, the government's version of the talks for the consumption of the people described them as having taken place in an atmosphere of understanding and sympathy." I must assume that the Stasi's "honest reporting" was designed to rile its leadership into applying even more pressure on Jaruzelski to step up greater anticommunist suppression. Of course, the East German regime would spur Moscow on to do likewise.

The evening mass in the soccer stadium on that first full day was attended by nearly a million people. It was "clearly a display of anti-socialist manifestations," the Stasi reported. "Again there were attacks by the pope against 'violations of human rights,' 'perversion of justice,' 'oppression'." The Holy Father called the Poles an "enslaved people" and compared them, especially the imprisoned, with a crucified Christ. According to the Stasi observer, the pope "made veiled attacks against the Soviet Union by saying the Polish people had a right for a 'sovereign existence'." Pope John Paul's weeklong visit, which took him to six cities, was meticulously chronicled by the East German secret police officers, concentrating almost exclusively on attacks against the government and communism and the reaction of the authorities.

The spiritual highlight of the pontiff's visit was the celebration of the 600th anniversary of one of Poland's most sacred icons, the Black Madonna of Czestochowa enshrined at Jasna Gora Monastery. The celebration had already been delayed for a year due to the political turmoil. The government had refused the pope's entry into Poland for fear of further aggravating the anti-government sentiments aroused by the introduction of martial law and suspension of independent organizations, such as Solidarity, which were officially sanctioned in August 1980. This is the East German report on the Jasna Gora ceremony:

"The events on June 18, 1983, and the anniversary mass on June 19 in which more than 2 million people participated, were again used extensively by the pope for anti-socialist manifestations. He continued in an aggressive manner to pursue his course toward ideological mobilization and activation of counterrevolution by:

- Severe attacks against the socialist state powers,
- Calls for resistance against the order of socialist society, for active struggle and proclamation of resistance on the basis of the Catholic conception of battling for 'law and liberty, human rights and freedom of conscience,'
- Propagating Catholicism as the only true ideology (his ideological demands were more comprehensive and confrontational),
- Emphasizing the 'contradiction' of State-People by citing 'injustice, oppression and suffering,'
- Approval of the events in 1980,
- Support of the underground, the imprisoned enemies, the interned, persons who were dismissed from their jobs, including the farmers Solidarity group,
- Renewed attacks against the Soviet Union."

In concluding the report on papal events, the Stasi writer offered this stunning criticism of the Polish Communist Party and the government, which must have shaken not only the East German regime but particularly Moscow where Foreign Minister Andrei Gromyko said the pope's visit was of a "religious character" and stressed his country would defend its "legitimate" interests in the region. "Poland has been and will remain an indivisible part of the socialist community."[4]

4. *Time* magazine, June 27,1983, quoting the Soviet news agency TASS.

Obviously, Comrade Gromyko had not yet seen what the East German comrade had written:

"After only a few days of the pope's presence in Poland, it is clear that the Party and government leadership suffered defeats through the Catholic Church and that further difficulties were created in the pursuit of stabilizing the political situation and in the political-ideo-logical activities, especially as these are aimed at influencing a broad circle of workers.

"By the fact that they found themselves unable to prevent this papal trip, they showed themselves inconsistent in important questions. That they retreated in the face of demands by the Church can lead to further significant damage to socialism in Poland, apart from the fact that this trip can be seen as encouragement of counterrevolutionary forces in their hostile anti-state activities. Without question, the pope's support of Solidarity and its ideology, as well as the massive public appearances of Solidarity members and sympathizers, will create considerable negative effects. Above all, it can result in stepping up further radicalization of anti-socialist activities by young persons, raising their readiness to stir up confrontations. The positions of counterrevolutionaries were further strengthened. Especially the extremists could feel energized to engage in new provocations.

"*It becomes increasingly evident that the demeanor of the pope concurs with the political line of USA imperialism vis-à-vis Poland and the increasing attacks of the reactionaries against socialism* [emphasis added]. Thus, it appears doubtful that expectations are realized that the pope's visit could contribute toward lessening the international isolation of Poland and toward easing the Western [economic] boycott policy."[5]

In a 12-page summary written four days after the pope's departure,

---

5. MfS Zentrale Auswertungs-und Informationsgruppe report Nr. 13371 dated June 20, 1983. BSTU Nr. 00001 – 7.

the East German Ministry for State Security's central evaluation group again expressed consternation over the Polish government's inability to rein in the pope's efforts to have the Church take a leadership position in "strengthening the *entire* [emphasis added] political opposition and cementing ideologically and morally the anti-socialist elements."[6] The attempts by the "Polish comrades to minimize as much as possible the negative effects failed, and . . . greater efforts of the counterrevolution toward building up their organizations must be expected." The urgency of exerting maximum pressure on the Polish authorities to resort to even more massive oppression of the population is glaringly evident in this and all other documents dealing with the papal trip. At the same time, the inability, or unwillingness, of the Polish leadership to maintain the upper hand is repeatedly lamented. "The pope's trip has created great damage to socialism, and the authority of the Party has sunk even deeper. Another noteworthy side effect came to the fore when a number of Communist Party [PVAP] members were unmasked as strict Catholics, including even members of the ZK [Central Committee] so that it is difficult for the party leadership to succeed in carrying through a unified line."

While in Czestochowa, the pope held a bishop's conference, which had either been infiltrated by a spy working for the East Germans or had been monitored with electronic listening devices. The top-secret report on this meeting covered 15 typewritten pages. "There, he laid out the long-range aims of the Vatican's battle against the socialist order and support of the counterrevolution," it said. "The pope was clearly oriented toward the active work of the Church in getting rid of socialism, the strengthening of the political confrontation with the state powers, and the defeat of the political-ideological aggression including, if necessary, by employing the 'official dialog.' He

6. MfS Zentrale Auswertungs-und Informationsgruppe report Nr. 13372 dated June 27, 1983. BSTU Nr. 00001-12.

demanded doubling the political activities and concentrating on the following main points:

- Genuine freedom
- Realization of human rights
- Ideological hegemony of Catholicism

"Regarding the pope's demand for a 'political offensive' of the Church and its means and methods, he, characteristically, emphasized that verbal agreements for 'dialog' did not call for assuring calm and order in the land, forgoing strikes, demonstrations, and street brawls. Instead he stood for demonstrative solidarity with elements, which, as a result of their provocative confrontations with security organs, are punished. He also emphasized assistance of the Church for imprisoned persons and those interned."

Lastly, the Holy Father expressed his concern that the Western contributions of food and other consumer goods are channeled wrongfully to government authorities for distribution and emphasized that the Church should insist on being the sole distributor in order to bolster the political and economic role of the Polish Church, including an aid program for private farmers, skilled workers, and shopkeepers. The report closed on a foreboding note: "The line enunciated by the pope is to be the basis for the anti-socialist activities of all opposition elements and to create a climate to place the Church into the leading role in the counterrevolutionary battle. At the same time, the Church is to become the power which would be in a position, in the 'spirit' of a rapprochement policy, to force political concessions that would lead step-by-step to the erosion of the socialist state power in the direction of a pluralist system. *And that will give rise to further danger for socialism*" [emphasis added]. By that time, the pope had spoken at 22 public gatherings and church masses in which, according to Polish officials, 6,650,000 persons had participated. In addition, hundreds of thousands packed the streets of Warsaw, Poznan, Wroclaw, Krakow, and Nowa Huta to cheer the pope as he passed in his "Popemobile." AP correspondent Victor Simpson quoted a government official, who asked not to be identified, as saying that authorities were surprised by the bluntness of the pope's remarks since arriving in Poland, and that the demonstrations he unleashed were also unexpected. "We are scared," the official was quoted as saying. "We thought it would be tranquil. Now we don't know what will happen."

Despite numerous statements by martial law authorities, including its head, General Jaruzelski, stating that Pope John Paul II would not be allowed to see Lech Walesa, they could not prevent a meeting. The two met in a country lodge near the Carpathian mountain town of Zakopane the morning of the pope's departure from Poland on June 23. Walesa was accompanied by his wife Danuta and his four children. The pope had flown to Zakopane by helicopter, accompanied only by his immediate staff. Only after the meeting was there an announcement that it had taken place, in private, and that no details would be given. Even the East German spies were caught off guard. Neither the pope nor Walesa would reveal what was discussed. Walesa said only that the meeting left him "moved and enthusiastic." Even now, after the pope's death, the Vatican would still not comment, said Simpson. But the mere meeting, according to the East German Stasi report, "must be judged as a successful attempt to enhance the status of Walesa as well as the former Solidarnosc, her ideology, and her anti-socialist aims."

Before boarding his plane in Krakow for the flight back to Rome, the pope shook hands with Communist Party and other officials who kissed his ring. In his farewell speech, he said: "I wish that good, under the care of the Holy Virgin of Jasna Gora, could once again turn out to be more powerful than evil on Polish land and be victorious. And I have been praying for this."[7]

7. *New York Times*, June 24, 1983.

As the pope was boarding his plane, his staunchest ally in the battle against communism, President Ronald Reagan, was mounting the dais 4,218 miles across the Atlantic in Chicago to address the Polish National Alliance and the Polish American Congress. Praising the "brave people of Poland" in their courageous struggle for freedom and independence, the president said: "Perhaps nothing more clearly demonstrates the repressive and insecure nature of communism than the tremor felt throughout the communist world as a result of Polish workers and citizens exercising inalienable human rights, the rights that are so fundamental to free Western societies and that we too often take for granted." Despite the brutality of martial law, the will of the people had not been broken. "And the papal visit to Poland, which ends today, is truly a ray of hope for the Polish and an event of historic importance. During these short eight days, the pope's message of hope and faith has helped to inspire millions of Poles to continue their struggle to regain the human rights taken from them by the Polish authorities 18 months ago."

President Reagan, who had met with Pope John Paul II at the Vatican a year earlier, said he was deeply moved by the pope's "outspoken defense" of the Polish people's human rights.'" His frequent statements of support for the interned, the imprisoned, and those dismissed from work for their political activities were poignant reminders to the Jaruzelski regime and the Soviets that they "cannot hope to erase the August accords [Ed.: establishing independents unions]. Freedom-loving people everywhere support his Holiness's call for social renewal, social justice, and reaffirmation of national sovereignty. I have long felt that many, if not all, of the problems faced by the Polish people could be resolved if Warsaw's neighbors would permit the beleaguered nation to work them out undisturbed. And you're aware of the neighbor particularly that we're talking about. The actions of the millions of Poles who attended the masses around the country, inspiring the spirit which gave rise to Solidarity, still flourish in Polish hearts. There is only one way for the Polish government to gain the confidence and trust of its own people. And that is to end martial law, to release political prisoners, to restore freely formed trade unions, and to embark on a path of genuine, national reconciliation."

In closing, the president told the assembly that the pope's visit to his homeland was an "inspiration to all who cherish freedom. It vividly showed that no one can crush the spirit of the Polish people. The moving words of the Polish national anthem, 'Poland has not died while we yet live,' are more true today than ever. The spirit of Solidarity that unites the Polish people with free people everywhere has never been stronger."[8]

A month later, Jaruzelski ordered the termination of martial law, and on October 5, Lech Walesa was awarded the Nobel Peace Prize in Norway. Fearing that he would not be allowed to return to his homeland, his wife Danuta flew to Oslo to accept the award. And at Christmas mass, Josef Cardinal Glemp announced that the regime would release 30 political prisoners and that the Church was also negotiating for the freeing of 11 prominent anticommunist rebels and former senior officials of the outlawed Solidarity union.

8. Reagan archive, University of Texas.

12 CURTAIN FALLS ON RED SPIES

Moscow's consternation over the growing strength of the anticommunist opposition as the result of the second papal visit to Poland and in conjunction with the success of Vatican spy-catcher Father Robert A. Graham, the Jesuit from San Francisco,[1] prompted an extraordinary conference in June 1984. The KGB summoned the secret police leadership and section chiefs from Bulgaria, Hungary, Czechoslovakia, Cuba, East Germany, Poland, and Romania. Purpose? "Preparing joint measures for combating the subversive activities of the Vatican."[2] The after-action report said that "according to the general assessment of its participants, the meetings were marked by a high political and operational standard." In other words, as was usual in dealing with Moscow, everyone ended on the same wavelength.

1. See chapter 6, page 99.
2. East German MfS translation XX/VK/5085/85 of secret KGB report. BSTU 000240-247. This document was not made available to the author until November 2007.

The conference established that "with the election of John Paul II, the policies of the Vatican vis-á-vis the socialist states assumed a markedly more aggressive position. Under the cover of the *infamous* [emphasis added] motto 'for the protection of the rights of believers,' the Vatican is attempting to meddle in the internal affairs of the socialist states." The Vatican was accused of initiating the development of anti-socialist propaganda campaigns. "The so-called 'Ostpolitik' developed by the Vatican is aimed at discrediting the social order of socialism in the eyes of the believers, and at inspiring them to overtly rebel against the organs of power of the socialist states. The Vatican is endeavoring to achieve the amalgamation of various elements of society on the basis of anti-socialism."

The recent anti-socialist activities of the Vatican, according to the KGB conference report, were "tightly intertwined with the policy of the imperialist states and the active support of the most reactionary elements poised against the communist workers and national liberation movements." Although Moscow's fears of the Vatican's political influence had been noted for many years, the purpose of this 1984 conference was to ascertain that its allies understood that their existence rested upon their determination to join the battle, no holds barred. It was astounding to learn that before outlining details of how the "battle" needed to be reinforced, the KGB felt it necessary to reiterate "the horrors" they were facing. "The Roman Curia supports especially the aggressive course of the U.S. administration in Latin America. It attacks priests who represent the 'Liberation Theology' and the so-called 'People's Church' and attempts to prevent Catholics in that region from participating in the revolutionary process."

In view of the "hostile course of the Vatican," the conference participants recommended the following "concrete measures" to combat the subversive activities. The communist bloc's intelligence services agreed to bolster their efforts in obtaining information on plans, forms, and methods of the Vatican and its affiliated organizations in opposing the communist states. Communist espionage was ordered intensified to achieve more detailed knowledge of:

■   the position of the pope and his closest advisers regarding important and current international problems such as East-West dialog, political and military easing of tensions, as well as the arms race and disarmament;

■   the relations of the Vatican with the "largest states of the capitalist world as well as with the People's Republic of China" and the coordination of policy, and the cooperation of the United States of America in particular, with the other NATO countries in undermining the positions of socialism, including their secret services;

■   the activity of the Vatican to broaden and strengthen the influence of Catholicism in the developing countries of Asia, Africa, and Latin America.

The participants agreed that their joint effort should be strengthened in "operational work," a.k.a. espionage, and counterpropaganda aimed at exposing and ending the subversive activities of the Vatican. "To this end, there must be a reinforcement of the unofficial [i.e., by spies] penetration and of operational-technical penetration [i.e., installing secret listening devices]." Specifically listed as targets were the secretary of state's office, Vatican Radio, international and national Catholic organizations, and educational institutions such as the Gregorian University "in which the policies of the Roman Curia vis-à-vis the socialist states are formulated."

The report devoted considerable attention to persistent rumors that influential cardinals were expressing "disagreement and dissatisfaction" with the policies of Pope John Paul II as they pertained to the Church's activities in communist countries. "These differences, especially those between the supporters of the hard line in the so-called Ostpolitik of the pope and the opposition, must be exploited. The reactionary activities of the right wing of Catholicism and the connection of the Vatican to the CIA, to the secret services of the other NATO states, and to the anti-socialist subversive elements of the West must be unmasked." It urged the unleashing of a smear campaign "about the treasonous work of the Vatican and the Catholic clergy," and recommended using "malleable publishers in capitalist and developing countries" for printing "material about the inquisition, connection with fascism during the Second World War, support of the reactionary regimes such as the Franco regime, connection with capitalist monopolies, etc."

Not surprisingly, blackmail had long been one of the communists' dastardly tools to force Church officials into cooperating with them in efforts to undermine the effectiveness of the religious leaders. Conferees agreed to pursue leading representatives of the Roman Curia and Vatican Radio to force them into stopping anti-socialist radio propaganda. "Thus, concentrating on collecting compromising material on members of Vatican Radio is vital in order to expose the mendacity of the provocative campaign about the 'alleged participation' of the Bulgarian citizen [Sergeji] Antonov[3] in the assassination attempt of the pope and the reprehensible position of the Vatican before the eyes of the world."

One cannot help but view this course of action as bordering on panic, especially in light of the repetitiveness in the five-page document of actions needed to defeat the influence of the Catholic Church in the communist bloc. Speaking loudly for this assessment are the invectives hurled against Pope John Paul II such as "lying protégé of the most reactionary circles of the West and his ferocious

3. See chapter 7. Antonov, 59, was found dead in his apartment in Sofia in August 2007. He had been in poor physical and mental health and had lived a hermit's life since his return from Italy in 1986.

anticommunism and anti-Soviet displays." The communists' rage called for intensifying pressure on emissaries, couriers, and missionaries of the Vatican and other Catholic centers who traveled under various guises to other countries to carry out their subversive work. "Among them are agents of the enemy. These must be found and, if possible, turn them [into double agents]." With Poland in uproar and anticommunist unrest intensifying throughout Eastern Europe, all with the pope's spy-catchers hunting full time, it would be safe to say that recruiting double agents was in vain, even if it was tried at all.

Finally, the KGB hosts called for improving the exchange of information between the security services of the communist countries to prepare for joint operations to "neutralize enemy actions" during celebrations of special anniversaries such as 600 years of Christianity in Lithuania (scheduled for 1985) and 1,000 years of Christianity in Russia, planned for 1988. In closing, it was stipulated that "the efforts by the individual security services in neutralizing the discussed chief targets will necessarily depend on the prevailing political situation in their countries." The latter statement obviously was based on the dire situations the governments in the various countries were facing from opponents inclined to demonstrations and street violence over which the Church had little or no influence. In studying the report, this author could not help but sense that the meeting had been a last-ditch effort to save Moscow's hides, as the tone of the discussions did not mirror the confidence displayed during past parleys.

The Moscow meeting and the continued debacle in Poland prompted the East German leadership to order the Stasi to produce an updated 31-page analysis of the Catholic Church's policies in dealing with communism.[4] As in the past, the Stasi was relying for secret information from its moles inside the Vatican. In the past, the Stasi analyses had concentrated primarily on the Vatican's activities in

4. Stasi assessment of 1984. Cover sheet missing. BSTU Nr. 000002-31.

European communist countries, but now it expressed alarm over how Pope John Paul II was pursuing his quest ever more actively. "It now has become apparent that Pope John Paul II pushes his anticommunist and anti-Soviet position not only as a vital part of his Ostpolitik, but has now taken on a global character." It pointed to Latin America and Africa, where this had become most evident. "Under cover of a legitimate desire to strengthen the Catholic Church throughout the world, all resources are consequently employed against progressive forces in the world, against socialism-communism. Increasingly, such anticommunist lay organizations, such as Opus Dei, known by its enemies as the 'Holy Mafia,' are used in these efforts." The bulk of the assessment dealt with Church history of anticommunist opposition.

Cardinal Casaroli, the pope's secretary of state, was no stranger to Washington, where he met with President Reagan and consulted with the National Security Council as well as with State Department officials. In November and December 1983, he was in Washington working with the White House and the State Department to prepare for the resumption of diplomatic relations between the United States and the Holy See on January 10, 1984. Three days later, Hungarian intelligence reported that "following the visit of Casaroli to America, the Vatican is of the opinion that in the 1970s the Soviet Union, as well as Western European states, misjudged the intentions of the USA."[5] The spy also reported: "The American strategic aims have not changed. The signs of readiness in the '70s on the part of the USA for negotiations did not result in a new American negotiating strategy, but were merely the manifestation of Washington's superpower crisis post-Vietnam. The USA wants to become again the world's first power and have set on a course from which they will not deviate in the foreseeable future regardless of whether President Reagan is reelected or not."

5. KGB report copy to Stasi Nr. 9026/84, classified top secret and originating with Hungarian intelligence. BSTU Nr. 000158-9.

Referring to U.S.-Soviet negotiations in the fall of 1983 on intermediate nuclear weapons involving Washington's decision to station Pershing II missiles in West Germany in response to Moscow's stationing the SS-20 intermediate missiles aimed at Western Europe, the report said:

"According to an assessment by the Vatican, the Soviet Union, one way or another, needed to refuse to continue to participate in the talks since, according to the Soviet view, the stationing of American rockets had violated the strategic balance of power between the two major adversaries. In such a situation, the Vatican is very careful when it comes to serving as a mediator between the two superpowers, and at this point does not feel it appropriate to offer concrete suggestions. Thus, the Vatican has limited its activities to determining how inclined the West European states are to contribute toward restoring confidence and how far Western Europe is in a position to exert pressure on the USA. The Vatican is extraordinarily worried that, because of the increase in accuracy of the nuclear weapons, there are a growing number of persons in military circles of the USA who consider it possible to achieve victory in a limited thermonuclear war. Because of the increasing danger to peace, the position of Casaroli has become somewhat stronger, but his activities are still curtailed because of the pope's pro-American course." In studying this report, one can conclude that communist intelligence officers had lost their professional touch, as they kept believing that poor Cardinal Caseroli's sympathies with Moscow's version of socialism were being suppressed by a wicked anticommunist pope. The Vatican's disinformation operation was working well.

Alleged machinations by a group of important cardinals to "weaken the position" of Cardinal Casaroli continued to be played up in espionage reports written in the spring of 1984.[6] Most attention was

6. Stasi translations of KGB/Hungarian intelligence reports classified top secret. Nr. 9221/84 and 9227/84 dated March 9 and March 14, 1984. BSTU Nr. 000186-87 and 000188-89.

focused on Cardinal Achille Silvestrini, who was described as being bent on taking over the foreign-policy function in the State Secretariat and pushing Casaroli into the background. "Casaroli is aware of this. It is believed that he had urged the pope to appoint Silvestrini as Archbishop of Bologna." None of this happened, and Casaroli remained a valued advisor to Pope John Paul II. The spy also reported that *Zo Giorni*, the publication of the Catholic laity organization Communione e Liberazione, Society and Liberation, had become the "mouthpiece" of the pope. "The Polish secretary [Stanislaw] Dziwisz maintains regular contact with the periodical. He personally relays the political directives for articles which increasingly are concentrated on socialist countries. The March edition will contain an article attacking the Czechoslovak regime over its treatment of dissidents." The arch-conservative Communione e Liberazione was founded by Monsignore Luigi Giussani, a professor of theology and one of the top personalities of contemporary Italian Catholicism. The leftist Catholic Action organization, which had been close to Pope Paul VI, was a bitter enemy of Msgr. Giussani's group. It was only a year before his death in 1978 that Pope Paul VI received a delegation of Liberazione. In 1982, Pope John Paul II instructed the Papal Council for the Laity to recognize the organization as officially sanctioned by the Church.

Pope John Paul II had been weighing a new attempt to establish formal diplomatic relations with Poland. "The pope has chosen Archbishop Luigi Poggi as the Papal Nuncio to Poland if relations are established this year on the basis of earlier agreements," a communist spy reported.[7] "However, the Vatican has become cautious because of the renewed deterioration of the situation in Poland, and the Polish episcopate also does not intend to support General Jaruzelski by speeding up diplomatic relations." The report added that the pope intended to continue to work toward establishing diplomatic relations

7. Top secret KGB report to Stasi Nr. 9476/84 dated May 5, 1984. BSTU Nr. 000222.

with communist countries, "including Prague, despite the attacks against him by the Czechoslovakians." The spy closed his report by saying that renewed talks between the United States and the Soviet Union expected in 1985 could create an atmosphere in Moscow for acceptance of a "proposal for a papal visit to the Soviet Union." The visit never took place, because of the Soviet government's enmity toward the Catholic Church and the decades of the Russian Orthodox Church's dispute with the Vatican, which also had a sizable presence in the region.

In 1984, the German monk Eugen Brammertz[8] was active again. Unfortunately, the detailed files of his contribution to East German intelligence on September 7, 9, and 26 were destroyed when the Stasi went out of business in early 1990. However, from registration sheets stored in the so-called SIRA data bank, one can determine the type of information the spying monk sent to East Berlin where, in turn, it was shared with the Soviet KGB. One report was titled "Information to a few aspects of the collaboration between the Reagan administration and traditional [Ed: conservative] Catholic groups and the relationship of the American bishops with the U.S. administration." Another report deals with the aftermath of the assassination attempt of John Paul II and the "changes in the political work of the Vatican, specifically in the Ostpolitik since the assassination [attempt], its background and repercussions." The third contribution was one which East Berlin and Moscow assuredly would have liked to have had years earlier. It described the "positions and operational methods of the BND [West German Federal Intelligence Service] and the American CIA in the Vatican and the entanglements between the Catholic Church and those secret services."

Although the communist intelligence services continued to focus chiefly on the Vatican's activities and policies in dealing with the

8. See chapter 8.

Polish unrest, the Holy See's dealings with the Hungarian regime were also under close scrutiny by the unholy moles. As in most East European countries, persecution of the Catholic Church in Hungary had been practiced for decades. It intensified during the Nazi period and became even uglier when the communists took the reins of government in the early 1940s. Father Guyla Havasa, a parish priest at Nagysap, spent many years gathering facts on the brutal oppression. He wrote of the arrest of some 600 priests, the detention of 800 monks and 2,000 nuns, and the abolition of more than 50 religious orders, resulting in the dispersion of some 10,000 nuns and 1,500 monks.[9] These atrocities prompted Father Gyorgy Bulanyi to form a non-violent movement in the mid-forties to cope with the persecution of the Church and its clergy. He named it "Bokor," or "Burning Bush" (Exodus 3: 2-4). The pacifist priest's movement was attacked by the government as illegal. The Hungarian communist authorities had Father Bulanyi arrested, "tried," and sentenced to life imprisonment. In 1961 he was released, and he subsequently revived his group. Concerned with the possibility of the Polish unrest creating the impetus of a new rebellion in Hungary, and possibly resulting in heavy casualties, Pope John Paul II sent Archbishop Luigi Poggi, a close associate of Cardinal Casaroli, to Budapest for consultation with church leaders. The archbishop, who was accompanied by his secretary Msgr. John Bukowsky, headed the Vatican's Council for Public Affairs, responsible for special tasks. His primary meeting was with Laszlo Cardinal Lekai. The Hungarian primate was close to the government and had been active in reconciling differences between the communist regime and the Church in line with the Ostpolitik as

9. The most prominent of the persecuted was Jozsef Cardinal Mindszenty, who in 1948 was subjected to a show trial and sentenced to life imprisonment. During the bloody 1956 uprising, the new premier, Imre Nagy, ordered the prelate's release. When the Soviet Army was sent in to crush the uprising, Mindszenty was granted asylum in the U.S. embassy in Budapest until 1971, when an agreement with the government allowed him to leave the country. He died in Vienna in 1975.

envisioned by the late Pope Paul VI but which his successor, John Paul II, abandoned soon after his election. Having seen the Polish people suffer under a totalitarian regime, Pope John Paul II was in no mood to continue appeasement with the Church's arch-enemy in Poland—or anywhere, for that matter.

As could be expected, Poggi's meetings with Cardinal Lekai, members of the episcopate, and theologians were either under electronic surveillance, or a Hungarian secret police informer was present, whose 500-word report was relayed to the Soviet KGB and East Germany's Stasi.[10] "During the talks with government officials, the representatives of the Vatican avoided questions which could have caused conflicts and endeavored to demonstrate continuity in correct relations based on mutual trust. During the talks with religious personalities, it was noticeable that the representatives of the Vatican were not prepared for these talks, but improvised and expected their interlocutors to come up with subjects they wish to discuss." Obviously, the pope's emissaries were sent to Hungary to "feel out" their Church brethren, many of whom, including their prelate, had become overly subservient to the authorities. The Holy See needed to know their stand vis-à-vis the communist regime if the Hungarian people decided to take the road of 1956. It is remarkable that the "listeners" were too obtuse to realize this. The report continued:

"However, the Vatican representatives asked questions about the everyday problems of the national Church. Within this framework, they inquired about the position of the illegal Bulanyi [Ed.: Bokor] movement, the relations within the Church, the question of religious instructions, and the participation of the laity in the religious life. Special attention was paid to the activities of the episcopate and ascertaining the position of individual bishops. The Vatican representatives showed special interest in the question of unity of the episcopate and

10. Stasi translation Nr. 9604/84 dated June 21, 1984, of top-secret KGB report. BSTU Nr. 000226.

the devotion of Cardinal Lekai vis-à-vis the state. The analysis of our investigation concluded that the Vatican representatives made no efforts to establish illegal contacts. However, during the talks with their Church partners, they tried hard to circumvent the technical controls [Ed.: bugging]. The establishment of diplomatic relations and a visit by Pope John Paul II were not mentioned during the talks." No question, Cardinal Poggi and Msgr. Bukowsky accomplished their reconnaissance mission well.

Following the lifting of martial law in Poland in 1983, the country enjoyed a relative calm it had not known for more than a decade, although the outlawed Solidarity union continued to operate underground. Its activities were still financed by the American CIA and the Vatican. Clandestine printing presses continued to produce anti-government leaflets, and secret radio periodically went on the air. Josef Cardinal Glemp, treading cautiously, maintained a relationship with General Jaruzelski, who pledged coexistence with the Church, easing repression, and even allowing more freedom for scientists, academics, and even artists.

In a top-secret report based on Vatican spies of Hungarian intelligence and informants, the East German Stasi said, on February 29, 1984, that the readiness of the Church leadership in Poland to cooperate with the government could enable the Church to strengthen its influence over the government.[11] This, the report said, was based on an assessment of West German government circles. "The view of the West is that the strengthening of the Church's influence in the country is significant, as it could affect the neighboring socialist countries." The report said the cardinal's "good" cooperation with the government was attributed to the cardinal's decision to visit Brazil and Argentina instead of the USA. "Glemp made a planned trip to the USA dependent upon Washington lifting the sanctions against

11. Stasi report Nr. 9174/84 of Dept. X. BSTU Nr. 000185.

Poland. Since this did not happen, a trip will apparently not take place this year." Whoever fed this information to the secret police was wrong. Cardinal Glemp visited the United States in September 1985. The sanctions were not lifted until 1987.

In closing, the secret police said: "The Vatican is mainly interested in maintaining constant relations with the Polish bishops and the Catholic masses in the country and to reinforce them. The pope and Casaroli continue to support Cardinal Glemp, although his position among the Polish bishops is relatively isolated. With Glemp's help, the Vatican wants to establish a channel in direction of the Soviet Union. A first step in this direction would be establishing relations with the Russian Orthodox Church through Glemp. In order to avoid having Catholics living in the Soviet Union turn away from him, the Holy See is urging Glemp that he, if only pro-forma, meet with representatives of the Catholic Church, especially with those in Lithuania. The Vatican hopes that the contacts with the Orthodox Church will have a positive effect on the situation of the Catholics. In view of the importance of creating channels leading to the USSR, there are no differences of opinion between the pope and Casaroli." If this information was correct, the Vatican was most likely trying to take advantage of the lull in the Polish turmoil to strengthen the resolve of Catholics in the Soviet Union, who had endured severe repression for nearly seven decades, to remain faithful, as better days were on the horizon.

The camouflaged peace in Poland was shattered on the night of October 19, 1984, by the murder of Father Jerzy Popieluszko. The 37-year-old priest drew many thousands to his masses as he preached against the communist tyrants, which made him one of the most famous priests in Poland. He was on his way home after visiting with miners in Bydgoszcz when his car was stopped by four security officers. He was beaten, and his unconscious body was dropped into a reservoir near the Vistula River, where it was found two days later. His body was returned to his church, St. Stanislaw in the Warsaw suburb of Zoliborz, where, according to the British Broadcasting Corporation, 250,000 people attended the funeral and sang the national church anthem "May God watch over Poland." The dimension of the people's outrage was such as to threaten new uprisings. To restore some measure of calm in the land, the government was forced to investigate and arrest the four secret police officers. They were tried, convicted, and sentenced to from 14 to 25 years in prison. Warsaw journalist Krzysztof Tomaszewski[12] said most Poles believed that besides maintaining a peace, however uneasy, "the convicted secret policemen were considered scapegoats for higher-ups in the interior ministry who ordered the killing."

Recognizing the enormous influence wielded by Pope John Paul II over events in Poland and in an effort to prevent a repetition in his domain, East German communist strongman Erich Honecker requested a meeting with the Holy Father in Rome after Father Popieluszko's murder. The Vatican announced its acceptance on February 11, setting the audience date for April 24. In preparation for this first meeting between the pope and an East European head of state, Honecker's secret police, the Stasi, prepared a four-page report based on information supplied by its moles in the Vatican.[13] "Several cardinals, archbishops, prelates, and other leading members of the Vatican's office of the secretary of state have held confidential discussions to prepare for the meeting between Comrade Erich Honecker and the pope," the report said. "Accordingly, the pope was well prepared for the encounter. The pope is adamant about discussing joint responsibility in maintaining the peace for humanity. Furthermore, also according to strictly internal information, the pope has received extensive material regarding the Church in the DDR [(East) German Democratic Republic] from the Berlin Bishop's Conference dealing with

12. Pseudonym.
13. Zentrale Auswertung und Informationsgruppe top secret report 172/85 dated February 17, 1985. BSTU 000001-4.

problems facing the Church." These problems included construction of new churches, increasing paper deliveries to church print shops, and obtaining permission for travel to Rome by young men studying for the priesthood. "The pope reportedly will not deal with these problems and will leave it to the East German leadership to settle."

Honecker was told that the Vatican State Secretariat, in judging the relations of the state vs. the Catholic Church in East Germany, observed the following: "In contrast to other socialist states, there have been no court actions against the Church, no imprisonments of Catholic priests, and no government interference in the pope's prerogative to name bishops." It is true that the East German regime became less overtly oppressive toward the Church and its 350,000 members after the Berlin Wall was built in 1961 to prevent the massive escapes that lowered the country's population from 18.388 million in 1950 to 16.624 million in 1985. In prior times, however, priests had been jailed and Church-related organizations were banned. To avoid government chicanery, nearly 500,000 Catholics joined over a million other countrymen in escaping to the West. The very man who once had vehemently urged an invasion of Poland to save its communist government, was now heading for the Holy City to make nice with the pope in an effort to burnish its standing among nations. As a gesture of magnanimity, feigned to be sure, the government announced that the dozens of East Germans who had sought refuge in the West German embassy in Prague, could return home to apply for permission to emigrate without fearing the usual punishment of imprisonment. While pushing for an audience with Pope John Paul II, the East Berlin regime also worked feverishly for an invitation to visit the United States and a "reception by Reagan."[14] Dr. William L. Stearman, a member of the National Security Council

14. Letter of Klaus Gysi, State Secretary for Church Affairs, to Erich Honecker, Communist Party General Secretary and Chairman of the State Council, dated January 15, 1985. BSTU Nr. 000007.

at that time, said the president never had any intention of boosting Honecker's international image by meeting with him. However, the papal audience scheduled for April 24 remained unchanged. To the consternation of the regime, seven days before the meeting, the West German newspaper *Die Welt* published a front-page report that before the Pope-Honecker encounter, the Holy Father would meet with a group of pilgrims that included three women who had been political prisoners in East Germany and were subsequently expelled to the West. "The women will ask the pope for help in getting the government to agree to allow the reunion of families," a Stasi report said, adding that this meeting would take place before Honecker's arrival.[15] Honecker's secret police commented:

"The report, judging by its content, definitely originated in the BRD [Federal Republic of (West) Germany]. Whether certain people in the Vatican played a role in this, is another question. The report fits imperceptibly into the malicious campaign, led by the Springer Company [Ed.: owner of *Die Welt*], as a provocation against the obvious results of our politics for peace and the church policies which were started in recent weeks. The 11th of February [Ed.: the audience announcement] was a heavy blow to these circles, and led immediately to positive consequences for us. For that reason, these circles in the BRD are trying to stop this development with confrontations and provocations. The article fits perfectly into the picture of these coordinated actions. An editorial in the same issue tries to dictate to the pope what he should discuss with Comrade General Secretary. At the same time, the report is designed to discredit the significance of this state visit." After discussing whether to react publicly to "this outrageous provocation," the decision was against it, saying "it is unlikely that the Vatican would issue a denial in such a situation." In a position paper to prepare Honecker for the meeting, he was told that it

15. Stasi report dated April 19, 1985. BSTU Nr. 000029-30.

was "unlikely that the pope will bring up questions of state-Church relations." However, it was pointed out that the pope "is an unpredictable personality so that one needs to be ready for anything, and it is possible that he will bring up a visit to our republic within the next years." Such a visit was termed as "not opportune." The latter remark to Honecker was almost comical, since he, of all people, knew the precariousness of his fiefdom where underground anticommunist cells had been growing since the early 1970s. And Honecker's secret police had been arresting citizens by the thousands merely for expressing the wish to emigrate westward. People were still being shot to death while trying to escape over the Berlin Wall. There had been at least 300,000 political prosecutions since the Wall went up in 1961.[16]

A terse record of the discussions between the pope and the East German communist leader noted that the subjects included "the search for reasonable, constructive solutions of those international problems which create conditions that allow the resolute continuance of a process for security and cooperation in Europe." On Honecker's return to East Berlin, the State Secretariat for Church Affairs, headed by Klaus Gysi, conducted what it claimed was a countrywide opinion survey for the regime's leadership.[17] "The majority of those questioned [Ed.: How many were mute?] rated this visit as an expression of the efforts of socialist states to include the Catholic Church in the world-wide struggle in preserving the peace and pointed to previous visits to the pope by politicians from other socialist states. The 'stopover' [emphasis added] was repeatedly described as an 'act of courtesy.'"

Although the number of reports from spies within the Vatican had

16. John O. Koehler, *Stasi: The Untold Story of the East German Secret Police* (Westview Press, Boulder, CO, 1999).
17. Survey by the State Secretariat for Church Affairs dated May 6, 1985. BSTU Nr. 000019-25.

decreased markedly since 1984 and none could be found covering internal Vatican discussions regarding Honecker's visit, it could well be that they were destroyed on arrival in Berlin, especially if they were critical of the communist leader. In any case, State Secretary Gysi's so-called survey, which was allegedly based on interviews with ordinary citizens and officials of the Catholic Church, reported these opinions: "It is politically savvy that the pope also has talks with nonbelievers. Officials of the Catholic Church and Catholic citizens, referring to the visit of Comrade Honecker with the pope, repeatedly expressed the hope that the state, especially in the area of public education, will become more tolerant and more understanding toward Christians. Among some progressive forces [Ed.: Communist Party members], the visit was met with astonishment, and in some cases it was out-right rejected on the grounds that it benefited the Catholic Church in the DDR more than our Party, to wit: the status of the Catholic Church in the DDR has been significantly enhanced; officials of the Church could be encouraged to interfere in societal affairs; the General Secretary of the Central Committee of the Party has talks with the head of the Catholic Church while the Party demands that its members stay away from the Church."

Considering his past behavior toward anticommunists, Honecker's groveling was a moment of sanctimony that most certainly was not lost on a pope so highly experienced in the deviousness of the communists. Within months of the meeting with the pope that was designed to bolster Honecker's international image, East Germany's top communist approved a mutual-cooperation agreement between his secret police chief, Erich Mielke, and KGB chairman Viktor M. Chebrikov.[18] The 24-page top-secret understanding was titled

18. Plan fuer die Zusammenarbeit zwischen HA XX des MfS der DDR und der V. HA des KfS (KGB) der Sowjetrepubliken fuer den Zeitraum 1986-1990. Kopie BSTU AR 8. Note: HA XX handled government, religious and cultural organizations, ditto KGB V Directorate.

"Combating the imperialist politics of confrontation, timely uncovering and foiling the subversive plans, intentions, and activities of the enemy." Although the list of entities to be attacked included various groups such as refugee organizations, publications, the American Radio Free Europe, and Radio Liberty, it aimed as well at religious groups, chiefly the Catholic Church, "which are actively engaged in subversive activities against socialist states." Since the hitherto-pliant East German Evangelical Church had increasingly begun to add its voice to a stirring anti-government movement, it was also included in the more active surveillance activities, thus reaffirming the communists' hostility toward any organized religion that tried to assert its own point of view and stand up for its faithful. These were "aimed at unmasking their subversive character, specifically to prove their collaboration with the intelligence service of the NATO states, as well as uncovering and elimination of communication channels and bases in the DDR and the USSR." It then named 16 organizations in West Germany, Great Britain, Holland, and Sweden. These included the Christian East Mission; Center for the Study of Religion and Communism; Mission Evangelica; Swedish Slavic Mission; Mission for Spreading Religion Light in the East, and Christian Aid for the East. Finally, the Stasi selected 18 IMs, the unofficial collaborators or informers listed only by code names, to infiltrate the organizations.

Despite many years of successful communist espionage penetrations of the Vatican, Mielke and Chebrikov pledged to boost efforts at the Holy See, undoubtedly a reaction to the outspoken anticommunist Pope John Paul II, its resulting repercussions in Poland and, increasingly, in Moscow's other satellites. Besides, counterintelligence experts in the Soviet Union and satellites noticed that reporting from the Holy See was becoming sparse, especially from those agents who had been reporting to the Polish service, testimony to the effectiveness of the Polish pope's spy-catchers. "Operational counter-intelligence activities against subversive actions by the Vatican have priority in connection with 'Ostpolitik'; uncovering and documenting compromising data regarding past and present policies of the Vatican (relations, among others, with fascist regimes) to the secret services of NATO states; influencing international religious organizations aimed at strengthening anti-Catholic sentiments; increasing pressure on emissaries, couriers, and missionaries of the Vatican and other Catholic centers and unofficial penetration of [i.e. spying on] Vatican Radio and Opus Dei." Just what had prompted the East Germans and the Soviets to seek an even greater ability to spy on the Vatican at this late date? As has been previously noted, there had been a noticeable decline in espionage reports reaching the communist services, especially from Polish moles who most likely had been uncovered and sidelined by the pope's American spy-catcher. Thus, even at a time when the survival of communism in Eastern Europe was more wishful thinking on the part of the functionaries than based on glaring reality, they acted almost like the Nazis in 1945—expecting the production of the *Wunderwaffe*, the magic weapon. When it didn't arrive, it was *Kaempfen bis zum bitteren Ende*, fighting to the bitter end.

About the time the Stasi-KGB agreement was signed, a top-secret report was sent to Comrade Honecker.[19] It was titled "remarks of responsible representatives of the Vatican regarding the relations of the Vatican with the socialist states." In view of the waves of extreme discontent of the vast majority of the East European population with their respective tyrannical regimes, one tends to question the sanity of the authors. To understand the mindset of these functionaries, here are the more salient portions of the document, as allegedly reported by a Stasi spy in the Vatican:

"From [the remarks] it is clear that a number of representatives are beginning to realize that the present course pursued by the leadership

---

19. Zentrale Auswertungs und Informationsgruppe, Ministerium fuer Staatssicherheit document Nr. Z 3527, 326/86 dated July 11, 1986. BSTU Nr. 000001-4.

of the Catholic Church in its relations with the socialist states is damaging the position of the Catholic Church. Thus, they say, one must strive toward returning to a mutually acceptable course for dialogues in relations with the USSR and other socialist states. Opposing this is the contradictory position of the pope. On the one hand, he is not ready to significantly modify his present course of relatively uncompromising behavior vis-à-vis the socialist states, but on the other hand, he must, for tactical reasons, consider a change of course in order to realize his planned trips to socialist states. According to the aforementioned remarks, primary speculations center on a planned papal trip to the USSR and a meeting with the General Secretary of the Central Committee of the Communist Party of the Soviet Union, Comrade Mikhail Gorbachev. The pope's aim is to combine the trip with a visit to Lithuania to help celebrate the acceptance of Christianity in that country and Latvia. The Soviet side is ready to permit the visit, so long as it is not in combination with one to Poland, which would create the impression that he is declaring Vilnius [Ed.: the capital in a region that had been part of Poland several centuries earlier] a Polish city. Other preconditions include that he not visit the city of Zagorsk, where progressive [Ed.: anticommunist] factions are concentrated, and that his visit is not accorded the character of a state visit.[20]

"In connection with the pope's planned trip to Poland in June 1987, Vatican officials say he will be very careful with political remarks or remarks that could be politically exploited. In this connection, it is worth noting that opinions from other sources say the pope intends that this visit to the People's Republic of Poland should serve as a basis for establishing diplomatic relations and the process

---

20. Pope John Paul II never was able to get the permission of the Soviet Union, and later the Russian Federation. He was not able to visit the Baltic States—Lithuania, Latvia, and Estonia—until 1993, two years after the collapse of the Soviet Union, after which the states regained their independence. The visit, as triumphant as had been his pilgrimages to Poland, was hailed as joyful as the liberation from 50 years of Soviet control.

of normalizing relations according to the principles of international law. Moreover, he believes that the settling of relations with Poland might become a serious impulse for progress in the dialog with other socialist countries. According to further remarks by Vatican dignitaries, relations between the Vatican and the DDR are generally viewed as positive. The position of the Catholic Church in the DDR is viewed as a 'sign of normality.'" The mindset of communist functionaries never ceases to amaze. When Honecker met with Pope John Paul II, he presented the Holy Father with a Meissen porcelain statue of the Virgin Mary, this one without a secret listening devise as had been the case with a similar "gift" to Cardinal Casaroli, as described in an earlier chapter. Here is how the Stasi's bootlickers used this present to appeal to the former roofer's vanity: "The visit of the Chairman of the State Council of the DDR, Comrade Erich Honecker, was then, and it is now, significant. His gift—a statue of the Virgin Mary of Meissen porcelain—is viewed as most positively in comparison with Federal President von Weizsäcker's gift of a gold wristwatch [Ed.: during the pope's visit to West Germany]. *This gesture is said to have shown statesmanlike astuteness and farsightedness*" [emphasis added]. Finally, Honecker was told that the pope was "said to be ready" to accept an invitation to visit East Germany in connection with the Catholic Assembly in July 1987, "because he was so favorably impressed by the meeting with Erich Honecker." Pope John Paul II never visited East Germany. It must be noted that this report to Honecker was not only marked "top secret" but also said it was only for "personal information because of extreme endangerment of the source"—in other words, "Eyes Only." Because of the information the report contained, the source most likely was either "Lichtblick," the code name for the treacherous German monk Eugen Brammertz, or his subaltern "Antonius," the Catholic News Agency correspondent Alfons Waschbuesch. Of course, considering the increasing public protests voicing dissatisfaction with the regime, it certainly could also have been completely "aus den Fingern gesogen," totally a product of thumb-sucking.

Polish workers, still cowed by their brutal oppression during martial law, kept the peace in factories and the streets. But the activities of underground Solidarity factions continued their agitation with leaflets and clandestine radio broadcasts. There were a number of arrests of the Regional Coordination Committee NSZZ "S," including Lech Walesa and eight others. Five were eventually freed. The other three were sentenced to between 2½ and 3 years in prison. But the "S" committee continued its work in factories and abroad, where it eventually obtained the recognition of the International Confederation of Free Labor Unions. Across the Atlantic, U.S. President Ronald Reagan ordered the lifting of economic sanctions against Poland on February 19, saying the regime had implemented steps toward human rights. At about this time, the Vatican and the Polish government announced jointly that Pope John Paul II would make his third trip to his homeland, visiting from June 8 to 14, 1987.

- The announcement prompted a two-day meeting between East German Stasi and Polish security service officials, each representing their respective religious affairs departments.[21] The Polish side, headed by a major general, informed their colleagues about the state of the Catholic Church in Poland. Of the 38 million Poles, 90 percent are Catholics, although the government admits to "only" 75 percent. At that time there were 98 Catholic bishops in the People's Republic of Poland, of whom 50% were appointed by John Paul II;

---

21. Stasi report: Consultations with Polish security services April 15/16, 1987, in Warsaw. Dated April 21, 1987. BSTU Nr. 000001-7.

22,000 priests; and 50,000 lay preachers. The East Germans were told that "at the beginning of the reign of Pope John Paul II, he waged an overtly aggressive policy toward the socialist states. Now, changes in this regard have become apparent as the pope supports in many situations the peace politics of Comrade Gorbachev. Comrade Gorbachev, on his part, had supported the pope's trip to South America." Mikhail Gorbachev, following the death of Konstantin Chernenko, was chosen as Secretary General of the Soviet Communist Party in March 1985, thus becoming the de facto head of the country. When this East German-Polish consultation took place, Gorbachev had already introduced his policies of *glasnost*, openness, and *perestroika*, restructuring, and was well on the way to seek changes in an effort to bolster the country's disastrous economy. While orthodox party functionaries decried the policies as too radical, they were hailed as enlightening in the West. Needless to say, neither the Polish leadership nor the arch-doctrinaire East German leadership voiced enthusiasm about these developments.

As the meeting progressed, the Polish comrades outlined what the regime expected to achieve by agreeing to the papal visit:

- Further normalization of the political situation;
- Achieving political stability and work against the political and economic boycott of the VR (People's Republic) Poland; strengthen the activities and economic goals, to overcome the economic crisis and confirm the credibility of the VR Poland;

- Weakening the propaganda activities against the VR Poland by the centers of political-ideological diversion;
- Exert influence over the 6 million native Poles abroad aimed at improving their relations with the homeland;
- Strengthen the disciplining of priests who are politically active against the VR Poland.

In connection with the pope's visit, Polish secret police officials told their East German colleagues that "the opposition intends to use the visit for its aims against the regimes by distributing copies of letters, lists of 'alleged' prisoners, of tortured persons and other defamations. The papal visit is to be used by the opposition to intensify the anticommunist activities." The East Germans were requested to relay any information regarding plans and intentions of "enemy" groups, to ban organized visits from, or transiting through, East Germany to Poland during the pope's presence, and tighten border security. In an obvious effort to avoid further aggravating the dissatisfaction of the population with the communist regime, the government decided not to arrest and try agitators "for the time being" and level "financial punishment" as well as confiscating printing presses and cars. *"There will be no religious prisoners"* [emphasis added].

The East German secret police officials informed their Polish counterparts that activities of Polish priests in East Germany were being controlled by requiring that they register with the government. The assignments in Poland of "IMs," informers, would be increased, and regular Stasi officers would be available for critical surveillance assignments. Regarding the latter, the East Germans were able to rely on the experience they had gathered during the earlier visits by Pope John Paul II, when several hundred East German "Spitzel," as the IMs were pejoratively called, were spread out over the country. In closing, the two sides agreed that any "further action vis-à-vis the Vatican will be based on joint consultations with the fraternal service in Moscow."

At this juncture, it had become clear that the spies in the Vatican had been neutralized or caught, or that those who had been "turned" to feed disinformation to their case officers in the East had become superfluous. In prior years, espionage reports from the Vatican abounded, particularly in later years when Pope John Paul II was preparing visits to countries hostile toward his Church. The curtain had fallen on Red spies.

Pope John Paul II arrived at the Warsaw airport on June 8, 1987, and was met by Church leaders and government officials as well as by the usual enthusiastic crowd of Polish Catholics. That same day, East Berliners witnessed the first major clashes between People's Police armed with clubs and tear gas and several thousand youth who wanted to listen to a rock concert in West Berlin being performed just on the other side of the Wall. There were many injuries and arrests. As usual, authorities kept the numbers under wraps. Unquestionably, the Polish government was kept up to the minute by the East German regime on the tense situation, but this time they lacked the spy reports that had previously provided functionaries with clues on what was on the Holy Father's mind regarding the situation in Poland. This may well be why General Wojciech Jaruzelski, the country's strongman who met with the pope immediately after the arrival, admonished the Holy Father not to question the "acceptance of the socialist principles of our state." In other words, don't use your visit to stir up the people, who, in the years since martial law, had been by and large cowed into submission. But the quiet was an uneasy one and their oppressors knew that it would not take much to re-kindle eruptions. As a precaution against anti-government demonstration, the Holy Father was surrounded throughout the week-long visit by scores of uniformed militia and plainclothes secret police goons.

In Lublin, a city 50 miles west of the Soviet border, Pope John

Paul II celebrated mass, during which he held up Father Jerzy Popieluszko, who was killed by Polish secret police in 1984, as a role model for priests who he had just ordained. He spoke of "our contemporary, sacrificing until his death, the young Father Popieluszko." The audience at the outdoor service, estimated by Vatican spokesman Dr. Joaquin Navarro-Valls at one million, erupted in prolonged applause. Earlier, he had told the new priests that their calling "makes demands and by doing so it liberates. You must serve the dignity of man, his liberation." Following the mass, the pontiff addressed academics at Lublin's Catholic University, where he had taught ethics for 24 years until he was elected pope. "It is an eloquent fact," he said, that "Lublin has the only free university" in the Soviet bloc.

The pope referred to Poland's location in Europe: he said Lublin "reflects the entire grand process of the meeting between East and West.[22] No one can relieve the people living here of the responsibility for the final result of this historic process at this place in Europe and in the world, in the spot of this difficult challenge." The pope spoke in the assembly hall of the whitewashed 18th-century building while his words were broadcast to some 3,000 people, mostly students, in the courtyard. When he appeared to speak to the assembled, a Solidarity banner was flashed for a moment in the crowd. A few minutes later, a sign espousing "Human Rights, Conditions for Peace" appeared and disappeared just as quickly, giving the secret police little chance to catch the "culprits." Earlier in the day, the pope had made a brief stop at a former Nazi death camp, Majdanek, located near Lublin. For seven minutes, he prayed silently next to a pile of ashes and bones of camp victims. Afterward, he spoke to a camp survivor, Wanda Ossowska. "Man cannot be an oppressor to another man," he told the 75-year-old woman. She, together with other survivors, were "symbols for future generations."[23]

22. Ibid.
23. Ibid.

Before the pope's arrival at his former archdiocese in Krakow, Polish police numbering between 400 and 600 appeared early in the morning at the homes of 40 people, arrested them, and hauled them off to prison. They were suspected of having played a leading role in a demonstration that witnesses said had numbered 3,000, while government spokesman Jerzy Urban said it was only 2,000 and that only 22 arrests were made at the scene, while witnesses placed the number at 56. The Krakow disturbances were small compared to those that occurred at other cities the pope visited. Confident that the pontiff's anticommunism had been reined in at least during this pilgrimage, General Jaruzelski allowed a visit to the ship-building cities of Gdynia, Gdansk, and Szczecin on the Baltic coast, where the Solidarity trade union movement was born. He had been banned from visiting there during his previous visits. In Gdynia, a crowd of 300,000 cheered wildly when the pope declared that "Solidarity is essential to the struggle for freedom." When he finished his address, the crowd chanted "Stay with us, stay with us," and many raised their hands to display the "V" for victory sign while a few held red-and-white Solidarity banners, risking arrest. It was illegal to even mention Solidarity, but Pope John Paul somehow used the word in clever ways so as not to incite his listeners, but to let it be known nevertheless whose side he championed.

At an outdoor mass in Gdansk, the pope, in extemporaneous remarks, told the more than 1 million faithful that "solidarity is a way of life . . . yes, solidarity purifies struggle . . . a struggle for human rights and his [man's] rights, for his genuine progress is in order . . . it is a struggle for a more mature human way of life." Inspired by the wildly cheering people, the pontiff continued: "Here along the shore of the Baltic Sea, I, too, pronounce this term 'Solidarity' because it is an essential part of the consistent message of the Church's social teaching. In the name of the future of mankind and of humanity, the word 'Solidarity' must be pronounced. This word was uttered right here, in a new way and in a new context. And the world cannot forget it." Earlier in the day, Pope John Paul had met for 40 minutes with Lech Walesa, the Solidarity chief, who would not reveal details of their talk, saying only that "the meeting was great."

Following the mass, 10,000 Solidarity supporters carrying red-and-white banners marched toward a monument honoring workers in downtown Gdansk. After they had marched for an hour, police stopped them at a bridge and told them to disperse. When 2,000 sat down and prayed, riot squads charged them with clubs and five-foot-long poles. "Don't beat your brother, be a Pole," yelled the protesters. But the police kept beating.[24]

There were no incidents when the pope visited Jasna Gora Monastery to pay homage to Poland's most revered icon, the Black Madonna. About 100,000 people expressed their delight with the Holy Father by chanting "Stay with us" and "Long live the pope." He stopped climbing the monastery steps and turned to the people. "As long as God lets me live, I will be here in my mind and heart," he said, adding with a smile "I barely managed to get here, and you already are calling on me to stay." After prayers, the Holy Father told his brethren: "In this land of Poland, there is such need of hope. I pray that all my fellow countrymen might have this hope which brings victory. I wish to summon here all my brothers and sisters who suffer privation, whose hunger for freedom is unsatisfied, who have no way of finding the truth."[25] The pope's meaning was not lost on his audience, which responded with enthusiastic applause. Nor was it lost on a jittery regime. Father Jerzy Tomzinski, a shrine spokesman, told the Associated Press that two ranking Communist Party officials had met with the pontiff and expressed concern about his vocal support for the outlawed Solidarity union. The officials, Kazimierz Barcikowski and Stanislaw Ciosek, told the pope that they were "concerned about the

24. Ibid.
25. Ibid.

tone of his speeches," Father Tomzinski said, adding that the Holy Father's remarks, including praise of the Solidarity movement, were "only expressions of the Church's social teaching." Barcikowski was a member of the Politburo and a top aide to General Jaruzelski, Ciosek a former labor minister who negotiated with Solidarity during its existence in 1980–81.

The evening prior to his departure on Sunday, June 14, Pope John Paul II was accorded a rousing reception by more than 2,000 artists and intellectuals at Warsaw's Holy Cross Church. Many had been members of Solidarity. "We offer you, Holy Father, our hearts beating in solidarity," declared Andrzej Lapicki, actor and rector of the city's Theater Academy. In his speech, the pope said "work is threatened when the freedom of man is not allowed to function correctly." It was followed by five minutes of rhythmic clapping. The crowd held up the red-and-white banner of Solidarity and one reading "Warsaw publishers in Solidarity with you in Truth and Hope." Earlier in the day, leaders of Warsaw's anti-regime activists sent a letter to Pope John Paul II signed by 12,000 factory workers calling for the right to re-form free trade unions which had been outlawed since 1981.

Before his departure for Rome, the pontiff met with more than 90 Polish bishops whom he told that he favored establishing diplomatic relations with the communist regime. "In the case of the so-called Catholic country, the Holy See considers relations with a state as a normal and right thing," he said. It was the first time that the pope raised the subject of church-state relations in public, although neither the pope's aides nor the government would reveal details of the conversation during the pope's meeting with General Jaruzelski. In a five-page report, Polish intelligence informed their East German colleagues about "current problems" in Polish-Vatican relations.[26]

26. MfS Zentrale Auswertung-Informations Gruppe report 13627 of October 2, 1987. BSTU Nr. 000031-35.

"The general expectations that agreement could be reached on establishing diplomatic relations during the pope's third visit of Poland were not fulfilled," the report said. "The Party and government have now concluded that establishment of diplomatic relations with the Vatican will take considerably more time because of the demands for such relations that the pope announced to the Polish Episcopate on June 12, 1987." In addition, the Polish regime objected to the inclusion of the Polish clergy in dealing with this matter, most likely because nearly all of Poland's leading Church officials were openly anticommunist and supportive of the Solidarity trade union. "Following the papal visit, the government has abandoned all official talks with the Vatican regarding this subject because the pope has the temerity to make demands that are under international practice totally wrong and cannot be accepted by the VRP [People's Republic of Poland]. Toward no other government has the Vatican applied such measures. Even though the Vatican knows that the VRP is for political reasons genuinely interested in such relations, it is, however, not ready to pay any price." Although the report did not mention specific conditions the pope had set for establishing diplomatic relations, it was clear that the Polish regime would not agree to establishment of a Nuncio, a full-fledged Church embassy with all its privileges and immunity, because "diplomatic practice of the Holy See clearly shows that its relations with other states have nothing in common with the 'national' Catholic Church." It was clear that the Polish government feared that a Vatican embassy in Poland might function to wield greater influence over the Polish Episcopate in opposing communism and afford protection, i.e., a safe haven, for clerics pursued by secret police authorities for real, or manufactured, "illegal actions against the states." Also, in a predominantly Catholic country such as Poland, the Apostolic Nuncio would automatically become the doyen of the diplomatic corps regardless of his length of service in the country to which he was accredited. "One possibility would be to agree to a Pronuncio," the report said, indicating the Vatican could have quasi-diplomatic relations, a step below a full ambassadorship, yet a safe haven for the politically pursued.

The remainder of the report impressed upon the East Germans that the Polish government had no intention of making any concessions to the Catholic Church in her demands for assuming pastoral welfare activities in the military, hospitals, and prisons, as well as for missionary and charitable work, and greater freedom for church publications. In other words, the government would maintain all restrictions it had imposed on the Church after the communist takeover in the late 1940s. The communist regime's intransigence was not lost on the country's workers. Dissatisfaction with working conditions had been simmering all along, but in the spring of 1988 it erupted again at the breeding ground of Solidarity, the Gdansk shipyard.

Just prior to the outbreak of new strikes, the Polish security service SB had another meeting with the East Germans.[27] As it turned out, it was to be their last before the anticommunist unrest in their countries and in the rest of the East Bloc assumed unstoppable dimensions. The two-day parley at the end of March provided an analysis on the pope's visit a year earlier. The analysis was provided the East German hierarchy. "While feigning religious motives, this visit had primarily a political character against the communist ideology and aimed at a change of the conditions of socialism in the VRP. The dialog with the VRP as practiced by the pope is primarily aimed at further strengthening the Church in Poland and winning back the people who had left the Church." Thus, the Polish government admitted it had failed in cowing Pope John Paul II into refraining from politicizing his flock. By installing secret listening devices at a location where the Holy Father met with leading clerics, the SB

27. MfS Directorate for Religious Affairs XX/4. "Consultations in Warsaw March 29-31, 1988", attended by Maj. General Paul Kienberg and Colonel Joachim Wiegand, with Polish security authorities. BSTU Nr. 000150-56.

learned that "the pope committed Polish Church leaders to organize variations of spiritual welfare organizations in order to develop the Church as the bastion for freedom, democracy, and justice." In this respect, it added that the Polish meetings were never held. All knew that the end was near. In Poland, the strikers' demands went beyond wages and working conditions: now they vehemently called for the lifting of the ban on Solidarity and for free elections. Within six months, the strikes had spread throughout the country's industrial centers, while leading activists, including Lech Walesa, met with government functionaries demanding talks on elections.

It was in this atmosphere of renewed tension that British Prime Minister Margaret Thatcher began her week-long visit to Poland on November 2. It was not only an obvious gesture of her solidarity with the Polish people, but also of her support of the efforts of Pope John Paul II and U.S. President Ronald Reagan in battling communism. The "Iron Lady" had her intelligence services operating in Poland hand in glove with the CIA. After attending a banquet hosted by Party leader General Jaruzelski, where she proclaimed her support for "freedom of expression, association, and the right to form free and independent trade unions," she made an emotional visit to the grave of Father Jerzy Popieluszko. The next day she visited Gdansk, where more than 10,000 workers had gathered to protest the announced closing just three days earlier of the Lenin Shipyards, where the Solidarity movement was born. Astonishingly, because of the new turmoil, she was the first Western leader to be permitted to visit the beleaguered city on the Baltic coast. Although suffering losses requiring more than $18 million requiring subsidies, the measure was obviously intended to destroy Solidarity by dispersing the workers to jobs elsewhere. Mrs. Thatcher braved possible criticism for trying to control labor unions in Britain. Instead of criticism, however, the journalist Tomasz Pompowski told me that the workers and many intellectuals were totally aware that the prime minister's legitimate powers had been granted her by democratic free election and not by dictators.[28] The yard remained open, but financial difficulties continued [see note 25]. While thousands chanted "Solidarnosc, Solidarnosc," Mrs. Thatcher met with Lech Walesa and other Solidarity leaders over lunch at the St. Brigit presbytery. There, she reiterated her support for freedom, particularly for free elections. Polish journalist Pompowski described the British leader's visit as "a wonderful morale-booster."

Meanwhile, it had become apparent that General Jaruzelski and his cohorts could not count on Moscow to renew its scare tactics. Mikhail Gorbachev, who had become the head of the Soviet Union in 1985, was struggling to have his Party's hardliners accept his policies of glasnost, openness to give the people greater freedom, and perestroika, the restructuring of the economy, which was in dire straits. Moscow's war in Afghanistan was on the road to nowhere, and a retreat was ordered (the last Soviet unit left on February 15, 1989, ten years after Leonid Brezhnev ordered the invasion). Most importantly, Gorbachev had emboldened the freedom-seekers in the Soviet bloc when he renounced the Brezhnev Doctrine, which called for the use of force by the Soviet Union if any Warsaw Pact country was moving toward abandoning communism.

After numerous heated debates with fellow bureaucrats, General Czeslaw Kiszczak, the minister of the interior who was in charge of the secret police, had met with Lech Walesa on August 31. It became a historic event when the general agreed that discussions should be held on the political future of Poland. In December, the Communist Party concurred in a plenary session, but only after a more realistic Party leader and head of state Jaruzelski threatened obstreperous hardliners with his resignation and those of most of his ministers.

---

28. The shipyard was not closed, but losses continued to be severe and finally, in 2007, it was sold to the Ukrainian firm Donbuss.

The so-called Roundtable Talks began in February 1989 and, after 94 sessions, ended in April with an agreement that political power be vested in a bicameral legislative body with a president to be the nation's chief executive. The Solidarity labor union was again legalized, and, more significantly, free and fair elections were mandated. In the June election, Solidarity won 99 of the 100 seats in the Senate and 35 percent of the 460 seats in Parliament. Tadeusz Mazowiecki became the first non-communist prime minister. Lech Walesa was elected president by a landslide.

From that point on, nothing could stop the fall of communism in Eastern Europe. This was reinforced by Soviet President Gorbachev, who told the Council of Europe in Strasbourg, France, on July 5 that the Soviet Army would not be used for "internal repression" such as the anti-government disturbances in East Germany. Herr Honecker had lost his guaranty for existence. Next to Poland, the demise of communist East Germany was the most spectacular. On August 13, the 28th anniversary of the erection of the Berlin Wall, Party boss Honecker arrogantly declared that his regime needed no reform and the "Wall will be standing in 50 and even 100 years if the reasons for building it are not removed." The people's reaction to these words was like a tiny snowball rolling down a steep slope to become an unstoppable avalanche. Three weeks later, on a Monday, some 1,000 people assembled at the Nikolai Church in the city of Leipzig. After praying for peace, they chanted demands for lifting travel restrictions to the West. This was the impetus for the "Montags Demonstrationen" which from week to week swelled to tens of thousands. Their demands were ignored, prompting thousands of East Germans, men, women, and children, to travel to Czechoslovakia to seek refuge in the West German embassy in Prague. While Czech police tried to keep the crowd from reaching the building, the pressure was so immense that the refugees broke through the lines and climbed over the wall. In less than a week, about 4,000 were camped in the embassy garden. At the end of September, they were put aboard special trains to West Germany, which had a common border with Czechoslovakia. The refugees kept coming. Within days, about 8,000 were again camped on the embassy lawns. Government and Party boss Honecker, under pressure from Czech and West German authorities as well as demonstrators throughout East Germany, authorized two more special trains. The East German authorities demanded that the trains, instead taking the direct route to the West, make a detour though East Germany. It was a decision that must have raised questions about the authorities' compos mentis. When the trains passed through the city of Dresden, a huge battle erupted between people who wanted to jump aboard the rolling trains and the "People's Police." Thousands were driven off the railbeds by police swinging Stahlruten, metal batons of steel springs topped with lumps of lead. There were many injuries, and hundreds were crammed on trucks and taken to internment camps. By the way, these batons were first used by the communists in their street battles with the Nazi brownshirts and SS stormtroopers during the 1920s and 30s. Shortly after the trains arrived in the West, the Hungarian government opened its border with Austria, allowing 15,000 East Germans to reach freedom. It was the forerunner to the end of communist rule in the land of the Magyars.

As communist regimes were tottering toward oblivion, Comrade Honecker insisted on pompously celebrating the 40th anniversary of the DDR on October 7, with a giant parade of his People's Army. Infantrymen goose-stepped past the reviewing stand of dignitaries including Soviet leader Gorbachev, the guest of honor who by this time had met three times with President Ronald Reagan. While the parade proceeded, the area around it was cordoned off by police to stop tens of thousands of Berliners from storming into the parade ground. Earlier in the day, a jeering citizenry besieged the ornate State Council building. As secret police chief Erich Mielke arrived, he was greeted by a general, whom he ignored to scream at police: "Club those pigs into submission!"[29] His ranting was ignored. When Gorbachev arrived, thousands of demonstrators waved and shouted: "Gorby, help us!" The people knew that their "leader" had rejected Gorby's glasnost and perestroika and had banned the sale of Soviet publications as subversive.[30] Inside, Honecker addressed his guests by extolling the virtues of the DDR as the "breakwater against neonazism and chauvinism, and the DDR cannot be torn from its firm embedment in the Warsaw Pact." Considering the tumult on his country's streets and in the surrounding communist nations, there was good reason to doubt the man's sanity. After the speech, Gorbachev told Honecker that he must institute reforms or "else." He arrogantly rejected the advice, whereupon the Soviet leader said: "Life will punish those who arrive too late."[31] Eleven days later, Honecker was forced to resign. The Politburo lasted until November 8. The next day, the Berlin Wall fell, unleashing an unprecedented euphoria among East Berliners. As they streamed through the former checkpoints, West Berliners welcomed them with cheers and tears. Less than a year later, East Germany quit the Warsaw Pact and after the communists' defeat, the country was reunited. The rest of Moscow's satellites fell in rapid succession. Nevertheless, Gorbachev was determined that communism retained its power in the Soviet Union, though with a "kinder and gentler face," through his policies of glasnost and perestroika, openness and economic restructuring.

En route to Malta for his first summit with U.S. President George H. W. Bush on December 3, the Soviet leader stopped in Rome for a meeting with Pope John Paul II. It was the first encounter of a head of the Catholic Church with a Soviet leader. The two met for an hour,

29. John O. Koehler, *Stasi: The Untold Story of the East German Secret Police* (Westview Press, Boulder, CO., 1999).
30. Ibid.
31. Ibid.

the first 10 minutes alone. At the time, the Supreme Soviet still had not repealed Stalin's inhumanely repressive religious law initiated in 1924, something the Holy Father had urged in a 1988 letter to Gorbachev, which Cardinal Casaroli delivered when he visited Moscow as head of a Vatican delegation. For this historical meeting, the KGB for the first time did not have an advance report for Gorbachev from a Vatican spy on what was on the pope's mind.

In a post-meeting statement, the pope said the Soviet president's visit "enables us to look with greater confidence to the future of the communities of believers in the Soviet Union." Though the Holy Father never lacked confidence, his position certainly was bolstered after learning that a poll taken a year earlier revealed that 40 percent of 286,717,000 Soviet citizens believed in God.[32] The pope continued: "The events of the past decades and the painful trials to which so many citizens were subjected because of their faith are widely known. Recent developments and the new perspectives which have opened up lead us to hope that the situation will change, thanks to the repeatedly affirmed decision of your government to proceed with a renewal of internal legislation in order to bring into full harmony the solemn commitments to which the Soviet world also subscribed. Mr. President, our meeting today will hardly fail to have a powerful impact on world opinion. Not only is it something new and unusual, it will also be interpreted as singular meaningful: a sign of the times that have slowly matured . . . a sign that is rich in promise." Gorbachev said his thoughts and concerns had been "duly appreciated" as well his assurance that the "problems that now exist in our country, including problems between the state and various churches, which we are addressing in a *spirit of democracy and humanism within the framework of perestroika* [emphasis added]." He added: "Respect for the people's national, state, spiritual, and cultural identity is an

32. *Time*, April 13, 1998.

indispensable condition for a steady international environment which Europe and the world now need to cross the historic watershed and attain a new period of peace. We proceed from these positions by initiating our dialogue with the Holy See—the dialogue which has now been consecrated by this summit meeting."

After the meeting, the pope invited Mrs. Gorbachev to join them. The Soviet leader, who had been born into a religious peasant family in Stavropol, paid his host a compliment that must have shaken his fellow communists to the core. *"Raisa, I introduce you to His Holiness Pope John Paul II, who is the highest moral authority on Earth, besides being a Slav like us."* It was an astonishing compliment, indeed, by a man who once had been one of the signers of an order to the KGB calling for the pope's "physical elimination, if necessary." Epiphany? Thomas P. Melady, who served as U.S. ambassador to the Holy See from 1989 to 1993, recalled Cardinal Casaroli telling him of his meeting with Gorbachev in 1987.[33] "While the two toured the Kremlin, Gorbachev told him about his mother having been a deaconess in the Russian Orthodox Church and that she had baptized him," Ambassador Melady said. "He said his mother had portraits of communist leaders hanging on the wall of the family's cottage and when the two were alone she would remove a portrait which hid an icon, took down the sacred picture and blessed him." This revelation was not known to the State Department or the CIA, and the ambassador was instructed to provide details of the discussion between the pope and the Soviet leader, as "the Bush administration was not yet sure to what extent Gorbachev could be trusted."

Before parting, the pope remarked on Gorbachev's meeting with the American president. "Tomorrow you will meet with the President of the United States of America, Mr. George Bush. For my part, I express cordial good wishes and pray that the forthcoming talks may

33. Interview with Ambassador Melady, October 16, 2006.

lead to a new understanding, one based upon a careful heeding of the needs and aspiration of peoples." Since the pope's intimate contacts with the White House continued after President Reagan departed, he was briefed by Ambassador Melady on President Bush's agenda at the Malta meeting. The two leaders signed a treaty for major arms reduction, agreed to work toward enacting a treaty on dealing with long-range nuclear weapons, and declared the Cold War over. And within one year, after a botched coup by hardliners and pressure from nationalists, turmoil on the streets and rebellion in the Soviet Republics, Gorbachev resigned, on August 24, 1991, his chairmanship of the Communist Party. His arch-enemy Boris Yeltsin had become president of the Russian Republic. On December 17, the two agreed to dissolve the Soviet Union. On Christmas day, Gorbachev resigned as president. The Soviet Union became history on January 1, 1992. The entire East European communist bloc, with its population of more than 409 million, was now ready to join the free world. The communists' Vatican spies were left out in the cold.

> *The claim to build a world without God has been shown to be an illusion.*
>
> —Pope John Paul II
> Prague, April 21, 1990

13 EPILOGUE

everal hundred devout Catholics braved the streaming rain outside the 14th-century St. John's Cathedral in the Old Town section of Warsaw on the morning of January 7, 2007. Inside the crowded church, the 11:00 mass was to be celebrated by the newly named Metropolitan Archbishop Stanislaw Wielgus, the replacement for the retiring Polish Primate Jozef Cardinal Glemp. But far from being a joyous occasion, the event became another stab into the hearts of Polish Catholics. Flanked by Cardinal Glemp, Archbishop Wielgus announced with much solemnity, and wiping a tear from the corner of his left eye: "After considerable reflection and assessment of my personal situation, I have put my office into the hands of the Holy Father." His words were met with a tumultuous reaction by those inside the cathedral. Polish President Lech

Kaczynski loudly clapped his hands with enthusiasm,[1] then stopped abruptly as if fearing he had violated the solemnity of the House. To the hundreds gathered outside, it must have seemed as if the rain was the tears of the heavens. There were shouts of "No, No," and "Remain with us." Was the archbishop's transgression so vile that he needed to quit? Yes. He was a spy for the communists, spying on his people, on his Church. One cannot imagine a more severe blow to the most revered religious institution in Poland which, in the main, had fought so valiantly for the people's freedom; it was the country's bulwark against communism.

The Vatican announced on December 6, 2006 that Pope Benedict XVI had chosen the son of poor farmers from eastern Poland, 67-year-old Archbishop Wielgus, to replace Cardinal Glemp. Within days, the conservative newspaper *Gazeta Polska* published a proverbial bombshell. The archbishop, the newspaper wrote, had been an informer for Sluzba Bezpieczenstwa (SB), the country's secret police, for more than two decades. Archbishop Wielgus immediately denied the accusation. He said, like many Polish clergymen, he had been approached by the SB, but that he never divulged information that "harmed anyone." He was quoted by the left-leaning newspaper *Gazeta Wyborcza* as saying he "greatly feared the publication of the files," adding: "The journalists started this media campaign to kill my reputation and to destroy me." He said he agreed with the Vatican's view that secret police files about a person should be released for publication only 50 years after his death. "Otherwise there will be unrest, disarray, and fear." He told the newspaper that he had "revealed everything" about his contacts with the secret police to

---

1. Lech Kaczynski's twin brother Jaroslaw is Poland's prime minister. Both are staunch anticommunist conservatives who had been demanding tough measures against communist functionaries who enriched themselves or otherwise had damaged the nation. For example, they have been pushing for a law to limit the monthly retirement pay of former SB officials to 600 Slotys (about U.S. $220) a month. They had been paid more than three times the average working teacher earning 1,200 Slotys or about U.S. $405.

Pope Benedict XVI. When he became rector of the Catholic University, he told the paper, he was "visited by the gentlemen from time to time." He said he should have put a stop to it at the beginning. "But at the time, I thought I would not be able to travel abroad. But that was naïve, and today I regret it." Pope John Paul II had appointed Wielgus to lead the diocese of Plock, a town near Warsaw.

The Catholic News Service circulated a statement issued by the Vatican press office which said the Holy See "took into consideration all circumstances of his life, including those regarding his past." This means, the statement said, that "the Holy Father has full trust in his Excellency Msgr. Stanislaw Wielgus and, with full awareness, entrusted to him the mission of Archbishop of Warsaw." Like the Vatican, Poland's church hierarchy also defended the new prelate-to-be.

Archbishop Wielgus obviously was confident that no implicating documents would come to light. He was relying on assurances made to Church officials many years earlier by General Czeslaw Kiszczak, the minister in charge of the SB, that all files on the clergy had been destroyed. But the general had overlooked the efficiency of his minions, who had stored the files on microfilm, which had been discovered by researchers of the Institute of National Remembrance. Incredibly, the same mistake was made by General Markus Wolf, the head of foreign espionage of the East German Stasi. At the Roundtable Talks over dissolving the Stasi in 1990, Wolf gleefully told anticommunist dissidents and politicians that all files of the Hauptverwaltung für Aufklaerung (HVA), his foreign spy service, had been shredded. A year later, the West German military took over a former East German Army base near Berlin and found cases of microfilm stored in a bunker. These were duplicates of complete HVA dossiers on its agents, including a Catholic monk and a Catholic News Agency reporter whose involvements are told in chapter 9. General Kiszczak refused to comment, and so did Markus Wolf before he died in 2006.

Wielgus's denial unraveled quickly. On Friday, January 5, three days before the scheduled initiation ceremony, Wielgus met with Church leaders who had been briefed by two independent commissions, who presented 68 pages of documents proving the archbishop's complicity. His contacts began in the late 1960s when he was studying at the Catholic University of Lublin. He was ordained in 1962, at age 23, and first tended to the spiritual welfare of students when he was recruited by the SB. Initially, he furnished reports on students. In 1969, he embarked on studying church history and philosophy at Lublin. He became an expert on medieval graphology and a scientific assistant. Four years later, the young priest was awarded a stipend by the prestigious West German Alexander von Humboldt Foundation to study at the University of Munich. It was at that point that his more serious involvement with the secret police began. To receive a passport and permission to leave Poland was conditioned upon signing the pledge to become an SB spy. Wielgus attended the Bavarian university from 1973 to 1975 and again in 1978, where he met Professor Josef Ratzinger, who would become Pope Benedict XVI. The SB found the contact so fruitful that in 1973 he was firmly recruited as a snitch and signed a one-page cooperation agreement which he signed with his code name "Grey." Over the years, he was given other pseudonyms such as "Adam Wysocki." At the meeting with the Church officials, he was given Pope Benedict's appointment document, but he was told that the decision to refuse the honor was left up to him. By then, the Sunday ceremony had already been announced. However, an hour before it began, the pope notified Cardinal Glemp that the appointment had been withdrawn and that Glemp should continue as the prelate for the time being.

One needs not be clairvoyant to know that the Holy See found itself in an incredibly awkward position, especially since it became clear that the outwardly conservative Wielgus has been less than candid in his revelations when questioned by Pope Benedict. A day after the former priest-spy resigned, an editorial in the newspaper *Rzeczpospolita* said: "The Polish Church cannot cope with the Archbishop Wielgus affair—instead of condemning his betrayals, certain bishops, priests, and Catholic commentators have vilified those with the courage to unveil the uncomfortable truth." The newspaper no doubt was referring to Cardinal Glemp's assertion that "the real need isn't for change in Church structures but for change in structures of our state, which needs to liberate itself from media pressure."

Earlier, according to press information, the newspaper *Gazeta Wyborcza* had sent to the Holy See a translation of the archbishop's SB dossier. It said President Kaczynski had had "discreet talks" with the Vatican and that he had spoken directly with the pope, whom he described as "extremely angry." However, Vatican spokesman Federico Lombardi termed the resignation of Wiegus "appropriate" because his authority has been "gravely compromised." He added that Poland's Catholic Church was undergoing a "moment of great suffering." The Holy See then reconsidered the earlier comments about the archbishop's resignation and the ensuing condemnations. According to Vatican Radio and the Polish Catholic Information Agency, the paper sent a letter on February 12 to Wielgus in which the pope assured him of his "spiritual closeness and brotherly understanding." The Holy Father also expressed a "wish" that the archbishop "resumes his activity in the service of Christ in a manner that will be possible for the good of the beloved Church in Poland." The day after his resignation, Wielgus sent a letter to Pope Benedict which prompted the Holy Father to express his thanks for the "confidence with which your Excellency opened your heart before me, showing the painful suffering of your heart." Obviously, this signaled, if not immediate, eventual forgiveness.

The exposure of the archbishop was followed by one wrenching revelation after another, shocking to the core a nation so sorely tried for nearly seven decades. On January 8, Father Janusz Bielanski, the dean of Krakow's famous Wawel Cathedral, resigned after being exposed as a secret police collaborator. He had been close to Stanislaw Cardinal Dziwisz, the Archbishop of Krakow and for 26 years the personal assistant to Pope John Paul II. Two weeks later, another priest of Cardinal Dziwisz's archdiocese, Mieczyslaw Lukaszczyk, handed in his resignation which, as in the case of Bielanski, was accepted without comment. Father Lukaszczyk was serving as dean of the parish of St. Catherine in Nowy Targ, a small town in the foothills of the Tatra Mountains. His alleged transgression was first reported in June 2006 by Jerzy Jurecki in the newspaper *Tygodnik Podhalanski*, and the Wielgus case brought it to the fore again. As he did earlier, Father Lukaszczyk denied that he had cooperated with the SB, though he admitted having been contacted by its officers and documents had been found showing he had been given the code name "Turysta." Reporter Jurecki wrote that while trying to "get rid of the secret police closing around him," Father Lukaszczyk nevertheless "accepted packs of coffee, bottles of cognac, and on his 25th anniversary of service to the Church he received an expensive German-made Pelikan fountain pen as a gift." To his credit, according to documents cited by the reporter, during talks with SB officers he had sharply criticized communism and the attitude of the Soviet Union toward the Catholic Church. Finally, another of Cardinal Dziwisz's priests, Father Miroslaw Drozdek, was unveiled as a collaborator. Drozdek was the custodian of the Sanctuary of Our Lady of Fatima at Zakopane, a small picturesque town in the Tatra Mountains famous for its winter sports. The unmaskings were especially painful to Cardinal Dziwicz, since Bielanski and Lukaszczyk were in his graduating class of seminarians.

Finally, another priest with the closest of ties to the late John Paul II was exposed by authorities. Father Mieczyslaw Malinski, according to the Institute of National Remembrance, had been spying for the SB since 1980 under the code name "Delta." Malinski became a friend of

Karol Wojtyla, the future pope, in 1940 while members of the "Living Rosary" group in Krakow. During World War II, both entered an underground seminary. Malinski was ordained a priest and after serving a parish, he became a writer for the Catholic weekly newspaper *Tygodnik Powszechny*. He wrote the first biography of Pope John Paul II. Father Malinski, now 83 years old, has denied the accusation.

As the church leadership was struggling over the events so damaging to their revered Church, an explosive book by Father Tadeusz Isakowicz-Zaleski titled *Priests in the Face of the Security Services* was published on February 26, 2007. He exposed 39 priests and four bishops who had been spies for communist Poland's secret police. One of the bishops was identified as Juliusz Paetz, who was recruited in 1978 and given the code name "Fero." He was another high-ranking cleric close to Cardinal Karol Wojtyla in Krakow, the future pope. Bishop Paetz was assigned to Rome to serve in the Synod of Bishops from 1967 to 1976. After returning to Poland, he served as Bishop of Lomza until 2003, when he resigned after being accused of sexual misconduct with young priests. Paetz denied the accusation of spying. In a written statement sent to this writer, the Polish investigative journalist Kryzsztof Tomaszewski said that "the book is a volcano which erupted, although until the last day it was not certain that it would be published. Cardinal Dziwisz criticized the publication." But the cardinal finally bowed to public protests. The journalist observed that he, and many of his colleagues and friends, believed that much of the scandal was kept from an aging Pope John Paul II until after his death so as not to embarrass him.

Father Zaleski's disdain for communism, the treasonous clerics, and the secret police was exacerbated by his horrible experience with the SB in December 1985. His home was invaded by a young woman and two men, who were dressed in paramedic uniforms. He was handcuffed, kicked to the ground, and beaten. Before leaving, the thugs ransacked and wrecked his home. It was the second attack on the priest. In the spring of 1985, at the height of martial law, he was ambushed by secret police thugs near his mother's home. One used a cigarette to burn on his chest the letter "V," which was the symbol of the banned Solidarity trade union that the priest publicly supported. In 2005, Father Zaleski was finally allowed to read the voluminous secret file that the SB had compiled on him. He learned that he had been under tight surveillance not just by secret police officers, but also by priests he thought of as friends and other acquaintances. After relaying Father Zaleski's story, the journalist wrote: "John, I come from a strong Catholic family. We, and all of our friends and relatives, are deeply affected by this horrible behavior of priests. The secret police files show that some did it out of fear, others, like Archbishop Wielgus, so they could study and travel abroad. But alcohol, money, and women also were the tools used to recruit and hold them. It will take some time for Poland to recover from this, but I believe there will be a great effort to make it a better country."

The Institute of National Remembrance revealed that about ten to fifteen percent of the nation's Catholic clergy had collaborated with the secret police. In 2006, Poland had 29,089 ordained priests, about 1,845 monks, and 23,105 nuns, by far the most of any European country.[2] Cardinal Dziwisz called for an all-encompassing investigation of the collaborator problem. At the same time, a Warsaw court agreed to investigate the Wielgus case. Although the clergy had been exempt from a law calling for screening of public figures, the court ruled that the archbishop had a right to attempt to clear his name. How long it will take to restore calm within the Catholic population is anyone's guess. There is an old saying: old millstones grind slowly.

The resilience of the Polish people and their happiness over at least having no longer to fear communist tyranny was displayed on July 4, 2008. Thousands of Poles celebrated their freedom by

2. Catholic News Agency, March 16, 2006.

exuberantly cheering the unveiling of an 11-foot bronze statue of the man who, together with Pope John Paul II and Margaret Thatcher, made it possible: Ronald Reagan. Earlier, the town Committee to Commemorate President Ronald Reagan's Merits voted to rename Constitution Square, Ronald Reagan Square, thus joining George Washington and Woodrow Wilson, who had plazas named after them. The town of Katowice renamed its Freedom Square, so named by the communists in honor of the Soviet Army for ridding the city of the Nazis in 1945. Now it bears the name "Ronald Reagan Freedom Square." Another Katowice honor for President Reagan was on the drawing board. The town fathers decided to replace the Soviet war memorial with a statue of the late American president.

On July 17, 2007, Jacek Klys and 60 of his fellow Polish freedom fighters gathered at the Ronald Reagan Presidential Library in Simi Valley, California. They cheered as Polish President Lech Kaczynski presented his nation's highest honor, the Order of the White Eagle, to Nancy Reagan, who accepted it on behalf of her late husband. A year later, Mrs. Reagan wrote Mayor Rafal Dutkiewicz expressing her "deepest gratitude to the people of Wroclaw" for naming a street for the late American president. In her letter of July 21, 2008, the former First Lady recalled how important it was to President Reagan that Poles should enjoy freedom and democracy.

ACKNOWLEDGMENTS

I wish to express my deepest appreciation to a number of sources for their support while I was researching this book. My thanks go to: Sergey A. Aleksandrychev, a contact within the Orthodox Church in Russia; David Alvarez, author of *Spies in the Vatican*; Peter Bartoszek, retired New York Police detective lieutenant with valuable contacts in Poland; Ferdi Breidbach, former Christian Democratic Party deputy in the German Parliament; Hal Baell, retired assistant general manager and director of photography, Associated Press; General Umberto Capuzzo, Senator to the Italian Republic, former Italian Army Chief of Staff and former Commander of the Carabinieri Corps; Felix Corley, editor and expert on religious persecution at the Keston Institute in Great Britain; Anne Cron, a trusted friend, fine editor, and adviser; Fritz W. Ermarth, a retired officer of the U.S. CIA and former chairman of the National Intelligence Council; Prefect Don Raffaele Farina, Biblioteca Apostolica Vaticana; the late Bernard Ficcara, M.D., former medical adviser to the Holy See and president of the Catholic Academy of Sciences of America; His Excellency Cardinal John P. Foley, former president of the Vatican Council for Social Communications; His Excellency Franco Frattini, Italian Foreign Minister and former chairman of the Italian Parliamentary Committee of Intelligence and Security Services; Joy Stellato Gabriella, Press Office of the Holy See; the late Theodor Hans, former U.S. Army counterintelligence officer; Paul Henze, former senior staff member of the U.S.

National Security Council and author of *The Plot to Kill the Pope*; Bishop Michel Hrynchyshyn, former director of the Vatican's Commission on Martyrs; Father Vjekoslav Huzjak, Secretary General of the Episcopal Conference of Croatia; Hetenyi Varga Karoly, expert of communist persecution of the Catholic Church in Hungary; Bishop Basil Osten, DD, retired Bishop of the Ukrainian Church of Stamford, Connecticut; Colonel A. F. "Fritz" von Marbod, retired U.S. Air Force counterintelligence expert and valuable partner in questioning a communist spy; Enrico Marinelli, former director of the Italian States Police Inspectorate for Public Security at the Vatican; Ambassador Thomas P. Melady, former chairman of Seaton University and Ambassador Plenipotentiary to the Holy See 1989-1993; Stefan Meining, Bavarian Radio/TV Munich; Bibliographer Michael M. Miller of the Germans from Russian Heritage Collection, North Dakota State University; Dr. Joachin Navarro-Valls, spokesman for Pope John Paul II; Christian Ostermann, director, Cold War International Project of the Woodrow Wilson Center, Washington, D.C.; Franscesco Pasanisi, Italian State Police assigned to the Vatican; Christo Petrov, former Bulgarian Telegraph Agency editor-in-chief in Rome; Thomasz Pompowski, a prominent journalist in Poland and a most helpful friend; Marco Politi, Vatican expert for the Rome newspaper *La Repubblica*; Gerald Praschl, chief reporter for SuperIllu newspaper in Berlin; Cristina Ravenda of the Vatican Press Office; Dennis Redmont, retired Associated Press bureau chief for Italy and the Mediterranean area; Father Thomas Reese, S.J., senior fellow at the Woodstock Theological Seminary at Georgetown University; Herbert Romerstein, one of America's top experts on communism and a good friend; Robert Royal, president of the Faith & Reason Institute in Washington, D.C., and author of *The Catholic Martyr of the Twentieth Century*; Dr. Bernd Schaefer, a top expert on communist persecution and oppression of religion in the former East Germany; Gustavo Selva, president of the Italian Parliament's Foreign Affairs

Committee; Ruediger Stang and associates Guenther Schreiber and Brigitte Richter at the archives of the former East German Secret Police Ministry for State Security, who were of great help in locating essential documents; Dr. William L. Stearman, retired high-ranking American diplomat who served on the National Security Council for 17 years and academician of the Catholic Society of Sciences of America; Father John Terletzki, Director of the Ukrainian Catholic Church Research Center in Stamford, Connecticut; Ivan Uspenski, librarian at the Goethe Haus in Moscow; Bishop Andras Veres, Bishop of Szombathely and Secretary General of the Hungarian Bishops' Conference; George Weigel, a Roman Catholic theologian and author of *Witness to Hope*, the acclaimed biography of Pope John Paul II; Father Christopher Lawrence Zugger, Albuquerque, New Mexico, pastor of the Byzantine Catholic Eparchy of Van Nuys and author of *The Forgotten*, a masterful chronicle of Soviet persecution of the Catholic Church. Lastly, I wish to thank those who were of vital help but who asked to remain anonymous because of their sensitive intelligence positions.

INDEX